Medieval Childhood:
Archaeological Approaches

Childhood in the Past Monograph Series

The monograph series was established to allow scholars from all disciplines a forum for presenting new, groundbreaking or challenging research into themed aspects of childhood in the past. The Society is happy to consider proposals for future monographs. Proposals should be submitted to the General Editor of the Monograph Series. Details for submission may be found on the Society's webpage at www.sscip.org.uk.

Dr Sally Crawford FSA
General Editor, SSCIP Monograph Series
The Institute of Archaeology
36 Beaumont Street
Oxford OX1 2PG
United Kingdom

sally.crawford@arch.ox.ac.uk

Childhood in the Past Monograph Series: Volume 3

Medieval Childhood:
Archaeological Approaches

Edited by

D. M. Hadley
and
K. A. Hemer

Oxbow Books
Oxford & Philadelphia

Published in the United Kingdom in 2014 by
OXBOW BOOKS
10 Hythe Bridge Street, Oxford OX1 2EW

and in the United States by
OXBOW BOOKS
908 Darby Road, Havertown, PA 19083

Paperback Edition: ISBN 978-1-78297-698-1
Digital Edition: ISBN 978-1-78297-699-8

A CIP record for this book is available from the British Library

Library of Congress Cataloging-in-Publication Data

Printed in the United Kingdom by Short Run Press, Exeter

For a complete list of Oxbow titles, please contact:

UNITED KINGDOM	UNITED STATES OF AMERICA
Oxbow Books	Oxbow Books
Telephone (01865) 241249	Telephone (800) 791-9354
Fax (01865) 794449	Fax (610) 853-9146
Email: oxbow@oxbowbooks.com	Email: queries@casemateacademic.com
www.oxbowbooks.com	www.casemateacademic.com/oxbow

Oxbow Books is part of the Casemate group

Contents

List of Illustrations

List of Contributors

Elizabeth Craig-Atkins is Lecturer in Human Osteology at the University of Sheffield. Her research has explored the character and provision of early Christian funerary practices, health, disease and disability in the past from both biological and social perspectives, and the skeletal analysis of populations from, in particular, the Anglo-Saxon and medieval periods. Her recent publications on these themes include: Chest burial: a middle Anglo-Saxon funerary rite from northern England. *Oxford Journal of Archaeology* 31 (3), 317–37 (2012); Investigating social status using evidence of biological status: a case study from Raunds Furnells (with J. Buckberry), pp. 128–42 in Buckberry, J. and Cherryson, A. (eds), *Burial in Later Anglo-Saxon England, c. 650–1100 AD*. Oxford: Oxbow (2010); and The diagnosis and context of a facial deformity from an Anglo-Saxon cemetery at Spofforth, North Yorkshire (with G. Craig). *International Journal of Osteoarchaeology* (forthcoming).

Sally Crawford, FSA, is Senior Research Fellow at the Institute of Archaeology, University of Oxford, and previously taught medieval archaeology at the University of Birmingham. Her research interests include the archaeology of childhood, and medieval attitudes to health, disease and disability. Her publications include: *Childhood in Anglo-Saxon England*. Stroud: Sutton (1999); *Children, Childhood and Society* (British Archaeological Reports International Series 1696) (ed. with G. Shepherd). Oxford: Archaeopress; and *Bodies of Knowledge: cultural interpretations of illness and medicine in medieval Europe* (British Archaeological Reports International Series 2170, ed. with C. Lee). Oxford: Archaeopress.

D. M. Hadley, FSA, is Professor of Medieval Archaeology at the University of Sheffield, and her research interests span aspects of early medieval identities relating to gender, ethnicity, social status and life cycle. Her publications include: *Masculinity in Medieval Europe* (ed.). London: Longman (1999); *The Vikings in England: settlement, society and culture*. Manchester: Manchester University Press (2006); *Everyday Life in Viking-Age Towns: social approaches to towns in England and Ireland, c. 800–1100* (ed. with A. Ten Harkel). Oxford: Oxbow (2013); Burying the socially and physically distinctive in and beyond the Anglo-Saxon churchyard, pp. 101–13 in Buckberry, J. and Cherryson, A. (eds), *Burial in later Anglo-Saxon England, c. 650–1100 AD*. Oxford: Oxbow (2010); and Microcosms of migration: children and early medieval population movement (with K. A. Hemer). *Childhood in the Past* 4, 63–78 (2011). She is also the editor (with S. Crawford and G. Shepherd) of the *Oxford Handbook of the Archaeology of Childhood*. Oxford: Oxford University Press (forthcoming).

Mark A. Hall is History Officer at Perth Museum and Art Gallery, principally responsible for the curation of the archaeology collections, which notably include the medieval excavation assemblages from Perth. His publications include *Playtime in Pictland: the material culture of gaming in early medieval Scotland*, Rosemarkie: Groam House Museum (2007); The Lewis hoard of gaming pieces: a re-examination of their context, meanings, discovery and manufacture (with D. Caldwell and C. Wilkinson). *Medieval Archaeology* 53, 155–203 (2009); Playtime: the material culture of gaming in medieval Scotland, pp. 145–68 in Cowan, T. and Henderson, L. (eds), *A History of Everyday Life in Medieval Scotland 1000–1600*. Edinburgh: Edinburgh University Press (2011); Making the past present: cinematic narratives of the

Middle Ages', pp. 489–512 in Gilchrist, R. and Reynolds, A. (eds), *Reflections: 50 Years of Medieval Archaeology, 1957–2007*. Leeds: Maney (2009).

K. A. Hemer is a British Academy Postdoctoral Research Fellow at the University of Sheffield. With a focus on early medieval western Britain, her research sees the integration of archaeological, historical, and funerary evidence with stable isotope data for diet and population mobility. Her publications include; Evidence of early medieval trade and migration between Wales and the Mediterranean Sea region (with J. A. Evans, C. A, Chenery and A. L. Lamb). *Journal of Archaeological Science* 40, 2352–9 (2013); A bioarchaeological study of the human remains from the early medieval cemetery of Cronk Keeillane, Isle of Man. *Proceedings of the Isle of Man Natural History and Antiquarian Society* XII (3), 469–86 (2012); Microcosms of migration: children and early medieval population movement (with D. M. Hadley). *Childhood in the Past* 4, 63–78 (2011).

Carenza Lewis, FSA, is a Senior Research Associate at the University of Cambridge, and Director of Access Cambridge Archaeology. She was previously an archaeological investigator with the Royal Commission on Historical Monuments of England. Her publications include: *Village, Hamlet and Field: changing medieval settlements in central England* (with P. Mitchell-Fox and C. Dyer). Manchester: Manchester University Press (1997); Childhood studies and the Society for the Study of Childhood in the Past (with Sally Crawford) (2008). *Childhood in the Past* 1, 5–17; Children's play in the later medieval English countryside. *Childhood in the Past* 2, 86–108 (2009).

Maureen Mellor, FSA, is a part-time tutor at Oxford University Department of Continuing Education and a specialist in post-Roman ceramics. She was the first John D. Rassweiler Curator of Medieval Collections at the British Museum and has worked for the Ashmolean Museum creating online resources in medieval ceramics. Her publications include: Oxfordshire pottery: a synthesis of middle and late Saxon pottery, medieval and early post-medieval pottery in the Oxford Region. *Oxoniensia* 59, 17–217 (1994); and *Pots and People that have shaped the heritage of medieval and later England*. Oxford: Ashmolean Museum.

Sally V. Smith is Research Development Manager at Queen's University, Belfast, and previously held research and teaching positions at the University of Otago, University College Dublin and the University of Auckland. Her research interests centre on the social archaeology of the late medieval English peasantry. Her publications include: Towards a social archaeology of the late medieval English peasantry: power and resistance at Wharram Percy. *Journal of Social Archaeology* 9 (3), 391–416 (2009); Materialising resistant identities among the medieval peasantry: an examination of dress accessories from English rural settlement sites. *Journal of Material Culture* 14 (3), 309–32 (2009); Houses and communities: archaeological evidence for variation in medieval peasant experience, pp. 64–84 in Dyer, C. and Jones, R. (eds), *Deserted Villages Revisited*. Hatfield: University of Hertfordshire Press (2010).

Kirsty E. Squires is an independent researcher and field archaeologist. Her doctoral research involved the osteological analysis and social investigation of the cremation practicing groups from Elsham and Cleatham. Her publications include: The application of histomorphometry and Fourier Transform Infrared Spectroscopy to the analysis of early Anglo-Saxon burned bone (with T. J. U. Thompson, M. Islam and A. Chamberlain). *Journal of Archaeological Science* 38 (9), 2399–409 (2011); Populating the pots: the demography of the early Anglo-Saxon cemeteries at Elsham and Cleatham, North Lincolnshire. *Archaeological Journal* 169 (forthcoming).

1. Introduction: Archaeological approaches to medieval childhood, *c.* 500–1500

D. M. Hadley and K. A. Hemer

The study of medieval childhood has been a vibrant field of research among historians over the last few decades (for reviews, see Orme 2008; Heywood 2010, 348–53). These studies have explored diverse aspects of childhood, including education (Orme 1973; 2001, 237–72; 2006; Bowers 1996; Clark 2002), work (Hanawalt 1986, 156–68; 1993), play (Orme 2001, 163–98), upbringing and socialization (Hanawalt 1977; 1986, 171–87; 1993; Shahar 1990, 21–32, 77–120; Goldberg 2008), experiences of religion (Orme 2001, 199–236), naming practices (Hanawalt 1993, 45–8), and adolescence and the transition to adulthood (Hanawalt 1993), drawing on the wealth of evidence from such sources as lawcodes, court records, saints' *Lives*, literary sources, and didactic texts, such as advice manuals. Archaeologists have also made important contributions to our understanding of medieval childhood, although the focus of their investigations has tended to be more narrowly restricted, with discussion dominated by the evidence from burials (*e.g.* Crawford 1993; 2007; 2008; 2011; Lucy 1994; Buckberry 2000; Lewis 2002; 2011; Lewis and Gowland 2007) and toys (*e.g.* Egan 1988; 1996; 1998; 2011; Forsyth and Egan 2005; Crawford 2009; Lewis 2009; McAlister 2013). This is, perhaps, inevitable because it is in these forms of archaeological evidence that children and their activities are most directly encountered – through their physical remains, which reveal aspects of lived experiences relating to health and diet, the manner in which they were treated in death, and the material culture with which they played. The aim of this volume is to broaden the focus of archaeological approaches to medieval childhood, and to highlight the manner in which archaeological evidence is capable of contributing to an understanding of medieval childhood that is just as wide-ranging and nuanced as that to have emerged from the investigation of written sources.

Archaeological interest in childhood emerged during the 1970s and 1980s, particularly among Scandinavian archaeologists (*e.g.* Gräslund 1973; Weber 1982), who were – perhaps not coincidentally – also among the pioneers of gender archaeology (see, in particular, Bertelsen *et al.* 1987, based on the proceedings of an important conference held at Stavanger (Norway) in 1979). In the late 1970s, Norwegian archaeologists were raising awareness of children in past human societies, most notably through museum displays created in response to the United Nations 'International Year of the Child' in 1979 (Lillehammer 1989, 97). Arguably the most influential early contribution to the emerging field of the archaeology of childhood was by the Norwegian archaeologist Grete Lillehammer, who pointed out in 1989 that for too long 'the child's world has been left out of archaeological research' (Lillehammer 1989, 89). Lillehammer was influenced by ethnographic studies that had revealed the diversity of the nature and duration of childhood, and she argued that the study of children and childhood would not only elucidate the experiences and contributions of the youngest members of communities, but it would also require archaeologists to grapple with such fundamental issues as 'the concepts of adaptation and acculturation' (Lillehammer 1989, 93–5). Lillehammer's review focussed on burial evidence and toys as the most direct means of exploring 'the child's world', and she suggested that archaeologists might fruitfully examine the child's relationship to both the environment and the adult world (Lillehammer 1989, 102–3). She concluded that '[t]he main obstacle to finding the child's world is neither the child nor the archaeological record, but the discipline's own understanding and knowledge of the adult world and her environment in past societies' (Lillehammer 1989, 103). This, indeed, remains an issue for archaeologists to address: if it is felt that children and childhood are difficult to study from archaeological evidence, then archaeologists should reflect on whether they are really uncovering *people* at all in any of their analyses (similar considerations were addressed in the emergence of gender archaeology: *e.g.* Tringham 1991).

Since this pioneering work, a plethora of edited collections have explored archaeological approaches to childhood (*e.g.* Sofaer-Derevenski 2000; Baxter 2006; Crawford and Shepherd 2007; Bacvarov 2008; Dommasnes and Wrigglesworth 2008; Lillehammer 2010; Lally and Moore 2011; Gläser 2012). However, most of these collections were multi-period in focus, typically including only a few medieval contributions. Among the handful of extended studies of the archaeological evidence for medieval childhood, are Mary Lewis's (2002) study of the impact of urbanisation on childhood health in medieval and early post-medieval England, a study of metal toys from London dating to *c.* 1200 to 1800 by Hazel Forsyth and Geoff Egan (2005; see also Egan 1996), and Sigrid Mygland's (2007) study of the diverse array of material culture associated with children that has been excavated from medieval contexts in Bergen (Norway), where the waterlogged environment permitted recovery of wooden artefacts and clothing. Preceding them all was Sally Crawford's (1999) influential volume on childhood in Anglo-Saxon England, which demonstrated the importance of interpreting the archaeological record within an inter-disciplinary context. There have also been a number of monographs focussing explicitly on the archaeology of childhood in later historical periods, particularly in north America (*e.g.* Baxter 2005), which have proven influential on approaches to the medieval archaeology of childhood. Aside from monographs and edited collections, there has been a proliferation of scholarly articles exploring the archaeological evidence for medieval children and childhood. In the discussion that follows, the key insights and debates that have emerged from two decades or more of scholarship on the archaeological evidence for childhood in the British Isles between *c.* 500 and 1500 are highlighted, and the lacunae identified. This serves to place the contributions to this volume in context.

The archaeology of medieval childhood: a review

Funerary archaeology

Children who were once invisible in the archaeological record are slowly coming into view. The primary data for the archaeology of childhood are the children themselves

Lewis 2007, 1

The 1980s saw a growing interest in the manner in which aspects of social identity were constructed through the burial record, and while the focus among medieval archaeologists was typically on gender identity (*e.g.* Pader 1980; 1982; Arnold 1980; Brush 1988) analysis of the funerary treatment of children was sometimes included in such studies (*e.g.* Pader 1982). Out of this scholarship emerged studies focussing specifically on the ways in which we might begin to understand childhood from burial evidence (*e.g.* Crawford 1993; Lucy 1994). Attention fell, in particular, on the inhumation cemeteries of the early Anglo-Saxon period, as this permitted exploration of the relationship between grave goods, on the one hand, and the age and sex of the interred, on the other. Simultaneously, the need to consider childhood in its historically-specific context began to be stressed, with Sam Lucy (1994, 29) arguing that 'the idea of what a "child" was may have been a far more flexible … concept than we can imagine'. Contrasting approaches were adopted, with some studies focussing on detailed contextual analyses of individual cemeteries (*e.g.* Pader 1980; 1982; Lucy 1998), while others surveyed the evidence on a regional or national basis (*e.g.* Stoodley 1999; 2000). The patterns that emerged from these analyses were then used to explore the ways in which childhood was constructed in a funerary context in the early Anglo-Saxon period.

Funerary evidence was the principal data set on which rested the pioneering research among medieval archaeologists interested in childhood, and this echoed the research focus of archaeologists working on other periods (*e.g.* Scott 1999; Rega 2000). Comparison of the deposition of grave goods with the age profile of skeletal remains, led Anglo-Saxon archaeologists to discuss the age categories that existed in the early Anglo-Saxon period and where the threshold between childhood and adulthood was to be found. This research was influential in exposing the mistaken assumptions that were inherent in earlier scholarship, which often failed to recognise that modern constructions of childhood were different from those of the Anglo-Saxon period. For example, Sally Crawford pointed out that claims that children were sometimes buried with adult grave goods were based on a belief that individuals aged between around twelve and seventeen years were still children, whereas, in fact, in Anglo-Saxon society adulthood was achieved, at least in terms of legal responsibility and capacity to marry, by around twelve years (Crawford 1991; 1999, 47–53; 2000, 170–2).

Research on early Anglo-Saxon burial practices has long debated the reasons for the disproportionately low numbers of burials of infants and young children in cemeteries of this period. A variety of factors that may explain this phenomenon have been discussed, including issues relating to taphonomy, biases in excavation, the nature of post-excavation procedures and selective exclusion of this demographic group from community cemeteries (Buckberry 2000; Crawford 2000, 169–70; see also Squires this volume). It is notable, however, that there is local variation, and while some cemeteries possess infant burials in varying numbers, others are completely devoid of infant burials, suggesting that in such cases infants 'were not acknowledged within the burial ritual as community members' (Stoodley 2011, 658). The discovery of infant burials in early Anglo-Saxon settlements has prompted particularly fruitful debate recently (*e.g.* Hamerow 2006, 14, 24; for continental parallels, see Beilke-Voigt 2008), and the notion that these were merely 'casual' deposits or of little significance, as was once thought, has been challenged (Crawford 2008, 202). There has been discussion of the potential symbolic resonances of burying infant remains beneath buildings or in the back-fill once they had been abandoned. It has been suggested that these infant remains were possibly ritual deposits, although it is acknowledged that interpretation is hampered by the nature of the recording of these burials, which are often not regarded as significant by excavators (Crawford 2008, 199–200). Yet, even as the analytical potential of the burials of children was recognised, it was also pointed out that we need to be careful not to assume the priority or agency of infant and child burials in all contexts. In particular, Crawford (2007) has suggested that when children were deposited in the same grave as an adult, the burial of the latter may have been the primary focus. She has gone as far as to argue that the child in such burial contexts was not necessarily regarded as having any agency at all: 'there is no good reason to suppose that the Anglo-Saxons always privileged all bodies in the burial ritual, nor that one or all of the bodies found within the multiple burial ritual should not have had a role as "objects", rather than as bodies' (Crawford 2007, 90).

Those regions and periods in which burial with grave goods was not normative, have, in general, attracted far less attention from funerary archaeologists until recently (Buckberry 2007; Hadley 2010; 2011; see also Hemer this volume). Accordingly, there has been only limited discussion of the funerary treatment of children in early medieval cemeteries from western and northern Britain (where poor bone survival is also a limiting factor; see Hemer this volume) and the cemeteries of the later medieval period. The feature of these cemeteries that has been afforded the most attention is the increased proportions of burials of infants and children, in comparison with cemeteries characterised by the early Anglo-Saxon furnished rite (Figure 1.1). This has been typically assigned to the influence of Christianity, which is presumed to have required all Christians to be afforded burial in consecrated ground, and examples of the burials of the very youngest members of the community adjacent to the walls of later Anglo-Saxon churches have been subject to particular scrutiny as potential evidence for the special place of children in the heart of Christian communities (*e.g.* Crawford 1999, 87–8; Page 2011; reviewed in Craig-Atkins this volume, where an alternative explanation is proposed). A recent study of later medieval churchyard burials in Britain by Roberta Gilchrist, which focussed on evidence for the use of magic in funerary rituals, noted that the graves of children 'make up a disproportionate number of those interpreted … as being linked with magic' (Gilchrist 2008, 148). The later medieval graves of children have been found to include a variety of objects with apotropaic attributes, such as beads, fossils and coins, which are argued as having been placed in the grave 'as protection against malevolent forces, and perhaps to deflect the evil eye' (Gilchrist 2008, 149). The clustering of burials of infants in some later medieval cemeteries has also been noted, and interpreted as evidence that 'age-cohorts were perceived as a distinct social group

Figure 1.1. Burial of a six-year-old child from the later Anglo-Saxon cemetery at Black Gate, Newcastle-upon-Tyne (Tyne and Wear) (reproduced courtesy of John Nolan; we are grateful to Dr Diana Mahoney Swales for assistance with identifying this image from the site archive).

or category' (Gilchrist 2012, 206). Baptised infants who died before the age of two years may, Roberta Gilchrist (2012, 207–9) has argued, have been likened to the 'Holy Innocents' – the infants massacred by Herod – who were expected to be the first souls saved at the Resurrection. She has also suggested that instances of infants buried in adult graves 'may have been regarded as spiritually efficacious material, while their spotless souls would have been desirable companions for adults journeying through purgatory' (Gilchrist 2012, 209). On the whole, however, the funerary treatment of children by medieval Christian communities has scarcely begun to be addressed.

Osteological evidence

By the 1990s there was increased recognition among osteologists that the remains of children were both worthy of study and survived in sufficient numbers to provide viable sample sizes for analysis (something which had previously been doubted; see reviews in Lewis 2007, 2–13; 2011, 3). As a consequence, numerous osteological studies of children emerged, with many drawing on medieval case-studies. Rather than continuing to emphasise the value of the study of children's remains for understanding such broader issues as demographic profiles of societies, fertility rates or societal adaptation to the environment, which had characterised earlier research (Lewis 2007, 10–13; 2011, 3), this research began to focus on what could be learned about aspects of children's lives and manner of death (Figure 1.2). Studies of child health, disease and mortality proliferated (*e.g.* Goodman and Armelagos 1989; Saunders 1992; Mays 1993; Anderson and Carter 1995; Ribot and Roberts 1996; Guy *et al.* 1997; Lewis and Roberts 1997; Sellevold 1997; Ortner and Mays 1998; Herring *et al.* 1998; Schurr 1998; Glencross and Stuart-Macadam

Figure 1.2. An osteologist examining the remains of a foetus from the later Anglo-Saxon cemetery of Kirkdale (North Yorkshire) (photograph courtesy of Dr Diana Mahoney Swales).

2000; Lewis 2000). This research into the osteological evidence for children has resulted in some of the fundamental principles of osteological analysis being challenged, particularly methods of assessing age. The importance of employing methodologies for ageing skeletons that are appropriate to the population under study has been emphasised, as it has been recognised that drawing on methodologies derived from the study of different populations may distort the age profile of the skeletal population being studied (Hoppa 1992; Saunders and Hoppa 1993; Liversidge 1994; Lampl and Johnston 1996; Hoppa and FitzGerald 1999; Gowland and Chamberlain 2002). The difficulty of ageing immature remains is further compounded by the fact that dental and skeletal development differs between male and female children, with girls reaching biological maturity up to two years in advance of boys (Lewis 2007, 39, 46). Attempts to develop an osteological methodology for identifying the sex of immature remains also received renewed vigour from the 1990s (*e.g.* Schutkowski 1993; De Vito and Saunders 1990; Molleson *et al.* 1998; Loth and Henneberg 2001; Rissech *et al.* 2003; Vlak *et al.* 2008), but these methods remain highly controversial, and unreliable (discussed in Cardoso 2010), while analyses based on the more reliable evidence of ancient DNA remain few, given issues of preservation and contamination, and the associated costs (Faerman *et al.* 1997; Brown 1998; Cooper and Poinar 2000; Mays and Faerman 2001; Brown and Brown 2011).

It has become apparent that determining age is not simply a matter of employing appropriate osteological methods. Indeed, a number of studies have argued that biological age is less crucial in dictating social attitudes to the very young than thresholds of activity – including the capacity to communicate or walk, and the weaning process (*e.g.* Wiley and Pike 1998; Kamp 2001; Lewis 2011, 1–3; Fahlander 2011, 17–18). Furthermore, drawing upon research into age identity undertaken in other disciplines such as sociology (*e.g.* Ginn and Arber 1995), Rebecca Gowland (2006, 143) has highlighted the varying ways in which age might be understood in past communities, including physiological/biological age (based on the physical ageing of the body), chronological age (the amount of time since birth), and social age (socially constructed norms concerning appropriate behaviour and attitudes for an age group). She has observed that osteologists have unhelpfully mixed up their terms, even in the context of studies that purport to be 'scientific', and have used culturally loaded terms – such as 'child' or 'adolescent' – to designate biological age categories, even though such terms can mean different things in different societies (Gowland 2006, 143). Osteologists also have a tendency to use the terms 'non-adult' or 'sub-adult' to refer to individuals below the ages of seventeen or eighteen years, and this also presents some culturally loaded assumptions, since in many cultures social adulthood commenced long before the age of eighteen years (Crawford 1991; 1999, 47–53; 2000, 170–2); moreover, these terms classify the youngest members of societies by what they lack – adulthood. The problems such issues present are compounded by the fact that osteologists do not use consistent age brackets and so one report's 'infant' is another's 'young child' (Lewis 2007, 5–7; Crawford 2011, 632). It has also been recognised that age cohorts are typically imbued by archaeologists with particular social norms, and that all members of an age group are typically seen as homogenous, with little regard for other factors that may influence age identity, such as status, gender and ethnicity (Gowland 2006, 145).

To account for the interaction between these different aspects of the social persona and age identity, Gowland (2006, 145) has encouraged archaeologists interpreting funerary evidence to consider 'the way that identities are played out over the entire life course', rather than focusing upon static, demarcated age groups and the biological age of the skeleton. She has applied such an approach to the funerary record from early Anglo-Saxon England, revealing that, for example, the deposition of 'feminine' grave goods varied across the life course, with the very youngest (<4 years) and the oldest (>35 years) female members of society receiving the fewest gendered grave goods (Gowland 2006, 147–51). Previous interpretations had drawn a correlation between such funerary provision and lesser social status, but Gowland (2006, 151) proposes, instead, that 'gender was simply not an over-riding characteristic of these stages of the life course'. Other studies have stressed the importance of studying not merely age categories, but rather 'the actual *process* of ageing' which should prompt us to ask 'when did significant age-related events occur, how did they impact on other social identities, and how were they expressed through material culture?' (Stoodley 2011, 642). The relationship between biological age and stage in the lifecycle was not consistent or necessarily predictable, as revealed by, for example, instances of older individuals buried with grave goods usually assigned to children, which may reflect something of the life experiences of that person; Nick Stoodley (2000, 468–9) has suggested that this reveals that 'for some individuals the lifecycle did not have a biological referent'.

The vulnerability of infants and children to disease and infection during the early years of life has been the premise behind the many studies seeking to investigate childhood health and disease in the medieval period. A formative study by Mary Lewis (2002) examined the remains of infants and children from four cemeteries dating from the ninth to the nineteenth century – Raunds Furnells (Northamptonshire), St Helen-on-the-Walls (York), Wharram Percy (North Yorkshire) and Christchurch, Spitalfields (London) – in order to compare the levels of morbidity and mortality of children from urban and rural environments, and to explore the impact of urbanisation and industrialisation on child health (Lewis 2002, 3). She concluded that identifiable differences in the morbidity and mortality rates of children were more likely to be due to the impact of industrialisation than urbanisation, with the former having the greatest negative impact on the health of children. Lewis and Gowland (2007) built on this study to investigate the contrast in infant mortality rates – defined as the number of infant deaths per 1000 births in one year – between the same two urban and two rural populations. The study set out to test the hypothesis that the processes of urbanisation and industrialisation would be reflected by a higher proportion of post-neonatal infant deaths (*i.e.* deaths between twenty-eight days and one year after birth) in the industrial population. Deaths up to twenty-seven days after birth (neonatal deaths) are widely regarded as being largely the result of maternal and genetic factors, such as low birth weight, congenital anomalies, and premature birth (Lewis and Gowland 2007, 118); in contrast, deaths of post-neonatal infants are regarded as reflecting wider socio-economic factors. The study found a higher rate of post-neonatal infant deaths for the sample from post-medieval London, indicating that factors such as poor sanitation and early weaning in the urban industrial environment had a detrimental effect on post-neonatal infant survival; lower numbers of neonatal deaths were interpreted as indicative of the wealth of the community and medical advances since the Middle Ages (Lewis and Gowland 2007, 127). This study also identified the fact that differing methods of calculating age on the basis of long bone lengths could affect the results generated by analysis of skeletal samples of infants (Lewis and Gowland 2007, 120–4).

The importance of contextualising osteological data within a wider archaeological and historical framework is a fundamental aspect of the so-called biocultural approach, which, in the words of Autumn Barrett and Michael Blakey (2011, 212), 'seeks to understand the dynamic relationship between biology and the culturally patterned environment in which life is lived'. The study of medieval childhood disease and disability has benefitted recently from such a holistic approach. For example, Elizabeth Craig-Atkins (formerly Craig) and Geoff Craig (2011) considered the burial of a six- to seven-year-old child displaying severe facial deformity from the Anglo-Saxon cemetery at Village Farm, Spofforth (North Yorkshire), which dates to between the mid-seventh and mid-ninth century. This child was affected by fibrous dysplasia, which resulted in a significant enlargement of the left jaw that was 'too substantial to have been hidden' (Craig and Craig 2011) (Figure 1.3). Given the visibility of the condition, and the potential responses it may have elicited from members of society, the authors examined whether this was reflected in the burial rites afforded to the child. It would seem,

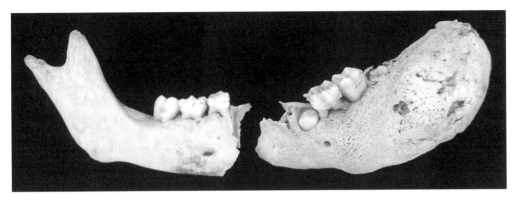

Figure 1.3. Mandible of a six- to seven-year-old child buried between the mid-seventh and mid-ninth century in a cemetery at Spofforth (North Yorkshire) (photograph courtesy of Dr Elizabeth Craig-Atkins).

however, that the child's simple earth-dug, west-east oriented burial was characteristic of normative funerary practice in this cemetery, and, therefore, despite a highly visible physical impairment, there was no evidence from the funerary record to suggest social differentiation, still less exclusion, of the child, at least not in death. Similarly, at the early medieval cemetery of Brownslade (Pembrokeshire), an infant, around two years of age, exhibiting characteristics attributable to achondroplasia, a form of short-limbed dwarfism, was afforded a normative burial in a stone-lined cist, close to other burials of children within the cemetery (Sables 2010, 53). Furthermore, the stone used for the construction of the cist had been brought to the site from another region suggesting that those responsible for the burial had invested both time and labour in obtaining the necessary resources (Sables 2010, 53). Yet, whilst this infant was buried alongside other members of the community, this was the only individual buried on their side. Achondroplasia is arguably more pronounced when an individual is laid on their back, and therefore the decision to bury the infant on their side may reflect an attempt to minimise its appearance (Groom *et al.* 2012, 144). By considering the evidence from the burial record and the wider cemetery context, these studies illustrate that despite visible, physically impairing conditions, infants and children were afforded normative burial rites suggesting that they took their place among the wider community in death, although in the case of the Brownslade infant their physical impairment seems to have prompted a variation in the way in which the child was placed in the grave.

The study of health, disease and physical impairment among children in past societies faces a number of challenges, including the issue of skeletal preservation, and the absence of diagnostic changes on the skeletons of children, amongst others (Wood *et al.* 1992; Lewis 2007, 20). However, certain conditions visible upon the adult skeleton can provide an indication of childhood health. For example, cribra orbitalia is commonly associated with anaemia during childhood but may remain visible upon the adult skeleton as pitting in the orbits (Stuart-Macadam 1985; 1992; Kamp 2001, 9; Gowland and Western 2012, 302) (Figure 1.4). A recent study has investigated the prevalence of cribra orbitalia amongst Anglo-Saxon populations, and the possibility that

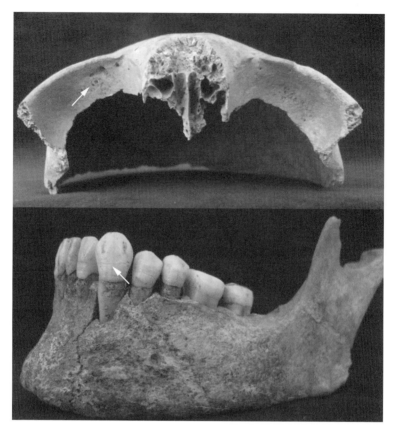

Figure 1.4. Frontal bone and mandible of an adult female aged twenty to twenty-five years from the later Anglo-Saxon cemetery at Black Gate, Newcastle-upon-Tyne (Tyne and Wear). Pitting in the orbits (marked with an arrow) is indicative of cribra orbitalia, a condition often linked with childhood dietary deficiency or illness. Dental enamel hypoplasia – the malformation of the tooth enamel, typically visible as linear or pitted defects (marked with an arrow) – is also an indicator of childhood stress. The survival of these skeletal markers on the adult skeleton enables osteologists to explore childhood experiences from adult skeletal remains (photographs courtesy of Dr Diana Mahoney Swales).

it was the result of malaria, which, while not leaving unequivocal skeletal markers, is strongly associated with anaemia (Gowland and Western 2012). The prevalence of cribra orbitalia amongst forty-six Anglo-Saxon inhumation populations was correlated with both geographic variables, such as the distribution of marshy locales, and historical accounts for occurrences in the nineteenth century of the malarial vector _Plasmodium vivax_, often termed 'ague'. It was revealed that cemeteries in lower-lying and fenland locations demonstrated higher levels of cribra orbitalia. Cribra orbitalia is not a conclusive indicator of malaria, but the distribution of this condition is not mirrored by that of other general indicators of childhood stress, such as enamel hypoplasia (Figure 1.4), and, thus, Rebecca Gowland and Gaynor Western (2012, 309) concluded that endemic malaria was a factor responsible for the observed prevalence among Anglo-Saxon communities of cribra orbitalia, which typically arises in childhood. This study illustrated the value of applying spatial analysis of cemetery location to the study of disease in past populations, and highlighted something of the regionally varying experiences of Anglo-Saxon childhood in terms of exposure to disease.

Stable isotope analysis

The proliferation of studies based on analysis of stable isotope evidence has revolutionised our understanding of both medieval diet and migration, and skeletal populations from across Britain dating to all parts of the medieval period have been subject to such investigation, which has provided an important counterpoint to studies based around analysis of grave goods which have tended, as we have seen, to focus on early Anglo-Saxon cemeteries. One particularly important area of recent investigation has been weaning patterns and breastfeeding practices in medieval populations (Jay 2009). Carbon and nitrogen isotopes from the diet are incorporated into collagen – the organic component of bone and dentine – via metabolic processes, and they reflect the primary source of protein consumed during life (Schwarz and Schoeninger 1991). Carbon isotopes (^{12}C, ^{13}C) are principally used to distinguish between the consumption of C_3 plants (such as barley, wheat) and C_4 plants (such as maize, sorghum), and marine and terrestrial proteins (Pate 1994, 172). Nitrogen isotopes (^{14}N, ^{15}N) primarily reflect the consumption of animal protein and form the focus of investigations into breastfeeding and weaning (Schoeninger 1985; Fogel *et al.* 1989; Schwarz and Schoeninger 1991; Schurr 1998; Fuller *et al.* 2006; Müldner and Richards 2005; Lee-Thorp 2008). Prior to the commencement of breastfeeding, the foetus or new-born infant will receive its dietary constituents from the food consumed by the mother, and will therefore share the same δ^{15}N value.[1] However, once breastfeeding commences, the infant is essentially feeding on its mother and is at a higher trophic position,[2] and as a consequence will have an enriched δ^{15}N value by comparison (Jay 2009, 169). As the infant is weaned and breast milk is gradually replaced by other foods, the infant's δ^{15}N value will decrease to reflect that of the new diet (Jay 2009, 169). Stable isotope analysis has permitted insights into the variability of breastfeeding practices, which has significant implications for the wellbeing of infants.

In addition to creating a bond between mother and child, breastfeeding can have a significantly positive impact on an infant's nutritional intake and health status (Knodel and Kintner 1977). Breastfeeding provides a primary source of nutrient-rich food, and prevents the infant from consuming contaminated food and water. Research on modern populations shows that infant deaths associated with various feeding practices could have been averted had the infants been breastfed exclusively for the first four to six months of life (Dettwyler and Fishman 1992, 176). In the medieval period, feeding bottles are known to have been used, in the form of, for example, cows' horns, which would, of course, have been unsterilised and have greatly increased the infant's exposure to infections such as gastroenteritis (Hagen 1992, 89).The duration and exclusivity of

---

[1] Isotope ratios are expressed using the delta (δ) notation, and values are given in parts per thousand (‰) relative to the isotopic composition of standard reference material (Pate 1994, 171).
[2] The position an organism occupies within the food chain.

breastfeeding, therefore, has an impact upon the infant's chances of survival. In studies of weaning practices at Wharram Percy it was discovered that weaning began around two years of age (Mays *et al.* 2002; Richards *et al.* 2002; Fuller *et al.* 2003). A similar weaning age for infants was also identified through isotopic analysis at the fourth- to sixth-century cemetery of Queenford Farm (Oxfordshire) (Fuller *et al.* 2006; for other studies on early medieval material see also Macpherson 2006; Macpherson *et al.* 2007; Haydock *et al.* forthcoming).

Stable isotope evidence is also increasingly employed in the study of migration, although the insights that this might provide about children have scarcely been addressed. An exception is a recent paper by the present authors that examined evidence for migration in Viking-Age Britain. Strontium and oxygen isotopes contribute to studies of migration as they reflect local geology and climate respectively, with strontium entering the food chain via groundwater and soil (Budd *et al.* 2004; Montgomery and Evans 2006; Evans *et al.* 2010), while oxygen isotopes in food and drink derive from meteoric waters, which is dependent on various factors including local climatic conditions, altitude and topography (Chenery *et al.* 2010). Both strontium and oxygen isotopes are incorporated into the enamel at the time of tooth mineralisation, which takes place between birth and twelve/thirteen years. Because enamel does not remodel, strontium and oxygen isotope signatures can therefore identify a person's place of childhood residence (Budd *et al.* 2003, 199). While this has long been recognised, in most studies the childhood place of residence has been accorded only passing significance, with the subsequent adult burial being typically accorded more attention (*e.g.* Budd *et al.* 2003; 2004; Lamb *et al.* 2012). A recent paper (Hadley and Hemer 2011) has, however, highlighted the potential for understanding migration during childhood by examining the stable isotope evidence from the teeth of children themselves, and also of undertaking analysis on multiple adult teeth, which form at different stages during childhood. The latter technique has the potential to identify whether children undertook multiple migrations, allowing archaeologists to explore the possible reasons for periods of mobility during childhood (see also Hemer this volume).

Toys and play

> Play is, *par excellence*, the defining activity of childhood, and toys are the defining artefacts that encapsulate the difference between 'childhood' and 'adulthood'
>
> *Crawford 2009, 56*

The other main area of investigation among medieval archaeologists interested in childhood has focussed on the evidence for toys and play. Until very recently, as Nicholas Orme (2008, 113) has observed, it was 'hardly conceived' that medieval toys existed to be studied, and it is the recovery of medieval toys only since the 1990s that has permitted insights into this aspect of the material culture of medieval children (Egan 1996; 1998; Forsyth and Egan 2005; McAlister 2013). Instrumental in the increased archaeological visibility of medieval toys were the creation of the *Portable Antiquities Scheme* in 1997, which provided a means for metal detector users in England and Wales to report their finds, and also the close working relationships of particular archaeologists

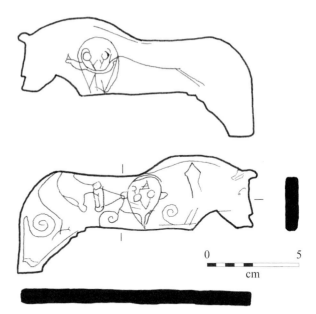

Figure 1.5. Schematic drawing of a wooden toy horse from Dublin (Ireland). The spirals and anthropomorphic figures have been interpreted as being drawn by a child (McAlister 2013; drawn by Dr Letty ten Harkel (after Gardela 2012, 237), to whom we are grateful for permission to reproduce the image).

with amateur collectors, such as the 'mudlarks' who recover finds from the Thames foreshore (Forsyth and Egan 2005, 14–25). Archaeological investigation has also added to the corpus in more recent times (Forsyth and Egan 2005, 26–31). Examples of medieval toys include base-metal figurines, miniature tableware and furniture, arms and armour, and tools (Egan 1996; Forsyth and Egan 2005). In addition, excavation in a range of waterlogged contexts, mainly urban, with good organic preservation has been instrumental in identifying wooden toys, such as toy boats, weapons and horses from Viking-Age Dublin (Ireland) and across the Viking diaspora as far as Russia (McAlister 2013) (Figure 1.5).

Analysis of play is important for our understanding of children in past communities; it is uncontroversial to identify it as an important aspect of childhood and an activity in which children are the principal participants (Baxter 2005, 62). It has been argued that the study of the material culture of play, of necessity, adopts a child-centred perspective. This is in contrast to other approaches to children's interaction with material culture, which tend to focus purely on their training as craft workers, and, while important, set children in the context of adult activities (Crawford 2009, 58). Yet, the initial publications on the emerging data set of medieval toys were, perhaps inevitably, largely descriptive as they sought to elucidate the range of evidence for medieval toys, and it has only been recently that the material culture of play has been both theorised and also set in its spatial context. Sally Crawford (2009) has, for example, drawn attention to the fact that the category of 'toy' needs to include not only items that were purpose made for use by children, but also a range of other artefacts that might be temporarily used by children in play. She has argued that 'this transient "toy" stage is not irrecoverable and invisible in archaeological terms if the role of children in the depositional pathway of objects into the archaeological record is reassessed with a child-centred theoretical framework' (Crawford 2009, 55). She reinforces this observation by citing a passage in the late ninth-century translation by King Alfred of Wessex of Pope Gregory's *Pastoral Care*, in which the king notes that 'we even warn our children from playing with our money' (Crawford 2009, 61; Sweet 1871, 391 for the quotation), which provides an example of children using for purposes of play items that would not be categorised normally as a toy, and, accordingly, she argues that we should regard a toy as much a concept as an object.

While it may be difficult to identify archaeologically the use for play of material culture that originated through the agency of adults, and was probably most frequently used by them, it is certainly not impossible if the contexts in which material culture is recovered are considered with the possibility of the agency of children in mind (see Crawford this volume). For example, the capacity of children to collect, curate and deposit artefacts that no longer have a use to adults has been highlighted as a potential factor in the distribution of broken artefacts in settlement contexts (Crawford 2009, 64–5). Pierced artefacts – spindle whorls, beads, animal bones, pottery – would have been appealing items for children's play, such as the use of pierced bones as musical instruments ('buzz bones'), and concentrations of such objects on rural settlements have been tentatively interpreted as indicative of the activities of children in moving artefacts around the site:

> These are tentative explanations, but even so, sensitivity to the role of children in collecting, retrieving and depositing used, worn and fragmentary artefacts which were transformed into play-objects at least allows a nuanced interpretation for the deposition of artefacts in the archaeological record
>
> *Crawford 2009, 65–6*

In a recent paper, Carenza Lewis (2009) has sought to develop the discussion about the importance to children of play through an examination of the spatial dimension of children's play in later medieval rural settlements. While the archaeological traces of children's play might initially appear to be difficult to discern, Lewis began her study by drawing on historical, anthropological, and folkloric sources to identify the range of games in which medieval children engaged and the form that these took. As she has pointed out, the games children played often involved the modification of the spaces around them – as they marked out a playing area of created bases and stations to run to and from – and they also often involved simple items, such as stones, wooden tops and marbles. There is, thus, some potential for these games to be traced archaeologically, even if the signals might be capable of multiple interpretations. To exemplify her argument, Lewis (2009, 97) drew attention to the famous 1560 painting by Pieter Bruegel, *Kinderspiele* (*Children's Games*), pointing out that:

> if all the children depicted in this scene departed, a range of physical objects would be left, some of which would be capable of survival into the archaeological record … From such evidence, it would be possible to reconstruct, or at least postulate the undertaking of a significant number of the activities in which the children had been engaged

With this observation in mind, Lewis (2009, 99–102) suggested that it was possible to reinterpret enigmatic post holes at rural settlements as relating to the activities of children and their games, in particular. Unusual, and otherwise unexplained, clusters of stones may also, she suggested (Lewis 2009, 103), have been the debris from children's games. While she acknowledges that her interpretation falls short of 'proof' that the archaeological evidence she has identified relates to children, she has, at the very least, posed some fundamental questions and called previous interpretations of nebulous features in to doubt, providing 'a much-needed shock to our established ways of thinking as we realise how completely we have wiped the sticky fingerprints of children off our views of the past' (Lewis 2009, 105).

Broadening the horizon

The foregoing review has highlighted the fact that there have been a number of important studies of the archaeological evidence for medieval children and childhood over the last two decades. However, this scholarship has been skewed towards particular issues and sources of evidence, and the current volume sets out to broaden the focus and to offer new ways of exploring the lives and experiences of medieval children through archaeological evidence. Sally Crawford examines the ways in which medieval archaeologists can begin to address the family, which she describes as the 'child production and nurturing unit', the study of which has hitherto been the preserve of historians. She suggests that one way of drawing on the archaeological record to understand the medieval family is 'to pay closer attention to the relationship between artefact, space and "maintenance activities" – the everyday use of space which can reveal social dynamics'. Rather than continuing to regard evidence for changes in the layout of buildings and their associated properties as indicative purely of social and economic developments, Crawford argues that they have much to reveal about families, as changes to domestic spaces impacted upon the 'daily practices and tasks ... carried out within and around these spaces'.

   Three chapters then explore aspects of work and play. Mark A. Hall takes a new approach to the study of children's play by exploring board and dice games, as he addresses the issue of how we can determine whether, and in what context, children played such games. As he notes, while there has been growing recognition of the material culture of play, through recovery of artefacts that were evidently toys, 'excavation reports remain wary of childhood, with toys and games often dealt with in a perfunctory, classificatory way, with the full implications of childhood for understanding both the archaeological record and the site side-stepped'. Yet, at the very least, miniature items are, on the whole, now readily regarded as the material culture of children's play, whereas board games are largely regarded as the preserve of adults. There is certainly documentary evidence to support the argument that skill at gaming was regarded as one of the attributes of men of high social standing, but how and in what context did they learn such skill at gaming? As Hall points out, there is archaeological evidence for gaming in school contexts, and written sources provide examples of adults looking back on their childhood and recalling the games that they played, which are often linked in some way to the adult activities that were to follow. Children played games for amusement, but board games also clearly played a part in elite contexts in training children for their adult roles, and in ritualising Christian beliefs. Play also provided adults with 'a rich source of metaphor on social, moral and religious behaviour'. As has already been noted in this introductory chapter, play can be a child-centred space, but, as Hall demonstrates, play can also be a 'serious' business in which adults encourage the training and development of children.

Sally V. Smith also grapples with the balancing act between studying children in their own right and in the context of their socialisation into the adult world. She explores the spatial dimension of childhood, and in doing so builds on the earlier work of Carenza Lewis (2009) discussed above. While Lewis focussed on the spaces of play, Smith explores children as 'actors in the social world' of medieval rural communities, and she argues that by considering the medieval countryside from the perspective of children we can begin to understand the processes of 'reproduction of particular aspects of medieval society'. Social reproduction has been of considerable interest to archaeologists, yet the role of children in this has been almost entirely overlooked. Smith's chapter is influenced by the insights to be gleaned from human geography, where the spaces of children's activities have been extensively explored. Human geographers tend to study contemporary societies, but, as Smith argues, the distinctions that they are able to identify between adult and child spaces may have relevance in the study of past societies. In particular, the reorganisation or removal of settlements could have particularly profound implications for children, whose social spaces were much more intimately associated with the home than were those of adults. Moreover, children's experiences of the spaces of the village community were arguably more communal than those of adults, and, again, changes to these spaces could impact on children in a much more acute manner than adults. It can also be suggested that medieval children would have been socialised in different ways according to the spatial organisation of the settlements in which they lived; this is a facet of medieval life on which archaeological evidence is especially informative, as documentary sources rarely permit insights into the physical form of settlements. As Smith suggests, perhaps it is the communal aspects of children's experiences of village spaces that plays a significant role in maintaining a sense of community identity over many generations, even in the face of pressures that emphasised the separateness of the household unit; perhaps it was in the communal spaces of the village community, and at the intersection between adult and child relationships that the village community was sustained. Smith's chapter also complements Lewis' (2009; and this volume) discussion of the potential for medieval archaeologists to draw on the insights generated by other disciplines.

Maureen Mellor explores the archaeological evidence for the involvement of children in the medieval workplace, focussing on the pottery industry. She draws on insights from ethnographic studies of pottery production to elucidate the potential contexts in which children may have contributed to this industry. As she argues, if we are to identify the contribution of children to the workplace, we need to know where to look. It is apparent from both ethnographic parallels and contemporary written sources that we should not seek the involvement of children in the pottery industry solely in the context of the manufacturing of the pottery products, but rather we need also to examine the broader setting of pottery production, and the reliance of the pottery industry on a range of ancillary activities to which children contributed. Children may also have played a part in producing the decoration and adding the details for some ceramic vessels; an interesting prompt for this suggestion is offered by the decorated fourteenth-century tiles from Tring (Hertfordshire), which depict scenes from the life of Jesus, including an image of the infant Jesus modelling a bird from clay. Mellor also identifies direct evidence for the involvement of children in ceramic manufacture in the form of their fingerprints, which, quite literally, trace the participation of children; Mellor cites examples of fingerprints of children around the parts of vessels to which the handles were fixed as indicative of one of the roles of children. In common with a number of the chapters in the present volume, Mellor highlights a form of evidence that needs to be more extensively studied and which has the potential to reveal much about the lives of medieval children. Fingerprints are commonly noted by ceramics specialists during their analysis of medieval pottery, but are rarely systematically recorded; it is to be hoped that this situation will be remedied now that the potential of this evidence has been highlighted.

The analysis of early medieval burials and osteological evidence has focused primarily on early Anglo-Saxon inhumations. In seeking to explore other aspects of the early medieval funerary record, the volume features three chapters that consider, in turn: the burial of infants in early Christian cemeteries in England; the treatment and disposal of infants and children in the cremation ritual of early Anglo-Saxon England; and childhood, children and mobility in early medieval western Britain, Wales in particular. Elizabeth Craig-Atkins considers the so-called 'eaves-drip burial' phenomenon, whereby infants and young children were buried in close proximity to structures in early Christian cemeteries. She draws on examples from a variety of published and unpublished sites, such as Raunds Furnells (Northamptonshire), Cherry Hinton (Hertfordshire), and Thwing (East Yorkshire). Previous interpretations of this funerary rite have imbued it with a baptismal significance, however as Craig-Atkins notes, the relevance of baptism amongst the general population is debatable, and, in any case, eaves-drip burials are not encountered in all early Christian cemeteries. Moreover, it would seem that the differential treatment of infants occurred across the Anglo-Saxon period, both prior to and after the conversion to Christianity. A significant observation is that the eaves-drip zone was not exclusively reserved for the very young, but rather, at most sites, a few adult females were buried amongst the clusters of burials of neonates and infants. Whilst some of these women may have died during or shortly after childbirth, Craig-Atkins suggests that it may also be a possibility that 'mother figures' were included to protect the groups of children after death, 'thus reflecting the linked identities of mother and child'.

In contrast to the large numbers of studies of early Anglo-Saxon inhumation cemeteries, there has been little investigation of the treatment and disposal of infants and children in early Anglo-Saxon cremation cemeteries, which are addressed in the present volume by Kirsty E. Squires. Through a consideration of cremated remains from several large early Anglo-Saxon cemeteries including Sancton I (East Yorkshire), Spong Hill (Norfolk), Cleatham and Elsham (both North Lincolnshire), Squires considers the demographic profiles and grave assemblages of these collections in order to redress the balance in studies of early Anglo-Saxon childhood. Consideration of the demographic data from cremation burials reveals that infants and children are equally underrepresented at cremation cemeteries as they are at inhumation cemeteries. Squires, thus, argues that the cremation of infants and children 'cannot, contrary to previous suggestions, account for the "missing" infants and children of inhumation practicing groups'. She also considers the inclusion of artefacts with the burials of infants and children from cremation cemeteries. A distinction on the basis of age was clearly made surrounding the inclusion of faunal remains, and it is suggested that the presence of these animal offerings with adolescents but not children may relate to rites of passage, and the roles and responsibilities afforded to older individuals. Other material culture recovered from infant and child cremations is seen as having distinctly domestic associations, reflecting the relationship between the deceased and their female carers. This chapter highlights that infants and children were perceived and treated in a similar manner in death despite their communities choosing to practice contrasting funerary rites.

K. A. Hemer then offers a complementary perspective to the study of Anglo-Saxon childhood, through a consideration of children and childhood in early medieval western Britain. Despite the paucity of skeletal remains from cemeteries in Wales, Hemer illustrates the significant contribution that stable isotope analysis for population mobility has made to the investigation of early medieval children, and highlights potential avenues for future research. She explores the concept of childhood and the lifecycle in early medieval Wales by drawing upon evidence from a range of documentary sources, including the Welsh lawbooks. The historical sources highlight the practice of fosterage and its potential impetus for the movement of children around the Welsh landscape. With this in mind, isotopic evidence and Late Antique funerary inscriptions are considered to investigate the mobility of children, and consideration is given to the use of multiple burials in this context. It is suggested that contemporaneous multiple burials could – in some cases – belong to migrant individuals who were afforded a multiple burial to reflect the fact that the individuals had travelled – and subsequently died – together.

Carenza Lewis rounds off the volume with an exploration of what archaeologists can draw from other disciplines and the approaches that they take to the study of childhood. She focusses on the evidence examined by historians, art historians, folklorists and literary scholars, and observes that the analytical perspective adopted by researchers in each of these disciplines has had a major impact on their capacity to examine childhood. Lewis argues that by looking across the disciplines, scholars of medieval childhood can better understand their own evidence. In particular, she draws attention to the fact that assertions based on analysis of one form of data, can be thrown into sharp relief when other forms of evidence are examined: her analysis reveals 'what a rich perspective different approaches can provide, and how inferences and ideas from one discipline can support, substantiate or illuminate those from other disciplines'. For example, it has sometimes been thought that the paucity of representations of children on later medieval funerary monuments reflects parental indifference, yet when set aside the parental mourning for the loss of a young daughter evident in the late fourteenth-century poem *Pearl* such a belief is shown to be implausible.

The archaeological study of children and childhood is a growing field of investigation, although, as we have seen, the focus among researchers of the medieval period has, until very recently, tended to focus on a comparatively limited data set and range of issues. This volume contributes to the broadening of the focus of archaeological research on medieval childhood. Archaeological evidence permits insights into aspects of medieval childhood that lie beyond the scope of the written record, and not only do archaeological approaches illuminate new aspects of medieval childhood, but they also serve to reveal how a focus on children can enhance our understanding of medieval society more generally.

Bibliography

Anderson, T. and Carter, A. 1995. An unusual osteitic reaction in a young medieval child. *International Journal of Osteoarchaeology* 5 (2), 192–5.

Arnold, C. J. 1980. Wealth and social structure, pp. 81–142 in Rahtz, P., Watts, L. and Dickinson, T. (eds), *Anglo-Saxon Cemeteries* (British Archaeological Reports British Series 82). Oxford: British Archaeological Reports.

Bacvarov, K. (ed.) 2008. *Babies Reborn: infant/child burials in pre- and protohistory. Proceedings of the XV World Congress UISPP* (Lisbon, 4–9 September 2006) (British Archaeological Reports International Series 1832). Oxford: Archaeopress.

Barrett, A. R. and Blakey, M. L. 2011. Life histories of enslaved Africans in colonial New York. A bioarchaeological study of the New York African burial ground, pp. 212–51 in Agarwal, S. C. and Glencross, B. A. (eds), *Social Bioarchaeology*. Oxford: Wiley-Blackwell.

Baxter, J. E. 2005. *The Archaeology of Childhood: children, gender and material culture*. Walnut Creek: Altamira Press.

Baxter, J. E. (ed.) 2006. *Children in Action: perspectives on the archaeology of childhood* (Archaeological Papers of the American Anthropological Association 15). Berkeley: University of California Press.

Beilke-Voigt, I. 2008. Burials of children in houses and settlements during the Roman Iron Age and early medieval period in northern Germany and Denmark, pp. 16–35 in Dommasnes, L. H. and Wrigglesworth, M. (eds), *Children, Identity and the Past*. Cambridge: Cambridge Scholars Publishing.

Bertelsen, R., Lillehammer, A. and Næss, J. (eds) 1987. *Were they all Men? An examination of sex roles in prehistoric society*. Stavanger: Stavanger Museum.

Bowers, R. 1996. To chorus from quartet: the performing resource for English Church polyphony c. 1390–1559, pp. 1–47 in Morehen, J. (ed.), *English Choral Practice 1400–1650*. Stamford: Paul Watkins.

Brown, K. 1998. Gender and sex: what can ancient DNA tell us? *Ancient Biomolecules* 2, 3–15.

Brown, T. and Brown, K. 2011. *Biomolecular Archaeology: an introduction*. Chichester: Wiley-Blackwell.

Brush, K. 1988. Gender and mortuary analysis in pagan Anglo-Saxon archaeology. *Archaeological Review from Cambridge* 7 (1), 76–89.

Buckberry, J. L. 2000. Missing, presumed buried? Bone diagenesis and the under-representation of Anglo-Saxon children. *Assemblage* 5 (available at: http://www.assemblage.group.shef. ac.uk/5/buckberr.html).

Buckberry, J. L. 2007. On sacred ground: social identity and churchyard burial in Lincolnshire and Yorkshire, *c.* 700–1100 AD, pp. 120–32 in Williams, H. and Semple, S. (eds), *Early Medieval Mortuary Practices* (Anglo-Saxon Studies in Archaeology and History 14). Oxford: Oxford University School of Archaeology.

Budd, P., Chenery, C., Montgomery, J., Evans, J. A. and Powlesland, D. 2003. Anglo-Saxon residential mobility at West Heslerton, North Yorkshire, UK from combined O- and Sr-isotope analysis, pp. 195–208 in Holland, J. G. and Tanner, S. D. (eds), *Plasma Source Mass Spectrometry: theory and applications*. Cambridge: Royal Society of Chemistry.

Budd, P., Millard, A., Chenery, C., Lucy, S. and Roberts, C. 2004. Investigating population movement by stable isotope analysis: a report from Britain. *Antiquity* 78 (299), 127–41.

Cardoso, H. F. V. 2010. Testing discriminant functions for sex determination from deciduous teeth. *Journal of Forensic Sciences* 55 (6), 1557–60.

Chenery, C., Müldner, G., Evans, J., Eckardt, H. and Lewis, M. 2010. Strontium and stable isotope evidence for diet and mobility in Roman Gloucester, UK. *Journal of Archaeological Science* 37 (1), 150–63.

Clark, J. G. 2002. Monastic education in late medieval England, pp. 25–40 in Barron, C. and Stratford, J. (eds), *The Church and Learning in Late Medieval Society*. Donington: Shaun Tyas.

Cooper, A. and Poinar, H. N. 2000. Ancient DNA: do it right or not at all. *Science* 289, 1139.

Craig, E. and Craig, G. 2011. The diagnosis and context of a facial deformity from an Anglo-Saxon cemetery at Spofforth, North Yorkshire. *International Journal of Osteoarchaeology* (preview available at: doi: 10.1002/oa.1288).

Crawford, S. 1991. When do Anglo-Saxon children count? *Journal for Theoretical Archaeology* 2, 17–24.

Crawford, S. 1993. Children, death and the afterlife in Anglo-Saxon England, pp. 83–91 in Filmer-Sankey, W. (ed.), *Anglo-Saxon Studies in Archaeology and History 6*. Oxford: Oxford University Committee for Archaeology.

Crawford, S. 1999. *Childhood in Anglo-Saxon England*. Stroud: Sutton.

Crawford, S. 2000. Children, grave goods and social status in early Anglo-Saxon England, pp. 169–79 in Sofaer-Derevenski, J. (ed.), *Children and Material Culture*. London: Routledge.

Crawford, S. 2007. Companions, co-incidences or chattels? Children and their role in early Anglo-Saxon multiple burials, pp. 83–92 in Crawford, S. and Shepherd, G. (eds), *Children, Childhood and Society* (British Archaeological Reports International Series 1696). Oxford: Archaeopress.

Crawford, S. 2008. Special burials, special buildings? An Anglo-Saxon perspective on the interpretation of infant burials in association with rural settlement structures, pp. 197–204 in Bacvarov, K. (ed.), *Babies Reborn: infant/child burials in pre- and protohistory. Proceedings of the XV UISPP World Congress (Lisbon, 4–9 September 2006)/Actes du XV Congrès Mondial (Lisbonne, 4–9 Septembre 2006) Vol. 24, Session WS26* (British Archaeological Reports International Series 1832). Oxford: Archaeopress.

Crawford, S. 2009. The archaeology of play things: theorising a toy stage in the 'biography' of objects. *Childhood in the Past* 2, 55–70.

Crawford, S. 2011. The disposal of dead infants in Anglo-Saxon England from c. 500–1066: an overview, pp. 75–84 in Lally, M. and Moore, A. (eds), *(Re)Thinking the Little Ancestor: new perspectives on the archaeology of infancy and childhood* (British Archaeological Reports International Series 2271). Oxford: Archaeopress.

Crawford, S. and Shepherd, G. (eds) 2007. *Children, Childhood and Society* (British Archaeological Reports International Series 1696). Oxford: Archaeopress.

De Vito, C. and Saunders, S. 1990. A discriminant function analysis of deciduous teeth to determine sex. *Journal of Forensic Sciences* 35 (4), 845–58.

Dettwyler, K. A. and Fishman, C. 1992. Infant feeding practices and growth. *Annual Review of Anthropology* 21, 171–204.

Dommasnes, L. and Wrigglesworth, W. (eds) 2008. *Children, Identity and the Past*. Cambridge: Cambridge Scholars Publishing.

Egan, G. 1988. *Base Metal Toys*. Finds Research Group Datasheet 10.

Egan, G. 1996. *Playthings from the Past*. London: Jonathan Horne.

Egan, G. 1998. Miniature toys of medieval childhood. *British Archaeology* 35, 10–11.

Egan, G. 2011. Ceramic toys and trifles: some medieval playthings and a Kingston-type ware knight, pp. 194–8 in Dunsmore, A. (ed.), *This Blessed Plot, This Earth. English pottery studies in honour of Jonathan Horne*. London: Paul Holberton.

Evans, J. A., Montgomery, J., Wildman, J. and Boulton, N. 2010. Spatial variations in biosphere $^{87}Sr/^{86}Sr$ in Britain. *Journal of the Geological Society* 167 (1), 1–4.

Faerman, M., Kahila, G., Smith, P., Greenblatt, C., Stager, L., Filon, D. and Oppenheim, A. 1997. DNA analysis reveals the sex of infanticide victims. *Nature* 385, 212–13.

Fahlander, F. 2011. Subadult or subaltern? Children as serial categories, pp. 14–23 in Lally, M. and Moore, A. (eds), *(Re)Thinking the Little Ancestor: new perspectives on the archaeology of infancy and childhood* (British Archaeological Reports International Series 2271). Oxford: Archaeopress.

Fogel, M. L., Tuross, N. and Owsley, D. 1989. Nitrogen isotope tracers of human lactation in modern and archaeological populations. *Annual Report of the Director, Geophysical Laboratory (1988–1989)*. Washington: Carnegie Institution of Washington.

Forsyth, H. and Egan, G. 2005. *Toys, Trifles and Trinkets: base-metal miniatures from London 1150–1800*. London: Unicorn Press.

Fuller, B. T., Molleson, T. I., Harris, D. A., Gilmour, L. T. and Hedges, R. E. M. 2006. Isotopic evidence for breastfeeding and possible adult dietary differences from late/sub-Roman Britain. *American Journal of Physical Anthropology* 129 (1), 45–54.

Fuller, B. T., Richards, M. P. and Mays, S. 2003. Stable carbon and nitrogen isotope variations in tooth dentine serial sections from Wharram Percy. *Journal of Archaeological Science* 30 (12), 1673–84.

Gardela, L. 2012. What the Vikings did for fun? Sports and pastimes in medieval northern Europe. *World Archaeology* 44 (2), 234–47.

Gilchrist, R. 2008. Magic for the dead? The archaeology of magic in later medieval burials. *Medieval Archaeology* 52, 119–60.

Ginn, J. and Arber, S. 1995. 'Only connect': gender relations and ageing, pp. 1–14 in Arber, S. and Ginn, J. (eds), *Connecting Gender and Ageing. A sociological approach*. Birmingham: Open University Press.

Gläser, M. (ed.) 2012. *Lübecker Kolloquium zur Stadtarchäologie im Hanseraum VIII: Kindhit and Jugend, Ausbildung und Freizeit*. Lübeck: Verlag Schmidt-Romhild.

Glencross, B. and Stuart-Macadam, P. 2000. Childhood trauma in the archaeological record. *International Journal of Osteoarchaeology* 10 (3), 198–209.

Goldberg, J. P. J. 2008. Childhood and gender in later medieval England. *Viator* 39 (1), 249–62.

Goodman, A. H. and Armelagos, G. J. 1989. Infant and childhood morbidity and mortality risks in archaeological populations. *World Archaeology* 21 (2), 225–43.

Gowland, R. 2006. Ageing the past: examining age identity from funerary evidence, pp. 143–55 in Gowland, R. and Knüsel, C. (eds), *Social Archaeology of Funerary Remains*. Oxford: Oxbow.

Gowland, R. and Chamberlain, A. 2002. A Bayesian approach to ageing perinatal skeletal material from archaeological sites: implications for the evidence for infanticide in Roman-Britain. *Journal of Archaeological Science* 29 (6), 677–85.

Gowland, R. L. and Western, A. G. 2012. Morbidity in the marshes: using spatial epidemiology to investigate skeletal evidence for malaria in Anglo-Saxon England (AD 410–1050). *American Journal of Physical Anthropology* 147 (2), 301–11.

Gräslund, A.-S. 1973. Barn i Birka. *Tor* 15, 161–79.

Groom, P., Schlee, D., Hughes, G., Crane, P., Ludlow, N. and Murphy, K. 2012. Two early medieval cemeteries in Pembrokeshire: Brownslade Barrow and West Angle Bay. *Archaeologia Cambrensis* 160, 133–203.

Guy, H., Masset, C. and Baud, C. 1997. Infant taphonomy. *International Journal of Osteoarchaeology* 7 (3), 221–9.

Hadley, D. M. 2010. Burying the socially and physically distinctive in and beyond the Anglo-Saxon churchyard, pp. 101–13 in Buckberry, J. L. and Cherryson, A. (eds), *Burial in Later Anglo-Saxon England, c. 650–1100 A.D.* Oxford: Oxbow.

Hadley, D. M. 2011. Later Anglo-Saxon burial, pp. 288–314 in Hamerow, H., Hinton, D. and Crawford, S. (eds), *The Oxford Handbook of Anglo-Saxon Archaeology*. Oxford: Oxford University Press.

Hadley, D. M. and Hemer, K. A. 2011. Microcosms of migration: children and early medieval population movement. *Childhood in the Past* 4, 63–78.

Hagen, A. 1992. *A Handbook of Anglo-Saxon Food: processing and consumption*. Hockwold: Anglo-Saxon Books.

Hamerow, H. 2006. 'Special deposits' in Anglo-Saxon settlements. *Medieval Archaeology* 50, 1–30.

Hanawalt, B. 1977. Childrearing among the lower classes of late medieval England. *Journal of Interdisciplinary History* 8 (1), 1–22.

Hanawalt, B. 1986. *The Ties That Bound: peasant families in medieval England*. Oxford and New York: Oxford University Press.

Hanawalt, B. 1993. *Growing Up in Medieval London: the experience of childhood in history*. Oxford: Oxford University Press.

Haydock, H., Clarke, L., Craig-Atkins, E., Howcroft, R. and Buckberry, J. L. 2014. Weaning at Anglo-Saxon Raunds: implications for changing breastfeeding practice in Britain over two millennia. *American Journal of Physical Anthropology* 151 (4), 604–612.

Herring, D., Saunders, S. and Katzenberg, M. 1998. Investigating the weaning process in past populations. *American Journal of Physical Anthropology* 105 (4), 425–39.

Heywood, C. 2010. *Centuries of Childhood*: an anniversary – and an epitaph. *Journal of the History of Childhood and Youth* 3 (3), 343–65.

Hoppa, R. D. 1992. Evaluating human skeletal growth: an Anglo-Saxon example. *International Journal of Osteoarchaeology* 2 (4), 275–88.

Hoppa, R. D. and FitzGerald, C. M. 1999. *Human Growth in the Past: studies from bones and teeth*. Cambridge: Cambridge University Press.

Jay, M. 2009. Breastfeeding and weaning behaviour in archaeological populations: evidence from the isotopic analysis of skeletal materials. *Childhood in the Past* 2, 163–79.

Kamp, K. A. 2001. Where have all the children gone? The archaeology of childhood. *Journal of Archaeological Method and Theory* 8 (1), 1–34.

Knodel, J. and Kintner, H. 1977. The impact of breast feeding patterns on the biometric analysis of infant mortality. *Demography* 14 (4), 391–409.

Lally, M. and Moore, A. (eds) 2011. *(Re)Thinking the Little Ancestor: new perspectives on the archaeology of infancy and childhood* (British Archaeological Reports International Series 2271). Oxford: Archaeopress.

Lamb, A., Melikian, M., Ives, R. and Evans, J. 2012. Multi-isotope analysis of the population of the lost medieval village of Auldhame, East Lothian, Scotland. *Journal of Analytical Atomic Spectrometry* 27 (5), 765–77.

Lampl, M. and Johnston, F. E. 1996. Problems in the aging of skeletal juveniles: perspectives from maturation assessments of living children. *American Journal of Physical Anthropology* 101 (3), 345–55.

Lee-Thorp, J. A. 2008. On isotopes and old bones. *Archaeometry* 50 (6), 925–50.

Lewis, C. 2009. Children's play in the later medieval English countryside. *Childhood in the Past* 2, 86–108.

Lewis, M. 2000. Non-adult palaeopathology: current status and future potential, pp. 39–57 in Cox, M. and Mays, S. (eds), *Human Osteology in Archaeology and Forensic Science*. London: Greenwich Medical Media.

Lewis, M. 2002. *Urbanisation and Child Health in Medieval and Post-Medieval England: an assessment of the morbidity and mortality of non-adult skeletons from the cemeteries of two urban and two rural sites (AD 850–1859)* (British Archaeological Reports British Series 339). Oxford: Archaeopress.

Lewis, M. 2007. *The Bioarchaeology of Children: perspectives from biological and forensic anthropology.* Cambridge: Cambridge University Press.

Lewis, M. 2011. The osteology of infancy and childhood: misconceptions and potential, pp. 1–13 in Lally, M. and Moore, A. (eds), *(Re)Thinking the Little Ancestor: new perspectives on the archaeology of infancy and childhood* (British Archaeological Reports International Series 2271). Oxford: Archaeopress.

Lewis, M. and Gowland, R. 2007. Brief and precarious lives: infant mortality in contrasting sites from medieval and post-medieval England (AD 850–1859). *American Journal of Physical Anthropology* 134 (1), 117–29.

Lewis, M. and Roberts, C. 1997. Growing pains: the interpretation of stress indicators. *International Journal of Osteoarchaeology* 7 (6), 581–6.

Lillehammer, G. 1989. A child is born. The child's world in archaeological perspective. *Norwegian Archaeological Review* 22 (2), 91–105.

Lillehammer, G. (ed.) 2010. *Socialization. Recent research on childhood and children in the past.* Stavanger: Stavanger Museum.

Liversidge, H. 1994. Accuracy of age estimation from developing teeth in a population of known age (0–5.4 years). *International Journal of Osteoarchaeology* 4 (1), 37–45.

Loth, S. and Henneberg, M. 2001. Sexually dimorphic mandibular morphology in the first few years of life. *American Journal of Physical Anthropology* 115 (2), 179–86.

Lucy, S. 1994. Children in early medieval cemeteries. *Archaeological Review from Cambridge* 13 (2), 21–34.

Lucy, S. 1998. *The Early Anglo-Saxon Cemeteries of East Yorkshire: an analysis and reinterpretation* (British Archaeological Reports British Series 272). Oxford: J. & E. Hedges.

Macpherson, P. 2006. *Tracing Change: an isotopic investigation into Anglo-Saxon childhood diet.* Unpublished Ph.D. thesis, University of Sheffield.

Macpherson, P., Chamberlain, A. and Chenery, C. 2007. Tracing change: childhood diet at the Anglo-Saxon Blackgate cemetery, Newcastle upon Tyne, pp. 37–43 in Robson-Brown, K. and Roberts, A. (eds), *BABAO 2004: proceedings of the 6th annual conference of the British Association of Biological Anthropologists and Osteoarchaeology, University of Bristol* (British Archaeological Research Reports International Series 1623). Oxford: Archaeopress.

McAlister, D. 2013. Childhood in Viking and Hiberno-Scandinavian Dublin, 800–1100, pp. 86–102 in Hadley, D. M. and Ten Harkel, A. (eds), *Everyday Life in Viking-Age Towns: social approaches to towns in England and Ireland, c. 800–1100.* Oxford: Oxbow.

Mays, S. 1993. Infanticide in Roman Britain. *Antiquity* 67 (257), 883–8.

Mays, S. and Faerman, M. 2001. Sex identification in some putative infanticide victims from Roman Britain using ancient DNA. *Journal of Archaeological Science* 28, 555–9.

Mays, S., Richards, M. R. and Fuller, B. T. 2002. Bone stable isotope for infant feeding in mediaeval England. *Antiquity* 76 (293), 654–65.

Molleson, T., Cruse, K. and Mays, S. 1998. Some sexually dimorphic features of the human juvenile skull and their value in sex determination in immature skeletal remains. *Journal of Archaeological Science* 25 (8), 719–28.

Montgomery, J. and Evans, J. A. 2006. Immigrants on the Isle of Lewis: combining traditional funerary and modern isotope evidence to investigate social differentiation, migration and dietary change in the Outer Hebrides of Scotland, pp.122–42, in Gowland, R. and Knüsel, C. (eds), *Social Archaeology of Funerary Remains*. Oxford: Oxbow.

Müldner, G. and Richards, M. P. 2005. Fast or feast: reconstructing diet in later medieval England by stable isotope analysis. *Journal of Archaeological Science* 32 (1), 39–48.

Orme, N. 1973. *English Schools in the Middle Ages*. London: Methuen.

Orme, N. 2001. *Medieval Children*. London: Yale University Press.

Orme, N. 2006. *Medieval Schools*. London: Yale University Press.

Orme, N. 2008. Medieval childhood: challenge, change and achievement. *Childhood in the Past* 1, 106–19.

Ortner, D. and Mays, S. 1998. Dry-bone manifestations of rickets in infancy and early childhood. *International Journal of Osteoarchaeology* 8 (1), 45–55.

Pader, E. J. 1980. Material symbolism and social relations in mortuary studies, pp. 143–59 in Rahtz, P., Watts, L. and Dickinson, T. (eds), *Anglo-Saxon Cemeteries* (British Archaeological Reports British Series 82). Oxford: British Archaeological Reports.

Pader, E. J. 1982. *Symbolism, Social Relations and the Interpretation of Mortuary Remains* (British Archaeological Reports British Series 130). Oxford: British Archaeological Reports.

Page, M. R. 2011. Ble mae'r babanod? (Where are the babies?): infant burial in early medieval Wales, pp. 100–9 in Lally, M. and Moore, A. (eds), *(Re)Thinking the Little Ancestor: new perspectives on the archaeology of infancy and childhood* (British Archaeological Reports International Series 2271). Oxford: Archaeopress.

Pate, D. F. 1994. Bone chemistry and palaeodiet. *Journal of Archaeological Method and Theory* 1 (2), 161–95.

Rega, E. 2000. The gendering of children in the early Bronze-Age cemetery of Mokrin, pp. 238–49 in Hurcombe, L. and McDonald, M. (eds), *Gender and Material Culture in Archaeological Perspective*. New York: Macmillan.

Ribot, I. and Roberts, C. 1996. A study of non-specific stress indicators and skeletal growth in two medieval subadult populations. *Journal of Archaeological Science* 23 (1), 67–79.

Richards, M. P., Mays, S. and Fuller, B. T. 2002. Stable carbon and nitrogen isotope values of bone and teeth reflect weaning age at the medieval Wharram Percy site. *American Journal of Physical Anthropology* 119 (3), 205–10.

Rissech, C., Garcia, M. and Malgosa, A. 2003. Sex and age diagnosis by ischium morphometric analysis. *Forensic Science International* 135 (3), 188–96.

Sables, A. 2010. Rare example of an early medieval dwarf infant from Brownslade, Wales. *International Journal of Osteoarchaeology* 20 (1), 47–53.

Saunders, S. 1992. Subadult skeletons and growth related studies, pp. 1–20 in Saunders, S. and Katzenberg, M. (eds), *Skeletal Biology of Past Populations: advances in research methods*. New York: Wiley-Liss.

Saunders, S. and Hoppa, R. 1993. Growth deficit in survivors and non-survivors: biological mortality bias in subadult skeletal samples. *Yearbook of Physical Anthropology* 36, 127–51.

Schurr, M. R. 1998. Using stable nitrogen isotopes to study weaning behaviour in past populations. *World Archaeology* 30 (2), 327–42.

Schoeninger, M. J. 1985. Trophic level effects on 15N/14N and 13C/12C ratios in bone collagen and strontium levels in bone mineral. *Journal of Human Evolution* 14 (5), 515–25.

Schutkowski, H. 1993. Sex determination of infant and juvenile skeletons: I. Morphognostic features. *American Journal of Physical Anthropology* 90 (2), 199–205.

Schwarz, H. P and Schoeninger, M. J. 1991. Stable isotope analysis in human nutritional ecology. *Yearbook of Physical Anthropology* 34, 288–321.

Scott, E. 1999. *The Archaeology of Infancy and Infant Death* (British Archaeological Reports International Series 819). Oxford: Archaeopress.

Sellevold, B. 1997. Children's skeletons and graves in Scandinavian archaeology, pp. 15–25 in De Boe, G. and Verhaeghe, F. (eds), *Death and Burial in Medieval Europe*. Bruges: IAP Rapporten.

Shahar, S. 1990. *Childhood in the Middle Ages*. London: Routledge.

Sofaer-Derevenski, J. (ed.) 2000. *Children and Material Culture*. London: Blackwell.

Stoodley, N. 1999. *The Spindle and the Spear: a critical enquiry into the construction and meaning of gender in the early Anglo-Saxon burial rite* (British Archaeological Reports British Series 288). Oxford: British Archaeological Reports.

Stoodley, N. 2000. From the cradle to the grave: age organization and the early Anglo-Saxon burial rite. *World Archaeology* 31 (3), 456–72.

Stoodley, N. 2011. Childhood to old age, pp. 641–66 in Hamerow, H., Hinton, D. and Crawford, S. (eds), *The Oxford Handbook of Anglo-Saxon Archaeology*. Oxford: Oxford University Press.

Stuart-Macadam, P. 1985. Porotic hyperostosis: representative of a childhood condition. *American Journal of Physical Anthropology* 66 (4), 391–8.

Stuart-Macadam, P. 1992. Porotic hyperostosis: a new perspective. *American Journal of Physical Anthropology* 87 (1), 39–47.

Sweet, H. (ed.) 1871. *King Alfred's West Saxon Version of Gregory's Pastoral Care* (Early English Text Society original series 45). Oxford: Oxford University Press.

Tringham, R. 1991. Households with faces: the challenge of gender in prehistoric architectural remains, pp. 93–131 in Gero, J. and Conkey, M. (eds), *Engendering Archaeology: women and prehistory*. Oxford: Blackwell.

Vlak, D., Roksandic, M. and Schillaci, M. A. 2008. Greater sciatic notch as a sex indicator in juveniles. *American Journal of Physical Anthropology* 137 (3), 309–15.

Weber, B. 1982. Leker eller? *Viking* 4, 81–92.

Wiley, A. and Pike, I. 1998. An alternative method for assessing early mortality in contemporary populations. *American Journal of Physical Anthropology* 107 (3), 315–30.

Wood, J. W., Milner G. R., Harpending, H. C. and Weiss, K. M. 1992. The osteological paradox: problems of inferring prehistoric health from skeletal samples. *Current Anthropology* 33 (4), 343–70.

2. Archaeology of the Medieval Family

Sally Crawford

It is relatively simple to study the *history* of the medieval family; the topic is a well-established area of research. Comparative information about the *archaeology* of the family is, however, more elusive and the subject is largely unexplored. Settlement archaeology tends to focus on economy, landscape, and building layout; burial archaeology focuses on ritual and religion; church archaeology on architecture and liturgy; and material culture, with rare exceptions, has not been discussed in the context of families. Archaeologies of life course have focussed on age, gender and status, but considerations of the private lives of men and women in relation to their family members, and of the relationships between family members through material culture evidence, have not yet been central to archaeological discussion and interpretation.

In this chapter I will examine more closely the absence of 'the family' as a topic in medieval archaeology compared to its recognised significance in medieval documentary sources, and will argue for the importance of recognising that family relationships form a core organising principle in aspects of medieval settlement and interpretation. 'Family', as it is used in this chapter and in histories of the medieval family, refers to the resident familial group alone, not the kinship network in general, nor any 'familial' relationships between distinct households (cf. Laslett and Wall 1972, ix), though, as James Casey (1989) has argued, too close an insistence on the meaning of 'family' may obscure cultural interpretations of 'family' and 'family dynamics'; see the introduction to his *The History of the Family* for a historiography of terminology and approaches to the concept of family.

Histories of the family

The history of the family has been a central strand in the study of medieval England for decades (*e.g.* Britton 1977; Goody 1983, 4, where the study of the European family and marriage is placed in a 150 year timespan). A grasp of family dynamics is seen as essential to an understanding of wider medieval social institutions and culture – indeed, for some historians, the shape of the medieval family defined and differentiated medieval culture from other societies: 'how was it', asked Jack Goody (1983, 5), 'that after about AD 300 certain general features of European patterns of kinship and marriage came to take a different shape from those of ancient Rome, Greece, Israel and Egypt, and from those of the societies ... that succeeded them?'. Family life has been studied by historians for insights into lordship, inheritance, religion, morality, politics, economics, agricultural change, demographic change, and education (see, for example, Houlbrooke 1984, 1–2; Fleming 2001, 1). Family is not just an accepted aspect of modern medieval historical investigation. It was also a matter of interest to medieval writers, too, in social, economic and religious terms. Medieval documents record births, deaths and marriages, the lives and interactions of families, ideal and less desirable families, and vagrancy and the breakdown of family ties (Razi 1980; Hanawalt 1986). History titles relating to the medieval family abound.

The perceived importance of 'family' to a study of society appears evident to historians: *Medieval Families: perspectives on marriage, household, and children*, edited by Carol Neel and published in 2004, brought together a collection of essays ranging in date from the 1970s to the 1990s, showing how, over a period of thirty years, the study of the family in medieval history, by historians, art historians, and literary scholars, had evolved and developed. Archaeology is absent from this collection.

The family in archaeological contexts has been largely unexplored. To highlight the absence of 'family' as a topic in medieval archaeology, entering 'history, family, medieval' into a search of *Amazon* recently produced 360 results. By contrast, entering 'archaeology, family, medieval' into *Amazon* yielded just six results, only one of which (*Medieval Lough Ce: history, archaeology and family* published in 2010 by Thomas Finan) was about archaeology or by an archaeologist, and none of which referred to the medieval family in England (Finan 2010; Rawson and Weaver 1999; Hill and Swan 1998; Redfield 2003; Keats-Rohan 1997; Lavelle 2007). Tom McNeill's (1992, 29) tongue-in-cheek comment that medieval castles were inhabited by two species – men and horses – still holds true throughout wider medieval society, as far as readings of the archaeological evidence are concerned. Archaeological discussion of the ways in which children and their carers interacted with the material culture around them, of the private lives of women and men in relation to their family members, and of the relationships between family members, is rare.

There is growing awareness, however, that this gap needs filling. A starting point for approaching the material culture of the family – in the sense of an interaction between parents and their children, or people who are associated with each other in a parallel of that relationship (parents and adopted or step-children, for example) – may be to consider how people organise their private, rather than their public, lives. As Simone Roux (2000, 695), in the entry for 'house' in the *Encyclopedia of the Middle Ages*, noted: '... the "house" is also the family that it represents in society. It is *par excellence* the setting for private life'.

Archaeological evidence for medieval houses is not lacking. It is disappointing, then, that archaeologists have given relatively little attention to private life and family in past discussions of medieval domestic buildings (see Smith 2010, 64 for a critique of the distance between archaeological and historical approaches to the study of medieval settlements). It is not that archaeologists are unaware of a direct relationship between society and the spaces people build and inhabit. Multi-period works on social archaeology and social space have emphasised the need to see buildings as frameworks which express the societies that use them (*e.g.* Hillier and Hanson 1984; Parker Pearson and Richards 1994; Locock 1994). Anthropologists have long recognised the importance to archaeology of understanding households, if not families: 'the degree of fit ... between households and their domestic buildings is an ethnographic fact and an assumption necessary for the reconstruction of past social organisation' (David 1971, 111). This view has been reiterated with passing decades: 'spatial structure is now seen not merely as an arena in which social life unfolds, but rather as a medium through which social relations are produced and reproduced' (Gregory and Urry 1985, 3). W. G. Hoskins noted in 1967 that: 'we ought to place all types of houses in their human background and relate them to the social and economic history of their immediate background' (Hoskins 1967, 94), and this view point was subsequently expressly recognised in works on medieval buildings (see, for example, Grenville 1997, 16–22).

One way of approaching the relationship between people and the buildings they live in is through access analysis, which allows space, architecture and society to be mapped. Openings, passageways and the difficulty or otherwise of accessing spaces within buildings can be used to articulate ideas about public and private space, and restriction and flow of movement. Principles of access analysis have been applied to a variety of medieval dwelling spaces, such as castles (Fairclough 1992), nunneries (Gilchrist 1994) and London houses (Schofield 1994), which for the first time encouraged archaeologists to consider the ways in which buildings were inhabited, as opposed merely to tracing structural development of buildings. Studies of architecture have also helped to define public and private spaces, as well as emphasising modifications of buildings and spaces over time. In her volume on medieval housing, Jane Grenville (1997, 67), for example, notes that the medieval hall was originally a public place for the lord, with private apartments 'to which the lord could withdraw'; by the later medieval period, 'the private dining-room of the lord and his immediate family moved yet again' (Grenville 1997, 115). In her index, Jane Grenville asks readers, under the entry for 'family', to refer to 'household', expressing the profound difficulty of separating the two words in archaeological interpretation. Yet, in fact, her discussion does argue for a cultural differentiation of 'family' and 'household' which she identified in the use of building space – while the lord (and his family) were in their private chambers, 'the household – that is, indentured retainers and senior servants – would be accommodated in lodgings ranges' (Grenville 1997, 116).

Where archaeologists refer to 'the family', it is frequently in terms of status and display, and 'family' is effectively being used as a synonym for 'male head of family' (*e.g.* Alcock and Woodfield 1996; Martin *et al.* 1993). This kind of interpretation, though saying much about domestic buildings in terms of economy and hierarchy, rarely yields any information about gender or family relations. This may be because, as Matthew Johnson (1997, 146–8) has noted, 'we could argue that it [the hall] deliberately fails to acknowledge this as an aspect of social relations'. Building morphology is readily linked by archaeologists to power and patriarchy, but the social experience of families is apparently more elusive (Johnson 1993; Johnson 2006).

It is hardly surprising that archaeologists have approached settlement sites from a spatial/functional/status perspective. Separating 'household' and 'family' has been an extremely difficult proposition for archaeologists, not least because of the fluidity of the terms: 'the nature of the relationship varies according to social, cultural, economic, and environmental factors, and the variation may be very great even within a limited area.

For these and other reasons archaeologists have fought shy of attributing households to houses' (Nicholas 1969, 111). Archaeologists may have 'fought shy' of the problem in the late 1960s, but the discipline has moved on. Out of American anthropological and archaeological studies, the archaeology of household has emerged as a discipline in its own right (see especially Bender 1967; Yanagiasako 1979; Wilk and Rathje 1982; Robin 2003), centring on the economic links between production, space and people (Hendon 2004, 272; for the archaeology of household see, for example, Meskell and Preucel 2004; Allison 1999; Samson 1990; Wilk and Rathje 1982). As such, the 'household' as a unit of production does not map directly onto 'the family', though there are areas of overlap (Hendon 2004, 272; see Birdwell-Pheasant and Lawrence-Zuniga 1999, 26 for an anthropological perspective).

Is there a value in being sensitive to the different nuances of 'household' and 'family'? Anita Guerreau's entry on 'family' in the *Encyclopedia of the Middle Ages* offers helpful insights. First, she establishes that the modern idea of a family – 'a group of persons united by recognised links of consanguinity and marriage' – chimes with what was understood by the term in the Middle ages, but then goes on to discuss the problem of understanding the family in terms of space and status:

> the way in which members of a network of this nature are distributed in space has to do with residence. The relationship between family organization and manner of residence is neither automatic nor constant: in one and the same society, the composition of residential units, domestic groups, varies according to social class … and the nucleus formed by those linked by kinship is in itself subject to various transformations in time, caused by births, deaths and marriages
>
> *Guerreau 2000, 531*

The family is central to place, space and status – but the family is also mutable. Families grow and diminish in size, members live together or separate, and extend their networks of affiliation across space – from village to town, from region to region.

In this sense, to understand changing domestic space only in terms of new technologies, ideologies, or changing power structures within society is to overlook the change in the physical requirements of buildings – how family members negotiate their places within the framework of space. Humans' physical needs and abilities change over time, and spaces may be modified to take dynamic family requirements into account, as babies are born or the elderly become infirm, for example. But families do not dwell in only one house – children and parents travel away from each other. What are the archaeological implications here for the movement of objects – and people – from towns to villages and vice versa? Guerreau (2000, 53) re-affirms the need for archaeologists to recognise the dynamic of 'family' and to incorporate it into their theories of interpretation: 'the family was the primary and ordinary setting of the transmission of property, status, or even a name or symbol of belonging'.

'The family' as a subject for discussion remains, however, elusive in medieval archaeology. Even as late as 2003, Chris Gerrard (2003, 223), in his review of the discipline of medieval archaeology, could only offer one sentence on the archaeology of the family: 'Large exhibitions of medieval and later toys were held in London in 1996 and again in Stratford in 1997 and placed childhood artefacts into a wider family and household context...'. Gerrard's general review was not the place to tackle the specific issue of family, but he offered a useful pointer for future approaches to the subject: 'As medieval archaeologists come to realise how incomplete their scholarship has been and adopt new analytical categories for their work, more research on the fuller diversity of medieval life will surely follow' (Gerrard 2003, 223).

In what follows, I am going to approach the topic of 'family' by taking two strands – gender and children – which may offer an avenue of research to tease out the relationship between settlement and family life. I am also going to look in more detail at specific sites, to see if this helps to elucidate the problem.

Gender and childhood

One strand of discussion, which has received increasing archaeological attention as an organising factor in settlement and material culture, is gender, which touches on, though does not directly address, family. In its widest sense, houses – living, eating and sleeping spaces – are often broadly categorised as 'domestic', in contrast to other structures (churches, barns and castles, for example) or other spaces – such as fields and heaths beyond the village. This identification of spaces as 'domestic' carries an implicitly gendered message, and indeed it has been argued that 'the house as a whole can be seen as gendered as feminine, as the woman's sphere of legitimate activities as opposed to the fields and the wider community of men' (Johnson 1997, 146). In terms of building organisation, the introduction in the later medieval period of 'private rooms' in yeomen's residences has, for example, been interpreted as bringing 'homosocial' relationships into the home: as Stewart (1995, 83) has argued, 'the male closet is not designed to function as a place of individual withdrawal, but as a secret non-public transactive space between two men behind a locked door'. This is not about privacy so much as locating a male-only centre of power within the house, and the exclusion of women from that power (Johnson 1997, 153).

Such discussion plays into much older theoretical approaches centred on a binary division of gendered spaces, where the internal, domestic world is female (*domus*) while the external world is male (*agrios*) (Hodder 1990; Hingley 1990; see also Whitehouse 2007 for a summary of gender theory in archaeology). This binary division has been contested, not least because it fails to take into account that the use of space is fluid, and perceptions of space may alter according to context: space that may be rigidly gendered during rituals may be less controlled in daily use, for example (Stig Sørensen 2000, 145).

Families were fundamentally important units, and children represented the most important part of that unit. Domestic space may be regarded as 'the women's legitimate spheres of activity' and the outside spaces as the 'legitimate' domain of the men, but where do children fit in to this space – children, the single and chief product that distinguishes the 'family' from the 'household'? When the later medieval yeoman retired to his private rooms for his private business with his male friends, where were the children? Did the sound of their high voices penetrate through the walls and disturb his private business? How did children and women negotiate their space and place in the hall house?

One approach to seeing the 'family' in the material culture of the village is to consider the relationship between settlement morphology and lived experience, as Sally Smith (2010) has done. Her comparative study of the Buckinghamshire villages of Great Linford, Tattenhoe and Westbury drew attention to the different social environments of their communities. The people at Westbury, for example, lived in a comparatively dispersed and straggling settlement, as a result of which, compared to Tattenhoe, it was not 'a fully functioning village community' (Smith 2010, 66). The scattered morphology of Westbury would not have served to draw a community together, and she argues that households here would, accordingly, have had relatively little social communication with other people. There is further corroboration of this lack of cohesiveness in the morphology of buildings, which is markedly individual, compared to that of Great Linford, where there is less distinctiveness in house layout, perhaps reflecting a more cooperative farming community.

The way space impacts on social movement and interaction – and on intergenerational memory and experience – is also relevant to understanding families in medieval settlement. As Henrietta Moore (2000, 320) argues, the meaning of space and structure is flexible, and the daily physical act of using and negotiating a space is evocative and significant. At the village of Tattenhoe, for example, because of the relative stability of the settlement, paths in and around the village remained in use for many years. Children would tread the same paths as their parents and grandparents, and would expect their own children to do the same, promoting, as Sally Smith (2010, 74) argues, a sense of 'embeddedness' and family history through day-to-day activities.

Children, like families and (though to a lesser extent) women, are effectively invisible in the archaeological record. Very few objects found during the excavation of settlement sites are ever attributed to child-use, nor is the agency of children in retrieving, modifying, collecting and caching objects recognised as part of the possible deposition patterns found for material culture at medieval sites (a situation discussed in Crawford 2009). The outstanding exception to the absence of children's material culture in medieval research is still the work of the late Geoff Egan (1996; 1998; Forsyth and Egan 2005).

Though a wealth of scholarship exists on the medieval child, most recently and impressively articulated in Nicholas Orme's (2001) volume on the medieval child, children continue to be absent from archaeological discussions of settlements and landscapes. *Medieval Villages in an English Landscape: beginnings and ends* (Jones and Page 2006), for example, has index entries on sheep, deer, dogs and cats, but nothing on family or children. I have selected this one volume as representative of many; the same absence is present in other archaeological publications on medieval villages.

Towards a settlement archaeology of the family

A consideration of the archaeology of two case study sites, at opposite ends of the social scale, offers insights into both the obstacles and the potential for identifying aspects of the family – the 'child production and nurturing unit' – within the archaeological record.

Barentin

The most complete excavation of a moated manor to date is that at Barentin (Oxfordshire) (Page *et al.* 2005). Excavations at the site provided complex evidence for the evolution of the manor. As the discussion of the site in the final publication illustrates, the archaeological evidence allows an analysis of Barentin's evolution in terms of expressions of status, and of the growing separation of social space in the thirteenth century between the gentry and the servants. Evidence was found for areas of craft activity, such as the bakery and the brewhouse. Children appear, in contrast, to be absent from the archaeological record of the site. The evolving use and regulation of social space at the site over time must, however, have had some impact on the experience of childhood, and it is possible to think about the changes in building function in terms of changing attitudes to the control of children's learning and socialisation. How did new walls, doors and ditches constrain the interaction between elite children and other children and adults at the site? Where did children play, and how did new structures confine or alter access to play spaces? Did the creation of walled spaces make children more or less visible, and how did their visibility or lack of it affect perceptions of the value of children and family in society?

These are not idle questions: it has been argued, for example, that the enclosure of patios and houses in Hohokam households in prehispanic Mesoamerica led to the women becoming 'invisible' in the public and wider social life of villages, leading to a consequent downgrading of their status and de-valuing of their economic activity (Hendon 2004, 274; Crown and Fish 1996), while a similar separation of gendered space in middle-class American houses during the first half of the nineteenth century has been linked to changing ideologies, shifting gender roles, and separation of women from the 'public' sphere (Christensen 2011, 159). Where the environment changes, so too does behaviour, levels of social contact, and social 'visibility'.

Children today have a significant impact on the organisation and use of public and private spaces, from the public provision of schools and playgrounds to the private use of babygates and stairguards, and it is worth at least considering that the same may have applied in the past. The medieval period saw changes in attitudes to children and child-rearing (see, for example, Nicholas Orme 2001 on play (164–97), weaning (66), sleeping arrangements (63–4, 77–9), and the influence of the Church (200–221)): it may be that these social and parental anxieties are reflected in medieval settlement structure. In this context, we might look more closely at the function of the garden at Barentin. Did the garden offer safe confinement for the elite children? Were the elite children kept separate from the other children on the site? And which, if any, of the artefacts found on the site can be linked to their games?

Gomeldon

Excavations at Gomeldon (Wiltshire) provide evidence for a settlement at a different point on the social scale to the Barentin manor complex. The dramatic thirteenth-century social shift leading to segregation of elite from servants and tenants marked by the change in building form and purpose at Barentin is missing at Gomeldon, but, nonetheless, the peasant houses show physical changes in their layout over time which may be linked to changing relationships between families, spaces, and interactions with buildings.

The site was excavated between 1963–8. Ten buildings were excavated, one dating from the twelfth century and the rest to the thirteenth and fourteenth centuries (Musty and Algar 1986). The houses of twelfth- to thirteenth-century date, showing a succession of buildings on at least two village tenement plots, chart the change from longhouse to farmstead through this period. As such, the Gomeldon houses are characteristic of peasant settlements across England, showing the development of settlement towards a courtyard plan with clearly-made distinctions between human and animal living spaces (Algar and Musty 1969; Platt 1978, 107). The houses have been described as belonging to the 'main' families of the village, with their development charting the emergence of 'a new class of yeoman farmer' (Platt 1978, 107).

Buildings at Gomeldon were arranged around a number of complexes. Complex one consisted of two buildings, one a longhouse dating to the twelfth century, and the second a similar structure dating to the thirteenth century. Complex 3/5 consisted of a longhouse, a barn, a yard, and an earlier building, re-used to construct an oven. Building 3 originally held animals at one end, with a living end with two hearths, one possibly an oven. Later the building was remodelled as the animals were shifted outside the building, and the hearths were moved towards the centre. The excavation report notes that: 'The consequence of these alterations was that animals were no longer living in – a long-house had been converted into a farm-house' (Musty and Algar 1966, 137).

This comment begs several questions, not addressed in the site report. Why had the animals moved out? What did people do with the additional space? How did the changing use of buildings reflect family dynamics? It may be that the movement of hearths reflects a chronological progression of the hearth from a central hearth to a hearth on a cross passage, leading eventually to a chimney. However, the placing of the hearths at the sites studied by Sally Smith (2010) does not follow this model, since different forms are visible in contemporary houses. In any case, the impact that such changes in the location of the fundamental heat source for the building will have had on children and parents is not irrelevant: small variations, as Ruth Tringham (1995, 95) has noted, may be treated by archaeologists as trivial, but in terms of lived experience and social organisation, they are not.

Families are not static – children grow, bring partners into the house, have children of their own. While the changing use of space in building 3 at Gomeldon may reflect pastoral, environmental or economic realities, is it out of the question that a growing family may have meant that space for people needed to be prioritised over space for animals? The location of the hearths also raises questions about children's access to the fireplaces during their life course, and the presence – or absence – of adults to look after them and prevent accidents. What I am trying to edge towards here is the suggestion that the physical aspects of buildings have a direct and meaningful impact on adults and children, in terms of access, safety, space – and that medieval adults and their children had an interactive, dynamic relationship with their physical space. People shape buildings, buildings shape people. Families change over time. How, then, can archaeologists 'read' buildings to see the forces of family dynamics at work within and upon them?

Evidence for the presence of children at Gomeldon

No child-related finds were identified at the site, but if one were actively engaged in arguing for children's presence, one might note the discovery of a strap-end buckle snagged in one wall. The loss of such a buckle – or the deliberate insertion of the buckle into the wall – reflects behaviours perhaps more likely to be associated with childhood activity than adult, though the same complex also yielded an almost mint gold quarter noble of Edward III (*c.* 1370) (Musty and Algar 1986, 142) , unique in its value (only a cache of 5 silver coins at West Whelpington (Northumberland) comes near it), raising the possibility that some of the objects found on medieval sites are evidence of ritual and superstitious deposition (Hinton 2010, 91, 95).

Building 5 was identified as a barn dating to the twelfth century, and was associated with some external hearths. Post holes for possible lambing hurdles were also identified, and one of these post holes contained part of an infant skeleton. Building 7b was described as 'an enigma'. An infant burial lay just under the inner edge of an early wall, one in a sequence of multi-phase walls associated with the structure. This building is unlikely to have had a domestic use, but intriguingly it is also the building in which the gold coin was found. Meanwhile, from the yards of complex 3/5 came a rib almost identical to one of the ribs from the building 7b skeleton.

The infant bones at Gomeldon are not an isolated case. Several other excavated sites in different parts of England have also revealed single infant burials. For example, at the end of the thirteenth century, a baby was buried under the southern wall of a building in Westbury. This was an *in utero* foetus of five to seven months of age, showing signs of gnawing marks from rodents, and was buried in association with a building on croft 13. Also within the building was a pit containing 'the remains of two intentionally-placed pots'. Whatever was happening at Westbury was outside any officially-sanctioned ritual behaviour; nonetheless, the sense of a deliberate, intentional and even purposeful burial was so strong that the excavator remarked that 'it is certainly possible that this burial represents some sort of foundation deposit' (Ivens *et al.* 1995, 145).

At the neighbouring village of Tattenhoe, the southern wall of building 4, archaeologically difficult to define, was marked by a line of pad-stones along the edge of an eaves-drip drainage gully. One pad stone sealed a shallow depression containing the remains of an infant, possibly a still-born baby, with three animal bones placed over it. Again, the sense of deliberate ritual was strong enough to promote the suggestion of a foundation deposit, or 'a more secretive burial of a perhaps illegitimate or deformed child' (Ivens *et al.* 1995, 33). In another part of England altogether, at the longhouse complex at Upton (Gloucestershire), the thirteenth-century burial of a three to six month old baby took place in the south-east passage corner of a room. The baby was buried with a spindle whorl and a large whelk shell, and a floor slab covered the grave (Rahtz 1969, 87).

How these infant bodies came to be interred within the settlement space, in an act contrary to religious and social laws, is an intriguing question. Setting aside the physical problems associated with finding a space and burying a baby, the question of whether the act was carried out with or without the knowledge and sanction of the family to whom the baby belonged is crucial. Small communities can provide large numbers of babies, and infanticide is not an absolute necessity as an explanation for the infant bodies. Also, although these baby burials did take place within publically-sanctioned contexts, nonetheless some of these private and (perhaps) familial burials carried elements of ritual, as at Upton.

How can the archaeology of these sites be interpreted in a family perspective? One promising way forward is to pay closer attention to the relationship between artefact, space and 'maintenance activities' – the everyday use of space which can reveal social dynamics. Maintenance activities have been defined by Sandra Montón-Subías and Margarita Sánchez-Romero (2008, 3) as 'a set of practices that involve the sustenance, welfare and effective reproduction of a social group … the basic tasks of daily life that regulate and stabilise social life. They mainly involve care giving, feeding and food processing, weaving and cloth manufacture, hygiene, public health and healing, socialisation of children and the fitting out an organisation of related spaces'. As the collection of papers in the volume edited by Montón-Subías and Sánchez-Romero's on maintenance activities illustrates, these activities tend to be performed by women. An approach to material culture from this perspective allows a different set of questions to be asked of the evidence from medieval settlements. Changes to buildings and re-location of hearths, wells, cess pits and walls need not be seen exclusively in terms of status and economy, but also in terms of their impact on, and reference to, the maintenance activities of the women and children whose daily practices and tasks were carried out within and around these spaces. At Upton, for example, the building containing the infant burial was assessed as not 'residential'; the excavators proposed, on the basis of the surviving archaeological evidence, that dairying or cloth-making took place here: it was, thus, a scene of day-to-day domestic activity (Rahtz 1969, 96).

Conclusion

Archaeologists can identify changes in buildings – new hearths, new doorways, new additions or demolitions – and these visible and identifiable alterations give the impression of distinct events separated by apparent periods of stasis or fixity. But, to quote Julia Hendon (2004, 276), houses, like people, have biographies, and there is an intimate connection between people and their families (see also Tringham 1994 and 1995). Some of the changes in buildings and spaces – the creation of walled gardens or separate private rooms – will have had a direct and immediate impact on families – on the visibility or invisibility of children and their carers, and on their socialisation through engagement or withdrawal from society. It is only by peopling medieval settlements with the crucial social dynamic at the heart of settlement – the family network of children, mothers and fathers, carers and relations – that a more comprehensive understanding and interpretation of the dynamic between buildings, artefacts, and society, will be achieved in medieval archaeology.

Bibliography

Alcock, N. W. and Woodfield, P. 1996. Social pretensions in architecture and ancestry: Hall House, Sawbridge, Warks and the Andrewe family. *Antiquaries Journal* 76, 51–72.

Algar, D. and Musty, J. 1969. Gomeldon deserted medieval village, Wiltshire. *Current Archaeology* 2 (3), 87–91.

Allison, P. M. (ed.) 1999. *The Archaeology of Household Activities.* London: Routledge.

Bender, D. 1967. A refinement of the concept of household: families, co-residence and domestic functions. *American Anthropologist* 65 (5), 493–504.

Birdwell-Pheasant, D. and Lawrence-Zuniga, D. 1999. Introduction: houses and families in Europe, pp. 1–35 in Birdwell-Pheasant, D. and Lawrence-Zuniga, D. (eds), *House Life: space, place and family in Europe.* Oxford: Berg.

Britton, E. 1977. *The Community of the Vill: a study in the history of the family and village life in 14th century England.* Toronto: Macmillan.

Casey, J. 1989. *The History of the Family.* Oxford: Blackwell.

Christensen, K. 2011. Ideas versus things: the balancing act of interpreting historic house museums. *International Journal of Heritage Studies* 17, 153–68.

Crawford, S. 2009. The ontology of play things: theorizing a toy stage in the 'biography' of objects. *Childhood in the Past* 2, 55–70.

Crown, P. L. and Fish, S. K. 1996. Gender and status in the Hohokam Pre-Classic to Classic tradition. *American Anthropologist* 98, 803–17.

David, N. 1971. The Fulani compound and the archaeologist. *World Archaeology* 3 (2) (*Archaeology and Ethnography* (Oct. 1971)), 111–31.

Egan, G. 1996. *Playthings from the Past. Lead alloy miniature artefacts c. 1300–1800.* London: Jonathan Horne Publications.

Egan, G. 1998. *The Medieval Household: daily living c. 1150–c. 1450.* London: Museum of London Stationary Office.

Fairclough, G. 1992. Meaningful constructions: spatial and functional analysis of medieval buildings. *Antiquity* 66, 348–66.

Finan, T. 2010. *Medieval Lough Ce: history, archaeology and family.* Dublin: Four Courts Press.

Fleming, P. 2001. *Family and Household in Medieval England.* Basingstoke: Palgrave.

Forsyth, H. and Egan. G. 2005. *Toys, Trifles and Trinkets: base metal miniatures from London 1200–1800.* London: Unicorn Press.

Gerrard, C. 2003. *Medieval Archaeology: understanding traditions and contemporary approaches.* London and New York: Routledge.

Gilchrist, R. 1994. *Gender and Material Culture: the archaeology of religious women.* London: Routledge.

Goody, J. 1983. *The Development of the Family and Marriage in Europe.* Cambridge: Cambridge University Press.

Gregory, D. and Urry, J. (eds) 1985. *Social Relations and Spatial Structures.* Basingstoke: Macmillan.

Grenville, J. 1997. *Medieval Housing.* Leicester: Leicester University Press.

Guerreau, A. 2000. Family, p. 531 in Vauchez, A., Dobson, B. and Lapidge, M. (eds), *Encyclopedia of the Middle Ages* (English edition). Cambridge: James Clarke and Co. Ltd.

Hanawalt, B. 1986. *The Ties That Bound: peasant families in medieval England.* Oxford and New York: Oxford University Press.

Hendon, J. A. 2004. Living and working at home: the social archaeology of household production and social relations, pp. 272–86 in Meskell, L. and Preucel, R. W. (eds), *A Companion to Social Archaeology*. Oxford: Blackwell.

Hill, J. and Swan, M. (eds) 1998. *The Community, the Family and the Saint: patterns of power in early medieval Europe* (International Medieval Research 4). Turnhout: Brepols.

Hillier, B. and Hanson, J. 1984. *The Social Logic of Space*. Cambridge: Cambridge University Press.

Hingley, R. 1990. Public and private space: domestic organization and gender relations among Iron Age and Romano-British households, pp. 125–48 in Samson, R. (ed.), *The Social Archaeology of Houses*. Edinburgh: Edinburgh University Press.

Hinton, D. 2010. Deserted medieval villages and the objects from them, pp. 85–108 in Dyer, C. and Jones, R. (eds), *Deserted Villages Revisited*. Hatfield: University of Hertfordshire Press.

Hodder, I. 1990. *The Domestication of Europe*. Oxford: Blackwell.

Hoskins, W. G. 1967. *Fieldwork in Local History*. London: Faber and Faber.

Houlbrooke, R. A. 1984. *The English Family 1450–1700*. London and New York: Longman.

Ivens, R., Busby, P. and Shepherd, N. 1995. *Tattenhoe and Westbury: two deserted medieval settlements in Milton Keynes* (The Buckinghamshire Archaeological Society Monograph 8). Aylesbury: Buckinghamshire Archaeological Society.

Johnson, M. 1993. *Housing Culture: traditional architecture in an English landscape*. London: UCL Press.

Johnson, M. 1997. Rethinking houses, rethinking transitions: of vernacular architecture, ordinary people and everyday culture, pp. 145–56 in Gaimster, D. and Stamper, P. (eds), *The Age of Transition: the archaeology of English culture, 1400–1600* (Society for Medieval Archaeology Monograph 15). Oxford: Oxbow.

Johnson, M. 2006. Houses, power and everyday life in early medieval England, pp. 285–98 in Maran, J., Juwig, C., Schwengel, H. and Thaler, U. (eds), *Constructing Power: architecture, ideology and social practice*. Hamburg: LIT.

Jones, R. and Page, M. 2006. *Medieval Villages in an English Landscape: beginnings and ends*. Macclesfield: Windgather Press.

Keats-Rohan, K. 1997. *Family Trees and the Roots of Prosopography of Britain and France from the Tenth to the Twelfth century*. Woodbridge: Boydell.

Laslett, P. with Wall, R. 1972. *Household and Family in Past Time, edited with an analytic introduction on the history of the family* (Worldwide Archaeological Series 9). Cambridge: Cambridge University Press.

Lavelle, R. 2007. *Royal Estates in Anglo-Saxon Wessex: land, politics and family strategies* (British Archaeological Reports British Series 439). Oxford: Archaeopress.

Locock, M. (ed.) 1994. *Meaningful Architecture: social interpretations of buildings*. Aldershot: Avebury Press.

Martin, E., Easton, T. and McKechnie, I. 1993. Conspicuous display: the extraordinary garden and buildings of a minor gentry family in mid-Suffolk. *Proceedings of the Suffolk Institute of Archaeology and His*tory 38 (1), 56–74.

McNeill, T. 1992. *Castles*. London: English Heritage.

Meskell, L. and Preucel, R. W. (eds) 2004. *A Companion to Social Archaeology*. Oxford: Blackwell.

Montón-Subías, S. and Sánchez-Romero, M. (eds) 2008. *Engendering Social Dynamics: the archaeology of maintenance activities* (British Archaeological Reports International Series 1862). Oxford: Archaeopress.

Moore, H. 2000. Bodies on the move; gender, power and material culture: gender, difference and the material world (reprinted from 1994), pp. 317–28 in Thomas, J. (ed.), *Interpretive Archaeology: a reader*. London: Leicester University Press.

Musty, J. and Algar, D. 1966. *The Excavations at the Deserted Medieval Village site of Gomeldon, Near Salisbury, Wiltshire* (Salisbury Museum Research Committee interim reports 3). Salisbury: Salisbury Museum.

Musty, J. and Algar, D. 1986. Excavations at the deserted medieval village of Gomeldon, near Salisbury. *The Wiltshire Archaeological and Natural History Magazine* 80, 127–69.

Neel, C. 2004. *Medieval Families: perspectives on marriage, household, and children* (second revised edition). Toronto: Toronto University Press.

Nicholas, D. 1969. Medieval urban origins in northern continental Europe: state of research and some tentative conclusions. *Studies in Medieval and Renaissance History* (old series) 6, 53–114.

Orme, N. 2001. *Medieval Children*. New Haven and London: Yale University Press.

Page, P., Atherton, K. and Hardy, A. 2005. *Barentin's Manor: excavations of the moated manor at Harding's Field, Chalgrove, Oxfordshire 1976–9* (Thames Valley Landscapes Monograph 24). Oxford: Oxford University School of Archaeology.

Parker Pearson, M. and Richards, C. 1994. Ordering the world: perceptions of architecture, space and time, pp. 1–36 in Parker Pearson, M. and Richards, C. (eds), *Architecture and Order: approaches to social space*. London: Routledge.

Platt, C. 1978. *Medieval Archaeology: a social history and archaeology from the Conquest to 1600 AD*. London: Routledge.

Rahtz, P. A. 1969. Upton, Gloucestershire, 1964–1968. *Transactions of the Bristol and Gloucestershire Archaeological Society* 88, 74–126.

Rawson, B. and Weaver, P. (eds) 1999. *The Roman Family in Italy: status, sentiment, space*. Oxford: Oxford University Press.

Razi, Z. 1980. *Life, Marriage and Death in a Medieval Parish. Economy, society and demography in Halesowen, 1270–1400*. Cambridge: Cambridge University Press.

Redfield, J. 2003. *The Locrian Maidens: love and death in Greek Italy*. Princeton: Princeton University Press.

Robin, C. 2003. New directions in Classic Maya household archaeology. *Journal of Archaeological Research* 11 (2), 307–56.

Roux, S. 2000. House, p. 695 in Vauchez, A., Dobson, B. and Lapidge, M. (eds), *Encyclopedia of the Middle Ages* (English edition). Cambridge: James Clarke and Co. Ltd.

Samson, R. (ed.) 1990. *The Social Archaeology of Houses*. Edinburgh: Edinburgh University Press.

Schofield, J. 1994. *Medieval London Houses*. New Haven and London: Yale University Press.

Smith, S. V. 2010. Houses and communities: archaeological evidence for variation in medieval peasant experience, pp. 64–84 in Dyer, C. and Jones, R. (eds), *Deserted Villages Revisited*. Hatfield: University of Hertfordshire Press.

Stig Sørensen, M. L. 2000. *Gender Archaeology*. Cambridge: Polity Press.

Stewart, A. 1995. The early modern closet discovered. *Representations* 50, 76–100.

Tringham, R. 1994. Engendered places in prehistory. *Gender, Place, and Culture* 1 (2), 169–203.

Tringham, R. 1995. Archaeological houses, households, housework and the home, pp. 79–107 in Benjamin, D. and Stea, D. (eds), *The Home: words, interpretations, meanings and environments*. Aldershot: Avebury Press.

Wilk, R. and Rathje, W. 1982. Household archaeology. *American Behavioral Scientist* 25 (6), 617–39.

Whitehouse, R. 2007. Gender archaeology in Europe, pp. 139–90 in Milledge Nelson, S. (ed.), *Worlds of Gender: the archaeology of women's lives around the globe*. Walnut Creek: Alta Mira Press.

Yanagiasako, S. 1979. Family and household: the analysis of domestic groups. *Annual Review of Anthropology* 8, 161–205.

3. 'Merely players'? Playtime, material culture and medieval childhood

Mark A. Hall

> It should be noted that children at play are not playing about; their games should be seen as their most serious-minded activity
>
> *Montaigne I: 23*

This chapter explores whether, and if so how, medieval play, especially board and dice games and toys, can be seen as specifically child orientated. It considers the ways in which games help us to chart the boundary between a child-determined view of childhood and an adult-determined view of childhood. The importance of board games to children as a performance mechanism (possibly with 'avatar'-like[1] implications?), both within and outside school, are considered as a means by which they negotiated a transition from childhood to adulthood. The chapter draws on a wide range of medieval material culture evidence, including archaeological, textual and art historical sources, and whilst the focus is on Britain, it recognises and draws evidence from the wider European context.

Children's play in context

In the summer of 1959, archaeologists discovered the interlocking tombs of a twenty-eight-year-old woman and a six-year-old boy underneath Köln cathedral in Germany. Both were members of the Merovingian royal family buried in the seventh century. Along with their grave goods their skeletons are on display in the Treasury of the cathedral and contemplating the display makes it clear that childhood is a cultural and social stage of development as well as a biological one. This is because the boy from Köln was buried with adult regalia, including a gold finger-ring, a wooden sceptre, bottles of oils and scents and weapons, and a child-sized helmet, shield, bed and chair (Doppelfeld and Weyres 1980). Thus, the boy was defined at the moment of burial both as a man or at least a man-to-be (through his weapons), as a prince (through his high-status regalia), as a boy (through his appropriately sized armour and furniture) and as a son (through the link to his mother's tomb).

---

[1] I use 'avatar' not in its classic sense of the human manifestations of the Hindu God Vishnu on earth (and extended to other spiritual beings such as Morgan Le Fey (Loomis 1958)) but in the more recently developed gaming sense of surrogate manifestations for game players in virtual gaming worlds (Britt 2008).

While this chapter is not about children's burial (a subject covered elsewhere in this volume), this example is offered as a reminder that the categories by which we define our evidence are not fixed. Indeed, I take it as axiomatic that childhood is contingent and contextual, as is play, which is a ubiquitous and fundamental aspect of human behaviour (Callois 1958). Indeed, if it is possible to define humanity by one characteristic then play is arguably a contender for that characteristic; play is an abiding human concern, which in different guises is pursued by most of us, from cradle to grave. For many, childhood and play are almost synonymous, which is certainly a factor in why both have been so lightly regarded by so many archaeologists; both are seen as transient and unimportant in comparison to the 'serious' pursuits of adults (Crawford and Lewis 2008; Orme 2008). While this is something of a post-Enlightenment reflex, it is, nonetheless, in some ways analogous to the medieval representation of childhood and games as the folly of mankind (Hindman 1981).[2] It was not, however, a universal medieval attitude. Several scholars, philosophers and ecclesiastics (including Isidore of Seville (*c.* 560–636), John of Salisbury (*c.* 1120–1180), Thomas Aquinas (1225–1274) and Erasmus (1466–1536)) endorsed the restorative value of play. It may be this restorative quality that provided the tolerant link between play and holiness. It was acceptable for saints to conduct miracles which related to games play: for example, John Combe reportedly made a miraculous recovery from a bat-and-ball game injury thanks to the intervention of the soon-to-be canonised Bishop Osmund of Salisbury (McLean n.d., 6), while a servant of the future saint, Thomas Cantilupe, Bishop of Hereford, reported a miracle in which his sight was restored enabling him to play once more at chess and dice (Hall 2009, 78). However, it seems to have been less acceptable for prospective saints to engage in such play themselves. Bede, writing in the early eighth century, says that St Cuthbert (d. 687) used to be an enthusiastic ball player with his friends, until he was divinely warned in the middle of a game to abandon 'vain play' (McLean n.d., 2). Bede also tells of a travelling party led by Bishop John of Beverley (d. 721), who came across a level stretch of ground suitable for horse racing. The bishop sees this as a waste of time but reluctantly agrees that a race can be held, and subsequently has to use his healing powers on his young acolyte who is injured during the race (Alcock 2003, 419). Children could also symbolise innocence – in art this often took the form of Christ as child, frequently holding or playing with a toy (Klapisch-Zuber 1998; Willemsen 2005). This chapter will now review something of the wider context of medieval childhood and play before concluding with a focus on the conjunction of education and play in childhood, taking into account gender and the transition to adulthood.

Some remarks on the wider context of childhood and play

Perceptions of Medieval children

In the modern era it is a readily observable phenomenon that concerns about children, their status, their rights and their welfare abound, both in the press and other media (of many studies see, for example, Postman 1996; Hendrick 1997; Heywood 2001;

---

[2] This representation was not of course restricted to children's games but was also applied to games (including board games) generally; see, for example, Hall 2009, 74–5.

Cunningham 2005; Sigman 2009), but in interpretations of the past it is important that the desire to privilege the child does not compromise a judicious analysis of the actual evidence. A particular concern, that has implications for the ways in which the public perceive medieval childhood, is the tendency for modern cinematic portrayals of medieval children to emphasise their innocence, their right to self-determination and their transition to adulthood. Generally they do this through linking their narrative to the life of an individual child, whether real (*e.g. Anchoress* (1993); *Lady Jane* (1986)) or imaginary (*e.g. Marketa Lazarova* (1967); *Navigator, A Medieval Odyssey* (1988); *The Virgin Spring* (1960); *Andrei Rublev* (1966)). Such films, of course, have the dramatic license to invent in their facilitation of the popular understanding of, and relationship with, the past. Some also commercialise that past. Several film-dramas set in the Middle Ages consciously appeal to the teen market (Finke and Shichtman 2009, 335–68), being aimed squarely at the youth culture of the years between thirteen and twenty. They commercially treat as one a hugely diverse social category and it has been argued that this diversity is such that the unified category of teenager is in reality fictitious – 'an invented transition between two carefully constructed norms, childhood and adulthood' (Finke and Shichtman 2009, 342, quoting Lang 1990, 156). It remains a recognised developmental category because a prolonged period of adolescence is economically lucrative, and many young people see themselves as having a shared teenage identity. Films tend to project this construction back into the past and are often roundly condemned for doing so on the grounds that the social category of teenager did not exist in the Middle Ages, although there was certainly a strong medieval concept of adolescence, as a long transitional phase between childhood and adulthood (Hanawalt 1986, 88–9; Lewis 2009, 88).

Perceptions of medieval childhood are sometimes used to justify a sense of progress in our contemporary attitudes to childhood. The supposed increase in our sentimentalisation of childhood is a key example, and yet there is sufficient evidence to show that sentimentality and emotion were important parental reflexes towards their offspring in the medieval period (Hanawalt 1986, 186–7). Medieval peasants may have had less time to devote to their children but they did seek to care for them, to teach them to talk and to work, and to discipline them:

> As the children grew up the parents continued to provide for them to the best of their abilities, arranging marriages, purchasing pieces of land and trying to establish them in their own households and families
>
> *Hanawalt 1986, 187*

In her analysis of the tombs of medieval royal babies in Westminster Abbey in London, Tanner (1953) accepts that elites may have been able to symbolise and memorialise their loss more effectively (as a demonstration of their wealth and power) but that this still reflects a love for lost children that many parents felt. Indeed, Princess Katherine, daughter of Henry III and Queen Eleanor, who died in 1257 at the age of three years, elicited disconsolate grief in her parents, according to the contemporary chronicler Matthew Paris (Tanner 1953, 26–8). Yet, such emotional investment in children was both ephemeral and open to exploitation. Tanner's study showed that all but two of the medieval children's tombs had been moved at least once during the Middle Ages, indicating the transient nature of that sorrow and its subservience to the needs of those in power in successive generations.

Further, striking, testimony to the medieval sentimentalisation of children is provided by the European-wide phenomenon of Christian children supposedly martyred by Jews. In England the earliest example is St William of Norwich, believed to have been martyred at the age of eleven/twelve years in 1144, and whose cult made Norwich a key pilgrimage destination. Over a century later, in 1255, the same fate was said to have befallen 'Little' St Hugh of Lincoln, whose shrine then flourished in the cathedral. Had Edward I not issued his Edict of Expulsion of all Jews from the kingdom of England in 1290 the trend of imaginary child murders by Jews may have continued longer. It did so on the continent. In Trento (Italy) the former fifteenth-century synagogue bears a seventeenth-century plaque recalling the murder of a child by Jews in the 1470s, the body found in the open drain in front of the synagogue. Twelve Jews were executed almost immediately and the 'victim', Simon, was so venerated as a saint that a church was built in his name. The annual procession of his supposedly uncorrupted body continued until 1966 when the Catholic Church relented and buried the body in an unmarked grave. With the turn of the twenty-first century the Church issued an official apology admitting its error in falsely executing the twelve Jews (for a discussion of this phenomenon of 'ritual murder', see, for example, Utz 2005).

The act of bestowing sainthood on these and other supposed victims was both a sentimentalisation and veneration of childhood (with strong parallels in the culting of the young Jesus and the biblical story of the Slaughter of the Innocents; Hanawalt 1986, 187), but also a cynical manipulation of childhood innocence to feed the persecution of the Jewish people. The sense of sentimentality drew on the perception of children as innocents, which had a long medieval tradition: in the year 697, Adomnán, abbot of Iona (Scotland), devised and promulgated the so-called 'Law of the Innocents', aimed at protecting women, clerics and children in times of war, and this was widely applied in early medieval Scotland and Ireland. That law defined children as innocent if they had not yet taken-up a weapon for the first time (Márkus 1997; Ní Dhonnchadha 1995). A late fifteenth-century engraving of Christ and John the Baptist jousting with windmills (Willemsen 2001, ill. 18.8) is a clear later expression of the innocence of children as expressed through them playing. Because of the belief in the dual nature of Christ, as both God and human, the latter was most readily signalled in medieval art through his depiction as a child, frequently a playing one, and in this way Christ validated childhood and children playing. A similar validation may be at work in those illuminations that link images of children playing with those of praying saints. A popular vignette was that of two boys spinning tops and frequently shown in front, or on the steps, of a church porch. There are two examples in the Book of Hours (books for personal, devotional meditations) of James IV of Scotland (d. 1513): fol. 18 carries this image at the beginning of St Mark's Gospel, alongside a small image of St Mark, while fol. 190 – the beginning of the Psalter prologue – shows the two boys alongside an image of St Benedict praying. Of course, the inherent multi-valency of medieval art means that such scenes also worked as vignettes of observable reality, a reality we find confirmed in the finds of playthings and the play-spaces in which they are found.

The meaning of play

The classic, older view of play was persuasively argued for by Johan Huizinga (1950) as pre-figuring culture and civilisation and as archetypically opposite to that which is rational, controlled and systematised. The alternative view is that proposed by Callois (1958), who described play as embedded in, and interwoven with, social structures. This perspective has a greater concern with particular forms of play and their social contexts. More recently a review of the evidence for board and dice games in medieval Scotland (Hall 2011) summarised play as primarily a free activity that creates an area of its own in space and time where it can unfold its own inner order. The amenability of play to these and other approaches is testimony to the ambiguous nature of play. In exploration of this ambiguity Sutton-Smith (1997) identified seven key, inter-disciplinary, overlapping narratives about the meaning of play which he labelled as the rhetorics of play:

- progress
- fate
- power
- identity (at a community level)
- the imaginary
- self-absorption
- frivolity

Three of these rhetorics (progress, the imaginary and the self) Sutton-Smith (1997) classifies as modern or individual rhetorics and the other four as ancient or communal ones. As a psychologist, Sutton-Smith (1997) pays particular attention to the role of play in children's lives, including the assumed – rather than proven – notion that play is adaptive and developmental for children (and animals), but not adults, a notion that misses the point of play's enjoyment. The rhetoric of progress dominates modern discussion of child-play and, as we shall see, the story is similar for medieval play. Sutton-Smith (1997, 111) comments that one of the negative consequences of this progress rhetoric (itself an adult tool) is that it has 'disguised' the understanding of what childhood is about as a means of maintaining adult power over children. He observed (Sutton-Smith 1997, 111) that 'there does not appear to be generally accepted power rhetoric or theory of play for children as there is for adults'. The medieval evidence has a contribution to make in addressing this issue.

Playthings

At the risk of over-simplification, we might observe that there are two basic forms of childhood play, both with varying material culture manifestations: games and toys. The earliest meanings of 'toy' are unclear. Textual evidence of the fourteenth to sixteenth centuries indicates that the word *toye* meant 'amorous plaything or sport, a piece of fun or entertainment and a trifle, a plaything of no value'. These meanings all appear to predate the meaning of 'child's plaything', which in English is first recorded in 1596 in Shakespeare's *The Taming of the Shrew*. However, this meaning may be of earlier origin if it was borrowed into English from the older Dutch, German and Danish cognates '*tuig*' ('tools, stuff, trash'), '*Speeltuig*' ('play-tool or plaything'), '*zeug*' ('toy, stuff, gear'), '*Spielzeug*' ('plaything, toy'), '*tøi*' ('stuff, gear') and '*legetøi*' ('playthings, toys') (Barnhart 1988, 1155). The word seems to evolve in the wake of the things, which in turn arise from the idea or concept, and again this confronts us with the question of ambiguity – are toys, for example, always miniature in form and are miniatures always toys?

The archaeological record of medieval North Britain and Scandinavia affords several examples of what can be claimed to be toys. Stummen Hansen and Larsen (2000) draw together details of several miniature quern/millstones, predominantly made of soapstone, from Shetland and from the Trondheim region of Norway. Previous studies had expressed uncertainty about the function of these objects but the authors posit toys, in preference to 'miniatures' or 'models', as the most likely identification on the grounds of logic and meaningfulness. They can be linked to other toy artefacts including swords, animals and boats, all echoing vital elements of daily life in the North Sea world. In the case of the mill- and quernstones, they illustrate the importance of growing and milling grain as a community, subsistence level activity. The toy versions would allow both boys and girls to learn techniques and the importance of milling, though repeated play (or practice) – traditionally rotary milling with a quern was female work and larger-scale milling was a male activity (Stummen Hansen and Larsen 2000, 115). More recently McLaren and Hunter (2008) have drawn attention to late Iron Age/early medieval miniature querns from mainland Scotland and the Western Isles. They accept toy as a possible explanation, but because of the paucity of clearly defined toys from the Scottish Iron Age they suggest that their size may be governed less by their use as playthings than by their utilitarian use by children expected to grind such material as seeds, herbs or minerals, which were required only in relatively small amounts. Such an explanation does not, however, allow for the adaptive culture of children which turns utilitarian scenarios into playful ones.

An uncertainty about identifying toys in the archaeological record also hovers around the wider miniature object tradition in British archaeology. Before the medieval period, miniatures tend to be seen as votives rather than toys. Hunter's analysis (in Armit 2006, 150 and colour plate 7) of a tri-lobed miniature bone sword from the Iron Age (second-third century AD) roundhouse of Cnip, Isle of Lewis, accepts either interpretation – toy or votive – as valid but leans towards the latter. He was persuaded by the seemingly greater attestation of votives in the Iron Age and Roman periods (certainly in southern Britain) as opposed to the harder to identify, definitive toys. But should we expect toys to be always definitive? Given the ritual element in play (in large part deriving from the imaginative repetition of actions) might not toys and votives have been interchangeable, indeed might not some toys have been offered as votives at times of transition, stress or illness within childhood or transition from childhood to adulthood? Miniature swords occur in various media: there is a late Iron Age bone example from Howmae (Orkney) (Armit 2006), a thirteenth-century wooden example from Braunschweig (Germany) (Leenen 2010, 361, cat. F3), several swords and other weapons (part of a large assemblage of wooden and clay toys and games) of tenth- to fifteenth-century date from Novgorod (Russia) (Khoroshev 2007, 344–53; Rybina 2007, 354–9) and a siltstone example recently excavated from the Viking levels (mid-ninth to mid-tenth century AD) of Old Scatness (Shetland) (Dockrill *et al.* 2010, 248) (Figure 3.1). Such Viking miniatures have been interpreted as magical devices (Duczko 2004, 131–3) but the later dates of the German material and some of the Russian material seem to make a toy identification (some of it part of a wider, aspirant-knight culture) more 'definitive', but given the commonality of votives in later medieval Europe (especially at saints' shrines) they may in reality have retained a fluidity of purpose. Like the Novgorod swords, the Scatness example comes from a site which also produced gaming equipment, spread across the Pictish and Viking sites, the mainly stone discs being suitable as counters, but with two distinct conical pieces suitable for a tafl-type game (Hall 2007; Hall and Forsyth 2011).

As a specialist material culture of childhood, toys are today a hugely profitable, commercial and consumer enterprise, but this does not stop many children playing, of necessity, of choice and of invention, with non-toy designated material – whether man-made or natural, such as stones, shells, sticks, water and snow – appropriating and re-defining it through use in play. During the medieval period, when capitalism was still in its infancy, and not withstanding that there were purpose-made toys, it seems self-evident that the imaginative adaptation and appropriation of non-toys as toys was even more common than it is today. It is an idea that applies beyond the medieval period, as Crawford (2009) has recently demonstrated in her exposition of the need for archaeologists to start recognising 'toy' to be a quality as much as a thing, a phase which many objects pass through, or in and out of, part of their social engagement or biography.[3] The concept was effectively widened by Carenza Lewis (2009) in her exploration of rural, medieval environments as play spaces, while Annemarieke Willemsen (2005, 429) finds a fruitful correspondence between manuscripts depicting children's play, archaeological examples of both the toys depicted and the urban spaces from which they were recovered. Spaces, like objects, are amenable to appropriation by children for the purpose of play; we may compare the late twentieth-century use of town streets as play environments despite the dangers of road traffic, indeed often incorporating those dangers. This rhetoric about spaces and things seems so obvious (and so recognisable from our own upbringings) that one wonders why archaeology has shied away from confronting it. In part it may be down to a 'taken-for-granted' sensibility, and in part a reluctance to sully site interpretation with mere and 'unserious' notions of play. But in reality can our interpretation of the medieval urban environment of, for example, Perth (Scotland) be complete without imagining how children moved through it, playing as they went, losing, hiding and sometimes stealing objects they made into toys? This role of children in site formation is hardly ever considered and even when synthetic analyses of the burgh are written (*e.g.* Hall 2002, which includes gaming material) they tend to posit only an adult presence as a default assumption.

Excavation reports remain wary of childhood, with toys and games often dealt with in a perfunctory, classificatory way, with the full implications of childhood for understanding both the archaeological record and the site side-stepped. The Winchester *Object and Economy* report is no different in this respect, but Martin Biddle (1990, 697–8) at least identifies context as important in helping to identify where toys and games were being used and left; by implication the reader might be prompted to consider that some

---

[3] Of course a strand espousing the opposite tack can be identified: the thirteenth-century anonymously written (but presumably by a cleric) Norwegian treatise, *The Kings Mirror*, advises that correct behaviour by a young nobleman should include shunning 'chess and dice, brothels and perjury, false testimony and other lasciviousness or filthy behaviour' (Larson 1917, KM part II, ch. XL). This 'duality' of purpose is the subject of a future paper by the present author.

0

10

20mm

Figure 3.1. The miniature sword
from Old Scatness (Shetland) (© and
reproduced with permission from S. J.
Dockrill, Department of Archaeological
Sciences, University of Bradford).

adult things may have been lost or placed somewhere by children, and there remain until found by archaeologists. The publication of a single volume (Mygland 2007) on childhood in the Bergen (Norway) excavation series suggests, however, that a change of approach may be underway. Whilst it does not tackle the question of ambiguity and artefact biography and ignores the possibilities of children playing board games (which it defines as an adult pursuit), this study nevertheless brings together much of the archaeological evidence – comprising 425 toys and 2,088 shoe soles – with a theoretical framework of childhood studies to ask illuminating questions about children in medieval (*c.* 1120–*c.* 1700) Bergen, particularly in relation to 'childhood as a separate stage of life and how archaeological artefacts may be interpreted to shed light on children's everyday life and presence' (Mygland 2007, 101).

Play as ritual, ritual as play

The foregoing discussion touched upon the overlap between play and ritual that merits further consideration. There is what we might characterise as a rituality of performance in children's play that reinforces both the repetition (or practice) leading to a learning reflex and the religious, predominantly Christian, cultural sub-text around such play. In her analysis of the repeated, ritual incisions of graffiti on religious wall paintings in the church of San Sebastiano, Arborio (Italy), Plesch (2002, 182) notes that many kinds of objects developed as devotional tools, helping to engage the believer in a physical way with their practice, including opening and closing the panels of a triptych, turning the pages of a book, handling rosary beads and 'playing with a Baby Jesus doll – a holy doll'. With reference to Klapisch-Zuber's (1998) work on the use of such holy dolls at the junction of play and piety in the fourteenth century, Plesch characterises this playing with Baby Jesus dolls as a trend of the fourteenth to sixteenth centuries, but in reality such holy or liturgical play is of much longer duration traceable from the sixth to the twentieth centuries. In his analysis of early twentieth-century photographs of Dutch Catholic children playing at the Mass, Post (1995, 193–4) notes that the tradition of such play in fact begins as early as the sixth century, as described in Christian narrative culture, including the *Pratum spirituale* of Johannes Moschus (Figure 3.2). In Brueghel's *c.* 1560 painting *Children's Games*, one of the scenes depicted shows children using a mock altar (Hindman 1981, 452), presumably not intended to be read as symbolic of folly (unless subversively) but of wise, devotional play.

Illuminated manuscripts are a further source of evidence for this intersection of play and religion. A particular group of Books of Hours from the Low Countries are profusely illustrated with scenes of children playing, primarily in the marginal spaces (Willemsen 2005; Randall 1972), and such scenes are echoed, again in marginal zones, on some Flemish burial brasses (Van Belle 1997). There are several reflexes at work here. In many of the Books of Hours the games being played are clearly linked to seasonality, and the images of playing children were used to recall feasts and customs of the months of the year as appropriate. Humour was also being deployed: many scenes were of play fights between children on hobby-horses, jousting with whirligigs. One example even places the play version beneath a scene of an adult jousting tournament, giving us a playful variant of reality that satirises the 'play' of knights but which also acts as a prefiguring of what children playing at knights will become, with a wider sense of children becoming adults by playing at adults. There may also be a note of censure, a warning that playful folly can become adult folly if not corrected. The motif of children on hobby-horses is also common on misericords, particularly continental examples, where typically the children are shown with adult faces (Bethmont-Gallerand 2002; Block 1999). Misericords also depict another game, *pannoy*, a form of wrestling. Invariably *pannoy* is shown as being played by men, and is an example both of 'life disguised as a game' (Block 1999, 51–2) and the use of child-like

Figure 3.2. Nineteenth-century liturgical toys for the Catholic Mass (photography by M. A. Hall, reproduced courtesy of the Spielzeugmuseum, Altes Rathaus, Munich (Germany)).

characteristics in non-children (Willemsen 2001). Other children's games depicted in the marginal arts, but especially manuscripts, include blind man's bluff and various buffeting games, including 'hot cockles'. Randall (1972, 246–57) has persuasively argued for such marginal scenes as supporting directly their main miniatures. Thus, in the Office of the Virgin sequence in the *Book of Hours of Jeanne D'Évreux* from the 1320s, the mock tilt and buffeting game marginalia are symbolically linked to widely known episodes in the Passion cycle; a clear reminder that the playing of such games was a salutary recollection of the mistreatment of Christ.

Playtime inside and outside the classroom

For decades the wider study of childhood play has been set by social sciences other than archaeology, including folklore studies (*e.g.* Gomme 1894; Opie and Opie 1959; Opie and Opie 2008) and interdisciplinary historical studies (including Orme 2003, notable for its cognisance of archaeological evidence). However, one area in which archaeology is making a key contribution is in and around the school space. The school space is a pivotal domain for childhood studies because it is contested ground where adult- and child-centred views of childhood vie, and where play was deployed on both sides to make their point.

In 1538 the Carmelite friary in Coventry (Warwickshire) was dissolved and became the town's free grammar school. Excavations in the 1970s recovered many objects that had fallen into the foundations beneath the choir stalls, at the time being reused as school desks, including arrowheads, buckles, buttons, pins, knife fragments, trinkets, marbles and counters (both stone and pottery). Notably some four hundred shoelace tags were found, probably used as currency in games, to measure gains and losses (Woodfield 1981; Orme 2003, 177). Coins were also found, and while undoubtedly valued as currency they could also have been used for the popular game of coin tossing or 'cross and pile', where the person who guessed the toss kept the money (McLean n.d., 104–5). Although the cultural context is a Reformation milieu transitioning the end of the Middle Ages, this assemblage of school boy bric-a-brac is similar to medieval assemblages, the majority of which have been excavated on the Continent. These have recently been brought together in a major work of inter-disciplinary scholarship, with a focus on the child's experience of school at its core (Willemsen 2008), particularly at the secularly controlled schools in the Netherlands between 1300 and 1600. It brings together a diverse array of medieval visual and written sources as well as the finds excavated at schools in Groningen, Leiden, Gorinchem and Zwolle. The evidence clearly demonstrates that though driven by adult rules and control, schools were contested spaces, which children sought to make their own. Within and around schools children had their own material culture (often improvised) of play which fell outside the formal structure of teaching; tolerated when played during breaks and when school had finished but not tolerated when played in class. This is indicative of behaviour which in more recent times has been labelled the power rhetoric of illicit play in the classroom, taking the form of 'doodling, note passing, whispering, making faces, giggling, mocking and satirising adults and play fighting' (Sutton-Smith 1997, quoting King 1987). Medieval schoolyards were also where the cruel play of bullying was carried out, while the power-play of physical violence was frequently deployed against children by teachers (Willemsen 2008, 181–90), so much so that in France, Michel de Montaigne (I: 26; Screech 2003, 186) writes of late sixteenth-century classrooms strewn with 'blood-stained birch rods'. To some degree this violence was reciprocated and there are depictions in medieval art showing children abusing teachers: St Felix was one of several saints and clerics martyred by their pupils, usually by pieces of school equipment (including pen tips and penknives) (Willemsen 2008, 139–40).

Throughout the medieval period formal education was a mechanism of social structuring in the control of secular and ecclesiastical elites. By the later Middle Ages pupils commonly deployed the playing of board games as a rejection of the boredom and strictures of the school day but for much of the medieval period the use of board games was a formal aspect of some teaching. Medieval social elites were always drawn to games as a demonstration of their status. Irish law codes of the seventh and eighth century, the sagas (e.g. Orkneyinga Saga) of the twelfth and thirteenth centuries and the values of the courtly culture of north-west Europe in the thirteenth and fourteenth centuries all set a high store on aristocratic proficiency at board games, always seen as a fitting attribute of a prince. The Irish law codes list the board games fidcheall and brandubh as games to be taught to boys of noble birth, along with how to swim, ride a horse and throw a spear: part of their training for a life of leisure, hunting and warfare (Hall 2011; Kelly 1997, 452; Ó Cróinín 1995, 132–4). In Orkneyinga Saga Earl Rognvald of Orkney lists board games as the first of nine skills needed by a nobleman (Caldwell et al. 2009, 177), and the Disciplina Clericalis of Petrus Alfonsi (c. 1100–1125) lists chess as one of the seven skills to be acquired by a good knight (Vale 2001, 171). In the late sixteenth century Montaigne (I: 26; Screech 2003, 185) recommends racing, wrestling, music-making, dances, hunting, arms and games as necessary to educate a man properly. As late as the seventeenth century, skill at tables, dice and cards was still part of the Gaelic panegyric code of 'great man poetry' (Caldwell et al. 2009, 177).

Some of this teaching was clearly a matter of household upbringing but archaeology also confirms that early medieval monastic schools had a role in teaching boys how (and why) to play board games. Excavations at St Marnock's chapel, Inchmarnock (a small island off the island of Bute, Scotland) uncovered some thirty-five graffiti gaming boards (plus several fragments and playing pieces) along with a number of other slates with graffiti designs, inscriptions and lettering. These are clear indications that the monastery at Inchmarnock included a school (Figure 3.3). The majority of the incised boards are for tafl type games (either hnefatafl and/or fidcheall) and probably date to the eighth or ninth century, but boards for merels and alquerque are also represented (Figure 3.4). The excavation report (Lowe 2008, esp. 114–75 and 257–63) suggests a pre-twelfth-century date for all of these but the difficult site stratigraphy does not permit certainty. The merels and alquerque boards are typically far more likely to date to after the twelfth century and the presence of other, later inscribed slates (including a fifteenth-century example) suggests that the school function continued with the apparent change from a monastic to a proprietorial church. One probable games board design missed in the report (Lowe 2008, 173, IS 71) is paralleled by a similar graffiti from the near-by St Blane's monastery, Bute (Anderson 1900, 313); both may be interpreted as practice attempts at circular variants of chess, merels or the Astronomical Game. Circular merels is an unwinnable game that goes on as long as the two players desire and so could potentially have supported teaching about eternity and social stasis.

Boys to men: children, adults, gender

'Within the culture of play the macro-world of adults is always being introduced into the micro-world of children's play' (Plesch 2002, 197), an observation implicit in much of the preceding discussion but particularly pertinent for this final theme concerning the transition of children to adulthood. All being well, children become adults (which play helps to facilitate) and large numbers of adults look back upon their childhood

Figure 3.3. Reconstruction painting of the Inchmarnock (Isle of Bute) monastic school (reproduced by kind permission of Chris Lowe, Headland Archaeology and the Society of Antiquaries of Scotland).

Figure 3.4. The double-sided slate hnefatafl *board from Inchmarnock (Isle of Bute) (reproduced by kind permission of Chris Lowe, Headland Archaeology and the Society of Antiquaries of Scotland).*

as determining their adult occupation, sometimes romancing their play in the process. Gerald of Wales in the early 1190s remembered his own childhood as including playing with his brothers, with sand and dust – presumably on the beach below their home, Manorbier Castle (Pembrokeshire); they made towns and palaces while he built churches and monasteries (Orme 2003, 175). Here we have a happy collusion of affirming, independent, imaginative play by children and the self-confidence of thinking about making decisions about one's future. Sometimes the adult recollection of play was a nostalgic reminiscence of happy times, which is evident in William Fitz Stephen's 1183 account of London boys playing Shrove Tuesday football, along with an affirmation that play transcended age boundaries:

> After dinner all the youth of the city goes out into the fields to a much-frequented game of ball. The scholars of each school have their own ball, and almost all the workers of each trade have theirs also in their hands. Elder men and fathers and rich citizens come on horseback to watch the contests of their juniors, and after their fashion are young again with the young
>
> *Orme 2003, 179*

Certainly in Scotland a more exclusive approach to the playing of football was applied in the sixteenth century (in part linked to the Reformation). In 1584 Andrew Maxton was admitted as a Master to the Perth Hammermen Incorporation, and included in his fee was being allowed to play at football. There are several entries to this effect in the *Hammermen Book* and in the *Perth Guildry or Lockit Book* just as there are entries indicating that servants and apprentices were not allowed to play football.

Several late medieval texts confirm that children had access to and enjoyed what are often mistakenly assumed to be adult games. A Scottish gentleman, Rait, wrote a poem in the fifteenth century, *Rait's Raving*, advising his son that tables, chess and dice were the games of children (Orme 2003, 178). The fourteenth-century Dutch literary text, *En beghinsel van allen spelen* ('A beginning to all plays [games]') counts amongst children's games dice, knucklebones, chess and other board games. Much earlier still, the partial remains of a Scandinavian child buried in the tenth-century Cloghermore Cave, Co. Kerry (Ireland) included amongst its grave goods two pegged playing pieces (one with the peg missing) typical of the type used in *hnefatafl* (Connolly 2010, 35, 41 and plate 8; for the wider Viking context see Connolly *et al.* 2005). In life these pieces may have belonged to an adult but the excavator infers that the gaming pieces would have served the child in the afterlife. Around the same time, but in a Christian context, in Mikulĉice (Moravia) a bone tablesman (decorated on both sides with an archer and animals) was committed to a ninth- to tenth-century child's grave beside the basilica (Poulík 1975, 18 and fig. 9.1; Kluge-Pinsker 1991, 160, no. B9). Of course, these various games were still also played by adults (Hindman 1981, 464) but by the fourteenth and fifteenth centuries those games that had been the preserve of a social elite, such as chess, were clearly being much played by children. Girls were not excluded from such play – indeed they contributed to the popularity of chess through its inclusion in strategies of Courtly Love, which permitted young women to play young men. Women and girls could also play against each other, as several illuminations in the thirteenth-century *Book of Games* of Alphonso the Wise of Castille show.[4] Below this elite level, however, it is less clear how much choice girls had in their play of board and dice games. Humanist writers, Erasmus and Vives included, advocated play as character forming, in particular for boys, 'restoring the body for further intellectual study' (Hindman 1981, 459), but Erasmus also wrote a colloquy entitled 'Knucklebones or the Game of Tali', tracing its history from ancient Greece, where it was played by men and boys, down to his own time where, by contrast, it had become 'only' a girls game (Hindman 1981, 452). Indeed, Breughel depicts it thus in his painting *Children's Games*, in which he also depicts girls playing with dolls (Roberts 1982, plate 5).

Parenthood has never been a uniformly held skill but we know from one exceptional individual, critical of his own parenting skills, Michel de Montaigne, writing in the mid-to-late sixteenth century, that parents did engage with their children in play. In his essay 'On habit: and on never easily changing a traditional law', he reveals that he played cards with both his wife and young daughter, to illustrate a point about honesty in play and not allowing children to learn dishonest ways that they will take into adulthood. It is, though, only in the context of the more informal domestic sphere that he talks of play in connection with girls and he has far more to say about the importance of play in bringing up boys. In recalling his own tutelage, he recounts how he learnt Greek like a game and so more effectively and compares this to those teachers who 'use certain board games as a means of learning arithmetic and geometry' (Montaigne I: 26; Screech 2003, 196) (a use to which games are still put today both in the home and at school, see for example Bell and Cornelius 1988).

Conclusion

In a necessarily wide-ranging survey we have seen, through the evidence of archaeology, of language, of text and of art, that medieval play as practiced by children is a fruitful field of study. Children were taught games as a matter of elite behaviour, as a means of learning other things and for their entertainment value; they played games for their inherent qualities of play (absorption, distraction, amusement and discovery), as a ritual practice and as an escape from life and its drudgeries and controls. Play marked out a future transition to adulthood, especially for boys, whom it could send awry if they learnt how to cheat. Play also helped to ritualise Christian beliefs and helped to define childhood in its own terms, giving adults, who were all once children, a rich source of metaphor on social, moral and religious behaviour. Conceptually play is unbounded: potentially children can take any space, any object, any piece of flora or geology and impart to it the quality of a toy or plaything. There are of course constraints – dangers in the environment and from certain objects (especially weapons) and from adult impositions – but play is arguably the fundamental strategy by which children advocate, perform and negotiate their agency. Closely interrogated there is clearly a wealth of material culture from the medieval period that evidences this agency of children; however inaccurate contemporary films dealing with children in the medieval past may be in some of their

---

[4] For an exploration of the female context to chess see Yalom 2004. There is no accessible translation of Alphonso's *Book* but a recent valuable study in German is readily available with all the illuminations reproduced: Schädler and Calvo 2009.

details they do at least share this recognition that past children had agency. This paper has only scratched the surface but enough to endorse Montaigne's opening comment, that children's games 'should be seen as their most serious activity'.

Abbreviations

Montaigne – Michel de Montaigne, *Les Essais* (Screech, M. A. (ed. and trans.) 2003. *The Complete Essays*. London: Penguin).

Bibliography

Alcock, L. 2003. *Kings and Warriors, Craftsmen and Priests in Northern Britain AD 550–850*. Edinburgh: Society of Antiquaries of Scotland.

Anderson, J. 1900. Description of a collection of artefacts found in St Blane's church, Bute. *Proceedings of the Society of Antiquaries of Scotland* 34, 307–25.

Armit, I. 2006. *Anatomy of an Iron age Roundhouse – The Cnip wheelhouse excavations, Lewis*. Edinburgh: Society of Antiquaries of Scotland.

Barnhart, R. K. (ed.) 1988. *The Chambers Dictionary of Etymology*. Edinburgh: Chambers.

Bell, R. C. and Cornelius, M. 1988. *Board Games Round the World: a resource book for mathematical investigations*. Cambridge: Cambridge University Press.

Bethmont-Gallerand, S. 2002. Le joute à cheval-bâton, un jeu et une image de l'enfance à la fin du Moyen Age. *The Profane Arts of the Middle Ages* 9.1–2, 183–96.

Block, E. C. 1999. Pannoy: a play for power. *The Profane Arts of the Middle Ages* 8.1, 45–56.

Biddle, M. 1990. The find spots of the dice, games-board and playing pieces, pp. 697–8 in Biddle, M. (ed.), *Object and Economy in Medieval Winchester, Winchester Studies 7ii: artefacts from medieval Winchester*. Oxford: Clarendon Press.

Britt, A. 2008. On language: avatar. *New York Times.com* for August 10, 2008, 1–3 (available at www.nytimes.com/2008/08/10/magazine).

Caldwell, D. H., Hall, M. A. and Wilkinson, C. M. 2009. The Lewis Hoard of gaming pieces: a re-examination of their context, meanings, discovery and manufacture. *Medieval Archaeology* 53, 155–204.

Callois, R. 1958. *Les Jeux et les Homes*. Paris: Gallimard (Barasch, M. (trans.) 1961. *Man Play and Games*. New York: Free Press of Glencoe).

Connolly, M. 2010. Plunder or funerary offerings? Burial, ritual and artefact deposition in Cloghermore Cave, pp. 33–44 in Murray, G. (ed.), *Medieval Treasures of County Kerry*. Tralee: Kerry County Museum.

Connolly, M., Coyne, F. and Lynch, L. G. 2005. *Underworld: death and burial in Cloghermore Cave, Co. Kerry*. Dublin: Wordwell.

Crawford, S. 2009. The archaeology of play things: theorising a toy stage in the 'biography' of objects. *Childhood in the Past* 2, 55–70.

Crawford, S. and Lewis, C. 2008. Childhood studies and the Society for the Study of Childhood in the Past. *Childhood in the Past* 1, 5–16.

Cunningham, H. 2005. *Children and Childhood in Western Society since 1500*. London: Longman.

Dockrill, S. J., Bond, J. M., Turner, V. E., Brown, L. D., Bashford, D. J., Cussons, J. E. and Nicholson,

R. A. (eds) 2010. *Excavations at Old Scatness, Shetland, Volume 1: the Pictish village and Viking settlement*. Lerwick: Shetland Heritage Publications.

Doppelfeld, O. and Weyres, W. 1980. *Die Ausgrabungen im Dom zu Köln* (Köln Forschungen 1). Mainz: von Zabern.

Duczko, W. 2004. *Viking Rus: studies on the presence of Scandinavians in Eastern Europe*. Leiden: Brill.

Finke, L. A. and Schichtman, M. B. 2009. *Cinematic Illuminations: the Middle Ages on film*. Baltimore: John Hopkins Press.

Gomme, A. B. 1894. *The Traditional Games of England, Scotland and Ireland*. London: Constable.

Hall, M. A. 2002. Cultural interaction in the medieval burgh of Perth, Scotland 1200–1600, pp. 290–301 in Helmig, G., Scholkmann, B. and Untermann, M. (eds), *Centre, Region, Periphery – Medieval Europe Basel 2002 Volume 1*. Hertingen: Archäologische Bodsenforschung Basel-Stadt.

Hall, M. A. 2007. *Playtime in Pictland: the material culture of gaming in first millennium AD Scotland*. Rosemarkie: Groam House Museum Trust.

Hall, M. A. 2009. Where the abbot carries dice: gaming-board misericords in context, pp. 63–82 in Block, E. C. (ed.), *Profane Images in Marginal Arts of the Middle Ages. Proceedings of the VI biennial colloquium of Misericordia International, Sheffield, 2003*. Turnhout: Brepols.

Hall, M. A. 2011. Playtime everyday: the material culture of medieval games, pp. 145–68 in Cowan, T. and Henderson, L. (eds), *A History of Everyday Life in Medieval Scotland 1000–1600*. Edinburgh: Edinburgh University Press.

Hall, M. A. and Forsyth, K. 2011. Roman rules? The introduction of board games to Britain and Ireland. *Antiquity* 85, 1325–38.

Hanawalt, B. 1986. *The Ties That Bound: peasant families in medieval England*. Oxford and New York: Oxford University Press.

Heywood, C. 2001. *A History of Childhood*. London: Polity Press.

Hendrick, H. 1997. *Children, Childhood and English Society 1880–1990*. Cambridge: Cambridge University Press.

Hindman, S. 1981. Pieter Bruegel's *Children's Games*, folly, and chance. *The Art Bulletin* 63 (3), 447–75.

Huizinga, J. 1950. *Homo Ludens. A study of the play element in culture*. Boston: Beacon Press.

Kelly, F. 1997. *Early Irish Farming: a study based mainly on the law-texts of the 7th and 8th centuries AD*. Dublin: Dublin Institute for Advanced Studies (School of Celtic Studies).

Khoroshev, A. S. 2007. Toys and miniatures, pp. 344–53 in Brisbane, M. and Hather, J. (eds), *Wood Use in Medieval Novgorod*. Oxford: Oxbow.

King, N. R. 1987. Elementary-school play: theory and research, pp. 143–66 in Block, J. H. and King, N. R. (eds), *School Play: a source book*. New York: Garland.

Klapisch-Zuber, C. 1998. Holy dolls: play and piety in Florence in the Quattrocento, pp. 111–27 in McHam, S. (ed.), *Looking at Italian Renaissance Sculpture*. Cambridge: Cambridge University Press.

Kluge-Pinsker, A. 1991. *Schach und Trictrac Zeugnisse mittelalterlicher spielfreude in Salischerzeit*. Simaringen: Jan Thorbecke.

Lang, J. 1990. Nightmare in the mirror of adolescence and the death of difference. *Social Text* 24, 156–66.

Larson, L. M. (trans.) 1917. *The King's Mirror (Speculum regale-Konungs skuggsjá)* (Scandinavian Monographs 3). New York: American-Scandinavian Foundation.

Leenen, B. (ed.) 2010. *Ritter, Burgen und Intrigen, Aufruhr 1225. Das Mittelalter an Rhein und Ruhr*. Exhibition catalogue of the Museum für Archëologie Westfälisches Landesmuseum Herne. Mainz: Verlag Philip van Zubern.

Lewis, C. 2009. Children's play in the later medieval English countryside. *Childhood in the Past* 2, 86–108.

Loomis, R. S. 1958. Scotland and the Arthur legend. *Proceedings of the Society of Antiquaries of Scotland* 89, 1–21.

Lowe, C. (ed.) 2008. *Inchmarnock. An early historic island monastery and its archaeological landscape*. Edinburgh: Society of Antiquaries of Scotland.

Márkus, G. (trans.) 1997. *Adomnán's 'Law of the Innocents', Cain Adomnáin: a seventh-century law for the protection of non-combatants*. Glasgow: University of Glasgow.

McLaren, D. and Hunter, F. 2008. New aspects of rotary querns in Scotland. *Proceedings of the Society of Antiquaries of Scotland* 112, 392–436.

McLean, T. n.d. *The English at Play in the Middle Ages*. Windsor Forest: Kensal Press.

Mygland, S. S. 2007. *Children in Medieval Bergen. An archaeological analysis of child related artefacts* (The Bryggen Papers Main Series 7). Bergen: Fagbokforlaget.

Ní Dhonnchadha, M. 1995. The Lex Innocentium: Adomnán's Law for Women, Clerics and Youths, 697 AD, pp. 58–69 in O'Dowd, M. and Wickert, S. (eds), *Chattel, Servant or Citizen: women's status in church, state and society*. Belfast: Institute of Irish Studies, Queen's University Belfast.

Ó Cróinín, D. 1995. *Early Medieval Ireland 400–1200*. London: Longman.

Opie, I. and Opie, P. 1959. *The Lore and Language of Schoolchildren*. Oxford: Oxford University Press.

Opie, I. and Opie, P. 2008. *Children's Games in Street and Playground* (reprint of 1969 edition). Edinburgh: Floris Books.

Orme, N. 2003. *Medieval Children*. New Haven and London: Yale University Press.

Orme, N. 2008. Medieval childhood: challenge, change and achievement. *Childhood in the Past* 1, 106–19.

Plesch, V. 2002. 'Memory on the wall': graffiti on religious wall paintings. *The Journal of Medieval and Early Modern Studies* 32 (1), 167–97.

Post, P. 1995. 'An excellent game ...': on playing the Mass, pp. 185–214 in Caspars, C., Lukken, G. and Rouwhuorst, G. (eds), *Bread of Heaven Customs and Practices Surrounding Holy Communion: essays in the history of liturgy and culture*. Kaupen: Kok Pharos.

Postman, N. 1996. *The Disappearance of Childhood*. London: Vintage.

Poulík, J. 1975. Mikulĉice: capital of the lords of Great Moravia, pp. 1–31 in Bruce-Mitford, R. (ed.), *Recent Archaeological Excavations in Europe*. London: Routledge and Keegan Paul.

Randall, L. M. C. 1972. Games and the Passion in Pucelle's Hours of Jeanne D' Évreux. *Speculum* 47 (2), 246–57.

Roberts, K. 1982. *Bruegel* (third edition). London: Phaidon.

Rybina, E. A. 2007. Chess pieces and game boards, pp. 354–9 in Brisbane M. and Hather, J. (eds), *Wood Use in Medieval Novgorod*. Oxford: Oxbow.

Schädler, U. and Calvo, R. (eds) 2009. *Alfonso X. 'der Weise' Das Buch Der Spiele*. Vienna and Berlin: LIT.

Screech, M. A. (ed. and trans.) 2003. *The Complete Essays*. London: Penguin

Sigman, A. 2009. *The Spoilt Generation: why restoring childhood will make our children and society happier*. London: Piatkus.

Stummen Hansen, S. and Larsen, A. C. 2000. Miniature quern- and millstones from Shetland's Scandinavian past. *Acta Archaeologica* 71, 105–21.

Sutton-Smith, B. 1997. *The Ambiguity of Play*. Cambridge, Mass.: Harvard University Press.

Tanner, J. D. 1953. Tombs of royal babies in Westminster Abbey. *The Journal of the British Archaeological Association* XVI, 25–46.

Utz, R. 2005. Remembering ritual murder: the anti-Semitic blood accusation narrative in medieval and contemporary cultural memory, pp. 145–62 in Østrem, E., Brunn, M. B., Petersen, N. H. and Fleischer, J. (eds), *Genre and Ritual: the cultural heritage of medieval rituals*. Copenhagen: Museum Tusculanum Press.

Vale, M. 2001. *The Princely Court. Medieval courts and culture in north-west Europe*. Oxford: Oxford University Press.

Van Belle, R. 1997. Woodland pastimes on the Cortschoof brass and other Flemish brasses. *Transactions of the Monumental Brass Society* XVI, 26–47.

Willemsen, A. 2001. Playing with reality. Games and toys in the oeuvre of Hieronymus Bosch, pp. 192–9 in Koldeweij, A. M., Vermet, B. and van Kooji, B. (eds), *Hieronymus Bosch: new insights into his life and work*. Rotterdam: Museum Boijmans Van Beuningen.

Willemsen, A. 2005. The game of the month. Playful calendars in Ghent-Bruges Books of Hours, pp. 419–30 in Dekeyzer, B. and Van der Stock, J. (eds), *Manuscripts in Transition. Recycling manuscripts, texts and images*. Leuwen: Uitgeven Peeters.

Willemsen, A. 2008. *Back to the Schoolyard. The daily practice of medieval and Renaissance education* (Studies in European Urban History 1100–1800 15). Turnhout: Brepols.

Woodfield, C. 1981. Finds from the Free Grammar School at the Whitefriars, Coventry *c*. 1545–*c*. 1557/8. *Post-Medieval Archaeology* 15, 81–159.

Yalom, M. 2004. *Birth of the Chess Queen. A history*. London: Pandora Press.

4. The Spaces of Late Medieval Peasant Childhood: Children and social reproduction

Sally V. Smith

Medieval childhood is a topic which has recently attracted the attention of a number of archaeologists. Significant studies have been carried out on a range of evidence related to the lives of medieval children, most notably toys (*e.g.* Crawford 2009) and skeletal remains (*e.g.* Crawford 1999; Jay 2009; Lewis 2007; Mays *et al.* 2002). Innovative work on childhood in the medieval countryside has also been undertaken by Carenza Lewis (2009). However, other than Lewis' study – which was primarily concerned with locating evidence for children's play activities – there has been limited engagement with spatial issues in the investigation of medieval childhoods. This chapter hopes to consider how archaeologists can start to think about space in order to elucidate the experiences of medieval children. The work of geographers may be helpful in this regard. Human geographers have developed a considerable literature on children's use and experience of space (see McKendrick 2000 for an annotated bibliography, and Philo (2000) for an excellent introduction to this literature). Geographical work on children tends to fall into two categories: studies which concentrate on children's spatial cognition and competencies, such as their ability to use and construct maps; and those which come from a more sociological perspective and which investigate children as actors in the social world (Holloway and Valentine 2000, 8; Matthews and Limb 1999, 65). It is this latter strand of work which has the greatest potential for archaeologists. This work has, in particular, focussed on the investigation of children's use of the everyday spaces of the home, school, street and playground, their habitual exploitation of various spatial 'ranges' – that is those spaces that are explored either regularly, occasionally, or rarely by children – and the diversity of childhoods as affected by class, gender and ethnicity.

While archaeologists of childhood do stress the importance of engagement with research from other disciplines (*e.g.* Baxter 2006a, 5), this often involves a focus on the potential of ethnographic and historical sources, rather than on the work of geographers. Engagement with the themes discussed by geographers, however, introduces the possibility of writing an 'historical geography' of medieval childhood rooted in the archaeological evidence. This chapter attempts to explore this possibility with respect to the archaeology of the late medieval English peasantry.

Context

The specific concern of this chapter is to explore the contribution that spatial evidence can make to an investigation of the process of socialisation and, therefore, of social reproduction – that is, the perpetuation of social structures over time. In other words, the chapter addresses the various ways in which the experiences of childhood were implicated in the continued reproduction of the late medieval world. However, before I go on to discuss this, it is important to highlight what appears to be a potential tension in the geographical and archaeological literature concerning children's use of space. Some scholars place considerable stress on the notion that children's work and play activities, and use of space in general, are a vital part of their socialisation into the adult world. Other scholars, in contrast, emphasise children's *distinctive* use of space, inasmuch as it appears to be different from that of adults. Of the first group, Nicholas Orme (2001, 307) and Shulamith Shahar (1990, 242–4), for example, mention the importance of childhood activity, which is intrinsically spatial, to the maintenance of gendered distinctions in the medieval period (on which I will have more to say later in the chapter). Katherine Kamp (2001, 18–19) draws attention to the way that play, in particular, is part of the way children learn social values. Similarly, Sally Crawford and Carenza Lewis (2008, 11) argue that studying childhood experiences in general is vital in understanding political, social and economic change, and, by definition, continuity. Jane Baxter (2005, 59), too, argues that 'children are enculturated and socialised in all aspects of their culture, and are taught the norms, values and behaviours deemed acceptable. Many of these behaviours and expectations concern the use of space'. She further suggests that 'As children begin to explore their environment they do not encounter spaces that are culturally "neutral", but rather each space is given a cultural context and meaning that shapes the types of behaviours and activities that take place there' (Baxter 2006b, 79).

Another group of scholars, however, emphasise the uniqueness and distinctiveness of children's use of space. Laurie Wilkie (2000) argues that children create and maintain spaces distinct from those of adults – for example, that they often seek out smaller and more secluded private spaces than do adults, which is a point made repeatedly in the literature on children's geographies. Sarah Holloway and Gill Valentine (2000, 10) also stress that 'young children use, experience and value space differently from adults'. Owain Jones (2000, 36) quotes the work of Robin Moore who suggests that children's patterns of interaction with a given terrain 'are more intimate, fluid, intense' than those of adults. Matthews and Limb (1999), in their work on children's geographies, also stress major differences in children's use of space from that of adults, which range from differences in risk-assessment of the landscape, to differences in heeding physical boundaries, to differences in identifying certain places as suitable for recreational opportunities.

There seem to a number of reasons for these different emphases. Firstly, the concern with difference – as in the difference between children and adults' use of space – seems to resonate with wider trends in the social sciences. In recent decades, there has been an attempt to give a voice to the 'other' in academic analyses (whether 'the other' be women, people of colour, non-heterosexual people, disabled people and so on). This attempt has meant that disciplines such as anthropology, geography, sociology and, indeed, archaeology, have been concerned with emphasising diversity and difference. Geographies and archaeologies of children can, therefore, be seen as a part of this general trend to highlight the specific experiences of an often-ignored social group. In a related manner, the emphasis on the distinctiveness of children's use of space also appears to be due to a desire to avoid discussing children in an instrumentalist way, that is, as if their activities and experiences only have analytical value because of what they can tell us about the adult world which they ultimately inhabit.

Secondly, it would seem that archaeologists, who of necessity are typically interested in investigating longer periods of time than scholars in other fields, are inclined to emphasise children's activities in long-term social reproduction. Human geographers, on the other hand, who less frequently take an explicitly historical perspective, may naturally emphasise the more fine-grained differences in the use of space between children and adults. However, while much of the specific detail of the geographers' work deals with contemporary society, it does seem likely that the very *fact* of difference in the use and perception of space between children and adults would be applicable to past societies and therefore cannot simply be dismissed by archaeologists.

A tension, therefore, does seem to exist between these two orientations, both of which, nonetheless, have intuitive appeal. It seems obvious that part of children's socialisation occurred via their use of space and through absorbing the social values connected with particular spaces. But it also seems self-evident that children use space, and probably did in the past, in a way differently from the way that adults do or did. So how did children use space both uniquely but also in such a way as to reproduce long-term, adult, social categories and values? It seems to me that a way to reconcile these two views is simply to accept that neither of these stances can offer the ultimate statement about children's use of space. Children (and, indeed, women, men, and the elderly) all use and used space differently from one another but this does not preclude the presence, learning and reproduction of dominant values. It may be that at times of social change these different perspectives played a part in refashioning the social environment, but it seems likely that, over the course of large chunks of historical time, they could be assimilated into the dominant discourse.

This chapter, therefore, is concerned with examining medieval children's use of space and related socialisation practices in order to determine what such an examination may be able to tell us about the reproduction of medieval society. It must be noted that I do not understand socialisation in the way outlined by Sofaer-Derevenski (1997, 194) as an essentially Freudian notion concerned with suppression. Rather, I follow Flordeliz Bugarin's (2006, 16) definition of socialisation as 'a process in which children, on their own, are learning how to satisfy their needs as well as the needs of their society'. While many archaeologists are concerned with the issue of social reproduction, and often draw on notions of *habitus* and structuration theory (*e.g.* Miller 1987), children's experiences are rarely mentioned. It is important to understand that such experiences also had a role in this process and that we, as archaeologists, are equipped to investigate this.

Social power

I would, first, like to turn to the issue of social power in late medieval England. While resistance to feudal power did occur and can be seen archaeologically (*e.g.* Smith 2009b), it must also be recognised that feudal power relationships were maintained,

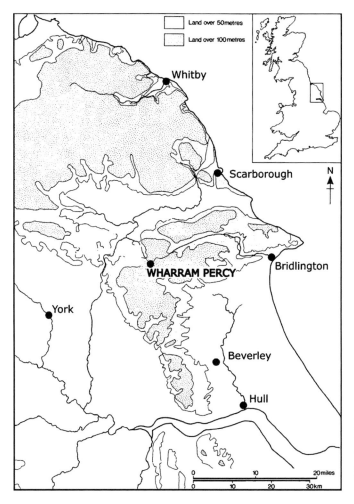

Figure 4.1. Location of Wharram Percy (North Yorkshire) (adapted from Beresford and Hurst 1990).

to a greater or lesser extent, for a number of centuries. Scholars have recognised the part that 'extra-economic' coercion played in maintaining these power relationships; in other words, that members of the seigneurial ranks did not retain their social position primarily due to their economic dominance – rather, political and ideological forces played a role in maintaining feudal relations of subordination (Rigby 1995). Ideological forces will often take material form, and attempts at maintaining feudal authority can be seen in entities as diverse as castles (Austin 1984, 71; Creighton 2002, 35), items of clothing (Hunt 1996, 307) and deer parks (Almond 1993; Marvin 1999). I would like to consider the part that childhood socialisation may have played in the maintenance of feudal authority, by turning to the village of Wharram Percy (North Yorkshire), the most archaeologically well-investigated late medieval settlement in England (see Figure 4.1 for its location). I have previously outlined the archaeological evidence for lordly power at this village (Smith 2009a) but I would here like to concentrate on just one aspect of that evidence, and to draw out the effects it would have had on the village's children in particular.

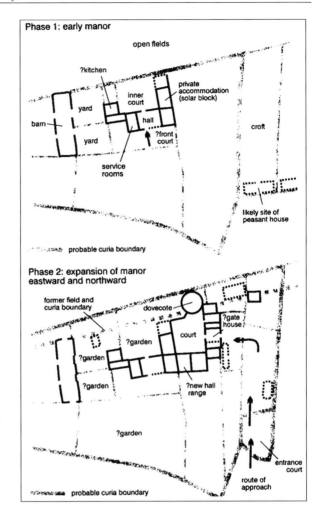

Figure 4.2. Interpretive phase plan of the North Manor, Wharram Percy (North Yorkshire) (after Oswald 2004; © English Heritage, National Monuments Record).

One of the most archaeologically-obvious examples of the exercise of lordly power at Wharram Percy can be seen in changes to the north row of the village, which occurred around the date 1245. This was caused by the construction of the North Manor buildings (Figure 4.2). It seems likely that this construction was initiated when the Percy family acquired the interest in the manor of the Chamberlains, the previous lords (Rahtz and Watts 2004, 295). The South Manor area (in Area 10) seems to have been the site of the Chamberlains' manorial buildings, although some of the dating of the structures in these two areas is disputed. What is important about the construction of the North Manor for our purposes here is that it seems likely that this dwelling and its associated outbuildings and ancillary structures were laid out over previously-used space, rather than empty land. In the first phase of construction, former open fields were built over (Oswald 2004, 30, 41) while the second major phase of building caused the destruction of at least one, and possibly two, peasant tofts in the north row and a further encroachment into an agricultural field (Oswald 2004, 45, 62–3; and see Beresford and Hurst 1990, 47, 80).

What is the significance of this evidence for the investigation of the archaeology of childhood and social reproduction? The initial issue to consider emerges from the work of both social geographers and medieval historians which points to the special and intimate familiarity that most children, both now and in the past, had with the spaces of their homes. Lewis (2009, 91) – using Barbara Hanawalt's data gleaned from medieval coroners' records – writes that 'In particular ... we can ... observe that the home and other private space occur with notable frequency in coroners' records for children of all ages and surmise that these were areas where children spent significant amounts of time'. Geographer Jeni Harden's (2000, 47) work on children's theorising of risk illuminates children's very strong association made between the home and feelings of safety due, in large part, to the fact of the home's private, enclosed space. Harden draws on the work of Irving Goffman who points out that 'walls, ceiling and floor tend to establish outside limits to a surround, the assumption being that these barriers are stout enough to keep out potential matters for alarm' (cited in Harden 2000, 47).While it may be possible that some of the strong associations with security that the children mentioned are due to the modern idealization of the private, the feelings of physical enclosure within the home would have been as true for the children of Wharram Percy as they would have been for the twentieth-century children who formed part of Harden's study. Indeed, Felicity Riddy (2003, 217) has pointed out that the medieval use of the word 'homly' did indeed 'cluster round ideas of familiarity, closeness, affection, privacy, intimacy and everyday-ness ... "home" is the focus of feelings associated with where you belong and what you are most attached to'. The profound familiarity that young children have with the home environment, therefore (see Philo 2000, 247), seems likely to have obtained in the medieval period.

Another issue of importance here is the idea that 'families are the primary agents of socialisation' (Baxter 2005, 30). What occurs within the domestic sphere will have very strong effects on the types of cultural knowledge that is imparted to children (for a modern example see Sebba 1991). The destruction of the entire built environment of the home by manorial lords, coupled with their parents' powerlessness, would have made a durable impact on medieval children who inhabited houses such as those in the north row of Wharram Percy. Such an act and the corresponding major disruption of their familiar environment would have been an expression of the power relations that existed within medieval society on an especially intimate and serious scale. Consequently, such experiences may have made a contribution to the social reproduction of feudal power relations, as part of the 'extra-economic' coercion employed by medieval lords.

While this example deals with the archaeological evidence for a small area of one village, it alerts us to the importance of looking at the spatial reorganisation of medieval settlements, particularly domestic structures, in terms of their effect on medieval children. While we must be very wary of attributing all such reorganisation to lordly efforts (see Dyer 1985; Lewis *et al.*1997), there are occasions, such as at Wharram Percy, where the hand of the lord can perhaps relatively uncontroversially be adduced. For example, Meaux Abbey (East Yorkshire) was responsible for the depopulation of two entire settlements (senior ecclesiastical officials such as abbots could act as manorial lords in the late medieval period, and could be owed labour services by peasants just as secular lords could). The chronicles of the abbey record that 'where the village of Meaux was sited there is now our grange which is called North Grange' (Waites

1962, 651n.). In addition, some time after 1200, the abbey had converted the hamlet of Myton (East Yorkshire) into a grange (Allison 1969, 11). Eaton Socon (Bedfordshire) suffered a similar fate in the twelfth century when the lord, desiring the site for his castle, relocated the entire village (Harvey 1989). These examples and the many others in which settlements were destroyed or removed for the creation of parklands and other seigneurial appurtenances can, therefore, when viewed from the perspective of rural children, be seen partially to be constitutive of the power relations of medieval society.

Gender

A key concern of those interested in childhood and socialisation has been the importance of juvenile experiences in the reproduction of a society's gender roles, and archaeologists have been urged to investigate this issue with respect to their data (*e.g.* Kamp 2001, 14). In this section, I aim to explore how archaeological data may offer insight into the gender identities of women in medieval England.

Social historians have carried out much work which, both directly and indirectly, has dealt with medieval countrywomen's sense of identity. Some of this has focused on practices which would have strengthened women's sense of group identity such as the process of birthing, churching ceremonies, and parish activities (*e.g.* McMurray Gibson 1996; French 1996; 2003; Houlbrooke 1986; Bennett 1981; van Houts 1999). Others, meanwhile, have stressed the importance of the household to the identity of medieval women. For example, Stephen Rigby (1995, 280) argues that 'in terms of a *subjective* sense of social identity and immediate economic interests, membership of a household was more important than gender'.

Noticeably absent, however, is the inclusion of archaeological – and particularly spatial – data in these discussions of countrywomen's identities. This is regrettable, as 'from the perspective of a life organised by physical existence … subjective consciousness is understood as an epiphenomenon of body' which involves 'barriers and distances and gestures' (Graves 2000, 15). Joanna Sofaer-Derevenski (1998) has argued that gender identity, in particular, is at least partly related to a cumulative identification with a repertoire of material forms and social practices (see also Ingold 1993). The use of space, therefore, can be seen as an important element in the production of identity including that related to gender.

To investigate this proposition, let us consider the earthworks of the village of Wawne in the former East Riding of Yorkshire. This village is situated near the east bank of the River Hull, and is located between the towns of Hull and Beverley (Figure 4.3). In 1984 Colin Hayfield published a detailed post-excavation report on the rescue excavation and survey work which had been carried out in 1961combined with the results of extensive historical research. During the course of these excavations, three types of building foundation that could be dated to the medieval period were identified and were described in the subsequent report as Types A, B and C. Here we will concentrate on the Type C houses, 16 out of the 18 of which were aligned along the southern side of the south road and all of which were of longhouse form. The ceramic evidence

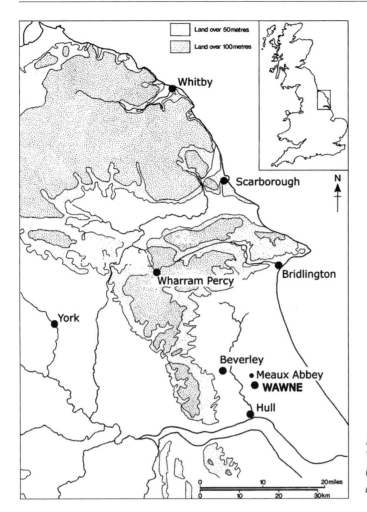

Figure 4.3. Location of Wawne (East Yorkshire) (adapted from Beresford and Hurst 1990).

indicated that the buildings were occupied from the middle of the fourteenth century into the early post-medieval period (Hayfield 1984).

Connected to the 18 Type C houses were only 10 fold-yards (a small enclosure for the keeping of livestock) (Figure 4.4), and it seems reasonable to surmise that these spaces were shared by the inhabitants of some of the houses. There is, in addition, no evidence that boundaries delineated the crofts (small piece of land surrounding the peasant houses) at Wawne (Hayfield 1984). These spatial arrangements could, it can be suggested, have particularly affected the closeness of *women's* interaction, because there is good documentary evidence that demonstrates that medieval women's taskscape included the space of the house and its surrounds more than did that of men (*e.g.* Hanawalt 1986, 145). The sharing of the fold-yards and the closeness of the crofts would, therefore, have meant that the women of this village would have interacted with each other on a very regular basis. The frequency and closeness of this interaction may have been greater at Wawne and similar villages than it would have been for women who

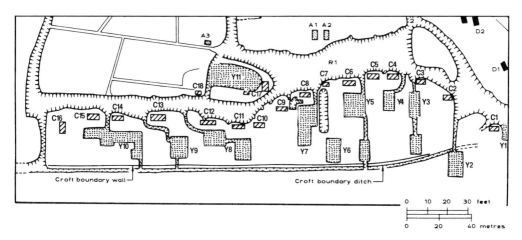

Figure 4.4. Type C houses and fold-yard features from Wawne (East Yorkshire) (adapted from Hayfield 1984 by permission of Landscape History*).*

lived in villages where clear toft boundaries were present. Moreover, women living in villages or nucleated settlements of any sort would have had greater opportunities for physical interaction (as well as for the parish and other activities outlined by historians) than would women who lived in dispersed settlements or hamlets. Given the statements on identity acquisition discussed above, which highlight the importance of physical practice and the affordances of space, there seems to be evidence for not inconsiderable variation in medieval women's gender, as opposed to family or occupational, identity. Interrogating archaeological data, therefore, allows us to give nuance to the general picture of medieval rural women's identities.

When we turn to the question of how these identities would have been reproduced through time, the importance of considering children's experience once again comes to the fore. In many societies, 'the tasks allotted to children tend to parallel the adult gender divisions of labour' (Kamp 2001, 16). Scholars of the Middle Ages have been among those suggesting that adult gender roles were reflected in the different behaviours expected of and encouraged in boys and girls. For example, Shulamith Shahar's (1990, 244) work leads her to conclude that 'girls usually worked more with their mothers and other women while boys worked with their fathers and the other village males'. Similarly, Nicholas Orme (2001, 307), again utilising the work of Barbara Hanawalt, writes that 'small girls followed their mothers in cooking or drawing water, while small boys were attracted to their fathers' work with tools and animals'.

Such evidence is important as children may be understood as 'learners and practisers of gender' (Sofaer-Derevenski 1997, 194) and one of the main ways through which they learn gendered behaviours is through imitative performance. Learning various tasks with the parent of the same gender would have taken place in conjunction with a host of other, unspoken and implicit, signals which would also have reinforced gender conventions (Baxter 2005, 30). Jane Baxter (2005, 30) has pointed out that 'cultural knowledge is acquired through multiple associations of learning including visual, aural and tactile experiences'. I would add to these kinetic experiences, that is, those concerning bodily movement through space. As girls followed their mothers around their taskscape, attending to the explicit lessons being imparted but also learning unconsciously from their movement around space and interactions with others, ideas about what it was to be female would have been absorbed. Such ideas would have been quite different for a girl moving around Wawne – working with her mother and sisters and encountering other mothers and daughters in the fold-yards, seeing her mother interact and converse with them there and on the streets – from the experiences of a girl living in a hamlet whose daily interactions would predominantly have been with members (of both sexes) of her nuclear family. In the latter case, the girl's sense of herself as member of a social group of *women*, as opposed to primarily being a member of a *family* group, would surely have been muted.

It is possible to understand, therefore, that the spatial configuration of settlements like Wawne is likely to have engendered a greater sense of gender-group identity for medieval women than at places with firmer physical boundaries between crofts or at dispersed settlements. Moreover, it seems likely that it was girls' emulation of their mother's use of space which would have played a part in the continuation of the variation in this aspect of women's identity. In a way similar to that of feudal power, it can be seen that looking at the spatiality of rural sites allows us to understand how the experience of medieval children was key to the maintenance of, and variation in, fundamental aspects of social organisation.

Village community

Settlement topography did not just affect the experience of gendered communities. Peasant experience of community *in toto* also varied according to different spatial affordances, particularly those connected to nucleated and dispersed settlements. For example, Christopher Dyer (1991, 48) has noted that a sense of community is likely to have been weaker in dispersed settlements and Brian Roberts (1983, 44–5) has argued in a similar vein that it is only in nucleated settlement that all the forces of 'communality' that he defines (of assent, to economise and by enforcement) would have been operative. The exploration of the maintenance of such communities in villages is once again advanced when we take into account issues of space, children's experiences and socialisation.

Firstly, it seems probable that medieval children recognised and experienced the spaces of their settlements in a similar way to adults; as a 'community', and an interim space between 'home' and the wider world. Harden's (2000, 50) work on modern children has shown that this intermediate sphere was particularly marked in rural children's perceptions 'where the village was perceived in some respects as an extended family or community with people watching out for each other'. In fact, and crucially, it is possible to see that children's use and perceptions of space in nucleated settlements may have been *more* communal than that of medieval adults. Here, I draw on the work of Owain Jones, a scholar who has researched the 'geographies of play' of children residing in modern English villages. Jones' observation of the children's play in the village of 'Allswell' demonstrated that younger children, in particular, 'seem much less clearly aware of the presence and/or significance of sharply defined boundaries of ownership, and private and public space. Consequently they may wander (or race) ... through the

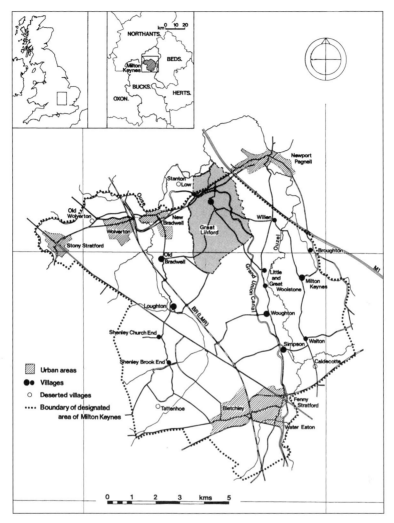

Figure 4.5. Map showing location of Great Linford (Buckinghamshire) in relation to modern Milton Keynes (adapted from Ivens et al. *1995 and reproduced by permission of the Buckinghamshire Archaeological Society).*

striated geographies of adult symbolic and material boundaries' (Jones 2000, 36). While parental attitudes did affect the extent to which children heeded these boundaries, what was critical was their permeability: 'If these boundaries are to some extent permeable to children, they have a chance to build their own geographies, to ... in effect create a dimension parallel to that of the adult space' (Jones 2000, 41). Lewis' (2009, 91) comment that medieval children 'ranged widely across both public and private areas of the rural landscape' lends support to the applicability of this point to the medieval context.

To turn to an archaeological example, let us look at the village of Great Linford (Buckinghamshire) (Figure 4.5). This was a nucleated village, which had developed

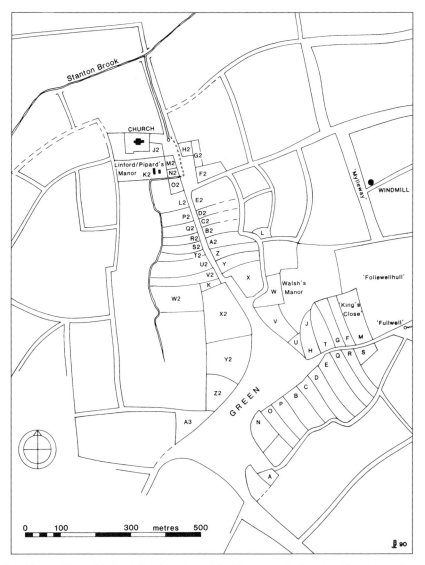

Figure 4.6. Plan of Great Linford (Buckinghamshire) in the early fourteenth century (reproduced by permission of the Buckinghamshire Archaeological Society).

around a green and, by the late thirteenth to fourteenth century, 'the village plan with regularly laid out crofts ... was fully developed' (Mynard *et al.* 1991, 17) (Figure 4.6). If we attend to the way that scholars have discussed the manner in which space, landscape and movement through it give expression to basic social values, categories and relations (see Lefebvre 1991, 143; Soja 1985, 90–127), we can see that the regularly laid out plan of Great Linford would have served to evoke meanings of cohesion and community (see Smith 2010). Given Jones' (2000) work, mentioned above, it is further possible to suggest that the 'community' experienced by the children of Great Linford would have

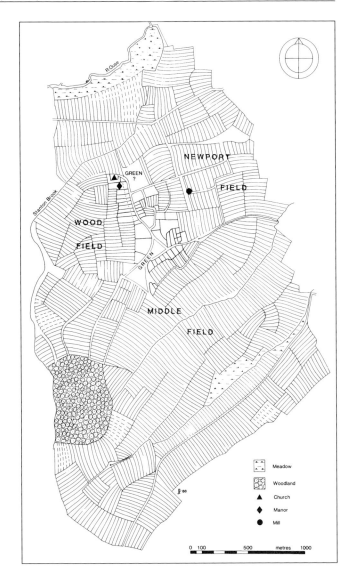

Figure 4.7. The medieval field system of Great Linford (Buckinghamshire) (reproduced by permission of the Buckinghamshire Archaeological Society).

been even stronger than that experienced by adults. If (as Lewis pointed out) children were swarming around both public and private spaces, it seems likely (especially given that the aforementioned croft boundaries all took the form of ditches, rather than walls; Mynard *et al.* 1991, 54, 60, 67) that the children of this village used space more freely than adults, and ignored boundaries that their parents are likely to have respected.

Let us consider another aspect of Great Linford which is relevant to a consideration of community: the evidence for the social practices connected to agricultural activities. Arable land at this village was allocated in what is often regarded as the 'classic' medieval fashion, with each tenant farming individual strips which were scattered through two large fields (Mynard *et al.* 1991, 8) (Figure 4.7). Land was therefore controlled in a communal way. In addition, there is evidence from the fifteenth century that suggests that the meadows were divided into portions called 'doles' and 'swathes', and from the sixteenth century of grazing also being communally and strictly controlled (Mynard *et al.* 1991, 9). It is widely accepted that the classic open-field agricultural system such as that which pertained in Great Linford would have necessitated and reproduced a strong sense of village community (*e.g.* Schofield 2003, 72). But, again, cognisance of the work of social geographers allows us to suggest that the agricultural landscape here would have produced particularly keen feelings of communality for the children of the village. Whether traversing the fields on a journey elsewhere or using the space for play (although presumably not during the period of crop growth), it is quite easy to envisage children moving around unconstrained, quite unaware of the small stones and other objects that may have marked out different tenants' selions, and which would have had great importance for their parents.

As mentioned above, many scholars have pointed out that nucleated settlements like villages did produce a higher degree of 'communalism' than, say, dispersed settlements. And yet, there was always a tension between the maintenance of the community and the upholding of individual rights to both space and resources and to individual privacy, both jealously guarded. Indeed, in some areas of England at this time there was even an offence, called 'hamsok', which involved the unacceptable impingement on another's private space (Müller 2001). Perhaps one reason why we see the continuity of the medieval village community, despite the material culture and legal structures which often emphasised the separate household unit, is connected to childhood experiences of this community, and particularly those of young children who had yet to pick up on adult strictures regarding ownership or privacy. Baxter (2005, 23) has written about socialisation as a dialogue rather than as a one-way transmission from adult to child. Similarly, geographers have discussed the 'street' (defined as outdoor public spaces) as 'thirdspaces' in children's lives, and they have outlined ways in which their use of space may reproduce adult norms but occasionally also challenge them (see Philo 2000, 251). The spaces of medieval childhood, therefore, and the knowledge created through encounters with them (see Barrett 2001, 141–64), may have acted in dialogue with some of the centrifugal forces of the adult world to sustain the village community.

Conclusion

This chapter has focused on the way that approaching the archaeological evidence of the medieval countryside from the perspective of children's experience can help us to understand the reproduction of particular aspects of medieval society. It might be said that this emphasis on socialisation fails to focus on children 'in their own right', a criticism made by Sofaer-Derevenski (2000) in her discussion of archaeological approaches to children. In one sense this would be an accurate appraisal of the current chapter, insofar as my focus has been on the reproduction of medieval society. However, if we conceptualise 'socialisation' as Bugarin (2006) does, as a process whereby children learn to satisfy their needs as well as society's, or as dialogue as Baxter (2005) suggests, such a focus can be seen to be investigating a key component of children's own experiences. Moreover, given that the world which is reproduced by the socialisation process became, in turn, the society which subsequent generations of children inhabited, this process can be considered central to the lives of medieval children themselves.

In addition to its focus on socialisation and social reproduction, this chapter has attempted to elucidate, as Chris Philo (2000, 245) writes, some of the 'differential *possibilities* for engagements with space, place environment and landscape' that medieval rural children lived out. In so doing, I have hoped to highlight the contribution that an investigation of space and spatiality, informed by the work of scholars in cognate fields, can make to the archaeological investigation of medieval childhood.

Bibliography

Allison, K. J. 1969. Medieval Hull, pp. 11–89 in Allison, K. J. (ed.), *A History of the County of York: East Riding volume I, the City of Kingston upon Hull*. Oxford: Institute of Historical Research.

Almond, R. 1993. Medieval hunting: ruling classes and commonalty. *Medieval History* 3, 147–55.

Austin, D. 1984. The castle and the landscape: annual lecture to the Society for Landscape Studies, May 1984. *Landscape History* 6, 69–81.

Barrett, J. C. 2001. Agency, the duality of structure and the problem of the archaeological record, pp. 141–64 in Hodder, I. (ed.), *Archaeological Theory Today*. Cambridge: Polity Press.

Baxter, J. E. 2005. *The Archaeology of Childhood: children, gender and material culture*. Walnut Creek: Altamira Press.

Baxter, J. E. 2006a. Introduction: the archaeology of childhood in context, pp. 1–9 in Baxter, J. E. (ed.), *Children in Action: perspectives on the archaeology of childhood* (Archaeological Papers of the American Anthropological Association 15). Berkeley: University of California Press.

Baxter, J. E. 2006b. Making space for children in archaeological interpretations, pp. 77–88 in Baxter, J. E. (ed.), *Children in Action: perspectives on the archaeology of childhood* (Archaeological Papers of the American Anthropological Association 15). Berkeley: University of California Press.

Bennett, J. M. 1981. Medieval peasant marriage: an examination of marriage license fines in 'Liber Gersumarum', pp. 193–246 in Raftis, J. A. (ed.), *Pathways to Medieval Peasants*. Toronto: Pontifical Institute of Mediaeval Studies.

Beresford, M. and Hurst, J. G. 1990. *English Heritage Book of Wharram Percy Deserted Medieval Village*. London: B.T. Batsford Ltd/English Heritage.

Bugarin. F. T. 2006. Constructing an archaeology of children: studying child material culture from the African past, pp. 13–26 in Baxter, J. E. (ed.), *Children in Action: perspectives on the archaeology of childhood* (Archaeological Papers of the American Anthropological Association 15). Berkeley: University of California Press.

Crawford, S. 1999. *Childhood in Anglo-Saxon England*. Sutton: Stroud.

Crawford, S. 2009. The archaeology of play things: theorising a toy stage in the 'biography' of objects. *Childhood in the Past* 2, 55–70.

Crawford, S. and Lewis, C. 2008. Childhood studies and the Society for the Study of Childhood in the Past. *Childhood in the Past* 1, 5–16.

Creighton, O. H. 2002. *Castles and Landscapes*. London: Continuum.

Dyer, C. 1985. Power and conflict in the medieval English village, pp. 27–32 in Hooke, D. (ed.), *Medieval Villages: a review of current work* (Oxford University Committee for Archaeology Monograph 5). Oxford: Oxford University Committee for Archaeology.

Dyer, C. 1991. *Hanbury: settlement and society in a woodland landscape* (Department of English Local History Occasional Papers Fourth Series 4). Leicester: Leicester University Press.

French, K. L. 1996. 'To free them from binding': women in the late medieval English parish. *Journal of Interdisciplinary History* 27 (3), 387–412.

French, K. L. 2003. Women in the late medieval English parish, pp. 156–73 in Erler, M. C. and Kowaleski, M. (eds), *Gendering the Master Narrative: women and power in the Middle Ages*. Ithaca: Cornell University Press.

Graves, C. P. 2000. *The Form and Fabric of Belief: an archaeology of the lay experience of religion in medieval Norfolk and Devon* (British Archaeological Reports British Series 311). Oxford: J. & E. Hedges.

Hanawalt, B. 1986. *The Ties That Bound: peasant families in medieval England*. Oxford and New York: Oxford University Press.

Harden, J. 2000. There's no place like home: the public/private distinction in children's theorizing of risk and safety. *Childhood* 7 (1), 43–59.

Harvey, P. D. A. 1989. Initiative and authority in settlement change, pp. 31–43 in Aston, M., Austin, D. and Dyer, C. (eds), *The Rural Settlements of Medieval England*. Oxford: Blackwell.

Hayfield, C. 1984. Wawne, East Riding of Yorkshire: a case study in settlement morphology. *Landscape History* 6, 41–67.

Holloway, S. L. and Valentine, G. 2000. Children's geographies and the new social studies of childhood, pp. 1–26 in Holloway, S. L. and Valentine, G. (eds), *Children's Geographies: playing, living, learning*. London: Routledge.

Houlbrooke, R. A. 1986. Women's social life and common action in England from the fifteenth century to the eve of the civil war. *Continuity and Change* 1, 171–89.

Hunt, A. 1996. *Governance of the Consuming Passions: a history of sumptuary law*. Basingstoke: Macmillan.

Ingold, T. 1993. The temporality of the landscape. *World Archaeology* 25 (2), 152–74.

Jay, M. 2009. Breastfeeding and weaning behaviour in archaeological populations: evidence from the isotopic analysis of skeletal materials. *Childhood in the Past* 2, 163–79.

Jones, O. 2000. Melting geography: purity, disorder, childhood and space, pp. 29–47 in Holloway, S. L. and Valentine, G. (eds), *Children's Geographies: playing, living, learning*. London: Routledge.

Kamp, K. A. 2001. Where have all the children gone? The archaeology of childhood. *Journal of Archaeological Method and Theory* 8 (1), 1–34.

Lefebvre, H. 1991. *The Production of Space* (translated by D. Nicholson-Smith). Oxford: Wiley-Blackwell.

Lewis, C. 2009. Children's play in the later medieval English countryside. *Childhood in the Past* 2, 86–108.

Lewis, C., Mitchell-Fox, P. and Dyer, C. 1997. *Village, Hamlet and Field: changing medieval settlements in central England*. Manchester: Manchester University Press.

Lewis, M. 2007. *The Bioarchaeology of Children: perspectives from biological and forensic anthropology*. Cambridge: Cambridge University Press.

McKendrick, J. H. 2000. The geography of children: an annotated bibliography. *Childhood* 7 (3), 361–87.

McMurray Gibson, G. 1996. Blessing from sun and moon: churching as women's theatre, pp. 139–54 in Hanawalt, B. A. and Wallace, D. (eds), *Bodies and Disciplines: intersections of literature and history in fifteenth-century England*. Minneapolis: University of Minnesota Press.

Marvin, W. P. 1999. Slaughter and romance: hunting reserves in late medieval England, pp. 224–52 in Hanawalt, B. A. and Wallace, D. (eds), *Medieval Crime and Social Control*. Minneapolis: University of Minnesota Press.

Matthews, H. and Limb, M. 1999. Defining *an* agenda for the geography of children: review and prospect. *Progress in Human Geography* 23 (1), 61–90.

Mays, S., Richards, M. R. and Fuller, B. T. 2002. Bone stable isotope for infant feeding in mediaeval England. *Antiquity* 76 (293), 654–65.

Miller, D. 1987. *Material Culture and Mass Consumption*. Oxford: Blackwell.

Müller, M. 2001. *Peasant Mentalities and Cultures in two Contrasting Communities in the Fourteenth Century: Brandon in Suffolk and Badbury in Wiltshire*. Unpublished Ph.D. thesis, University of Birmingham.

Mynard, C., Zeepvat, R. J. and Williams, R. J. 1991. *Excavations at Great Linford, 1974–80* (Buckinghamshire Archaeological Society Monograph Series 3). Aylesbury: Buckinghamshire Archaeological Society.

Orme, N. 2001. *Medieval Children*. New Haven and London: Yale University Press.

Oswald, A. 2004. *Wharram Percy Deserted Medieval Village, North Yorkshire: archaeological investigation and survey* (English Heritage Archaeological Investigation Report Series AI/19/2004). York: English Heritage.

Philo, C. 2000. 'The corner-stones of my world': editorial introduction to special issue on spaces of childhood. *Childhood* 7 (3), 243–56.

Rahtz, P. A. and Watts, L. 2004. *Wharram: a study of settlement on the Yorkshire Wolds Volume IX: the North Manor area and North-West enclosure* (York University Archaeological Publications 11). York: University of York.

Riddy, F. 2003. Looking closely: authority and intimacy in the late medieval urban home, pp. 212–28 in Erler, M. C. and Kowaleski, M. (eds), *Gendering the Master Narrative: women and power in the Middle Ages*. Ithaca: Cornell University Press.

Rigby, S. H. 1995. *English Society in the later Middle Ages: class, status and gender*. Basingstoke: Macmillan.

Roberts, B. K. 1983. Nucleation and dispersion: towards an explanation. *Medieval Village Research Group Annual Report* 31, 44–5.

Schofield, P. R. 2003. *Peasant and Community in Medieval England*. Basingstoke: Palgrave Macmillan.

Sebba, R. 1991. The role of the home environment in cultural transmission. *Architecture and Behaviour* 7 (3), 205–22.

Shahar, S. 1990. *Childhood in the Middle Ages*. London: Routledge.

Smith, S. V. 2009a. Towards a social archaeology of the late medieval English peasantry: power and resistance at Wharram Percy. *Journal of Social Archaeology* 9 (3), 391–416.

Smith, S. V. 2009b. Materialising resistant identities among the medieval peasantry: an examination of dress accessories from English rural settlement sites. *Journal of Material Culture* 14 (3), 309–32.

Smith, S. V. 2010. Houses and communities: archaeological evidence for variation in medieval peasant experience, pp. 64–84 in Dyer, C. and Jones, R. (eds), *Deserted Villages Revisited*. Hatfield: University of Hertfordshire Press.

Sofaer-Derevenski, J. 1997. Engendering children, engendering archaeology, pp. 192–202 in Moore, J. and Scott, E. (eds), *Invisible People and Processes: writing gender and childhood into European archaeology*. London: Leicester University Press.

Sofaer-Derevenski, J. 1998. *Gender Archaeology as Contextual Archaeology*. Unpublished Ph.D. thesis, University of Cambridge.

Sofaer-Derevenski, J. 2000. Material culture shock: confronting expectations in the material culture of children, pp. 3–16 in Sofaer-Derevenski, J. (ed.), *Children and Material Culture*. London: Routledge.

Soja, E. W. 1985. The spatiality of social life: towards a transformative retheorisation, pp. 90–127 in Gregory, D. and Urry, J. (eds), *Social Relations and Spatial Structures*. Basingstoke: Macmillan.

van Houts, E. 1999. *Memory and Gender in Medieval Europe 900–1200*. Basingstoke: Macmillan.

Waites, B. W. 1962. The monastic grange as a factor in the settlement of north-east Yorkshire. *Yorkshire Archaeological Journal* 40, 627–56.

Wilkie, L. 2000. Not merely child's play: creating a historical archaeology of children and childhood, pp. 100–13 in Sofaer-Derevenski, J. (ed.), *Children and Material Culture*. London: Routledge.

5. Seeing the Medieval Child: Evidence from household and craft

Maureen Mellor

This chapter reviews the evidence for the contributions made by the medieval child to the labour force and economy within the context of the pottery industry. In particular, the chapter reviews our understanding of the ceramic craft environment, identifying tasks that would be within the skill and strength capacity of a child, and exploring evidence for a range of competences within a workshop that might also be a clue to the involvement of a wide age range of craft workers and labourers. The chapter also argues that ceramics have a unique potential to capture the activities of the individual medieval child through fingerprints, which are typically recorded during pottery and tile analysis but tend not to be accorded much significance in the ensuing reports. Recent scholarship by archaeologists has done much to illuminate the roles and experiences of the medieval child, particularly with respect to funerary evidence (*e.g.* Lewis 2002) and, more recently, the settlement record (*e.g.* Lewis 2009; Smith this volume). This chapter contributes to this growing field of study of medieval childhood by focussing on the working environment.

This chapter considers clay industries from the re-emergence of towns in England at the end of the ninth century through to 1700. Given the nature of the available evidence, it is necessary to draw on sources from across this period. While the dangers of aggregating evidence from diverse periods and places must be acknowledged, there is sufficient consistency in potting practices across those centuries for this approach to be valid. Indeed, many areas saw the continuation of medieval patterns of land use and settlement over this period, with towns retaining their medieval layouts and character (Wood *et al.* 2006/8, 23). In the much better documented period of later industrialised pottery manufacture children were an integral element in the manufacturing processes; for example, in 1861 out of an estimated total workforce of *c.* 33,000 manufacturing fine tablewares, 4,605 children under ten worked in the Staffordshire potworks, 593 of whom were children aged five (Baker 1991, 10, 66–7). The present chapter seeks to elucidate whether children similarly played such an important role in medieval pottery manufacture.

The medieval pottery industry

Pottery is an industry well represented in the archaeological record, which often acts as a signal of major change or of continuity of settlement (Grenville 2004, 33; Jones and

Page 2006, 79–104, 117). In the late Anglo-Saxon period, many pottery workers sought out the security of defended towns to set up in business, as at Stafford in the West Midlands, and Stamford and Lincoln in the East Midlands (Ford 1998/9, 11–36; Cotter 2009; Kilmurry 1980; Young and Vince 2005, 41–69). Under a lordship, these potters and their families would have participated in the life of the town: in renting land, selling goods in the market and benefiting from a community with other craftsmen, learning new technologies and exchanging ideas. A pottery kiln at Lincoln shared the same street as glass and iron production – all anti-social smoke-producing industries where skill with fire and furnace were needed (Miles _et al._ 1989). Other potters in this period, however, set up in more isolated areas, closer to their clay, fuel and water supplies, as at Michelmersh (Hampshire) (Brown and Mepham 2007).

The late eleventh century saw the beginning of a gradual shift towards pottery production in the countryside, coinciding with the re-emergence of hand-made wares that competed with the established urban wheel thrown products, a change that is visible in both London and the south Midlands (Blackmore and Pearce 2010, xvi; Mellor 2010, 64). Greater regional variability with new styles and decoration were evident (Mellor 2005, 150, 160–1), suggesting that some craft workshops were becoming more organised. Greater division of labour in a less congested rural setting with a smaller geographical distribution range may, therefore, have favoured the use of children, in a craft supplying the growing population of urban and rural consumers (Dyer 1997, 63).

The potter families that served this industry rarely appear in censuses, taxation returns, court rolls, inventories and wills, although rentals are more frequent after the Norman Conquest, recording, in particular, the right to extract clay, sand and fuel, mostly on the lord of the manor's land (Le Patourel 1968; McCarthy and Brooks 1988, 59, 69–70). Potters sometimes paid in kind, with pots (and, on at least one occasion, eggs) as part payment (Page 1907, 251–2). In many parts of England, complaints against the potter also increase – especially for not infilling the clay pits, which then became hazardous to animals and the wider community (Le Patourel 1968, 101–22; Draper and Copland-Griffiths 2002, 11–12) – suggesting that some potters had a somewhat independent spirit. Women and children are not mentioned with any consistency in medieval documents, but where they occur they are often recorded amongst the 'reserve workforce', with women taking a secondary position to adult males. If a male is recorded as receiving a similar wage to women, it indicates that they were a child or elderly or disabled person. Children's contribution to the labour force in agriculture or the building trade fluctuated over time. Boys and girls took up labour shortfalls when adult men were in short supply, for example at harvest time or immediately after the Black Death (Langdon 2010, 120–1, 125).

The impact that the pottery industry had on rural communities is evident in a variety of sources. For example, significant human activities are often reflected in English place-name patterns (Cole 2010, 22), and it is notable that in the thirteenth and fourteenth centuries some Midland communities, probably with manorial sponsorship, were sufficiently proud of their craft that the names of their hamlets and villages evolved to reflect this service. Examples include the forest potteries of Potters Lyveden (Bryant and Steane 1969; 1971) and Potterspury (both Northamptonshire) (Jones and Page 2006, 125). Other settlements, equally involved with pottery production, were not, however, re-branded, including Boarstall/Brill and Olney Hyde (both Buckinghamshire) (Farley

1982, 107–17; Ivens 1982, 144–70; Mynard 1984, 56–85), nonetheless the impact of the potters is sometimes evident in other ways, including in the layout of the settlement. Many of these villages had individual workshops set up for potting, with the kiln at the back of the croft, suggesting a regulated community with a coherent layout (Jones and Page 2006, 196). These were clearly small-scale family concerns where a potential role for children should not be underestimated, as the family was the basic economic unit for working the land (McCarthy and Brooks 1988, 79), and also for socialising the children (Hanawalt 1986, 3). Once established, these 'nucleated rural workshops' might last several generations (Foard 1991, 13), with inheritance customs helping to keep the enterprise together. However, it should be noted that other potters worked in dispersed settlements, as in the Savernake forest (Wiltshire) (Birkbeck 2000), serving as a reminder that the impact of potting on rural communities was diverse.

Archaeological evidence suggests that in the countryside there was a variety of working relationships between tile-makers and potters; some shared space when firing the kiln and some workshops appear to have combined the making of pottery and tiles, for both the roof and floor (Moorhouse 1981, 108; Meddens *et al.* 2002/3, 3–43), while elsewhere the two crafts were practiced as specialist enterprises (Cotter 1997; Stopford 2005, 10–24). Documentary evidence suggests that the potters shared raw materials with other craft workers operating in close proximity, particularly in the environment of the forest (*e.g.* charcoal burners and iron smelters), while the resourceful potter did not rely solely on pottery making but combined it with agriculture, lime burning (for making mortar) and forestry (Johnston *et al.* 1997, 13–42).

Children and production: archaeological approaches

Studying children archaeologically is an inherently interdisciplinary endeavour
Baxter 2006a, 5

Studies of childhood in the archaeological record have drawn on ethnographic research to provide valuable insights about processes of production (Baxter 2006b, 77–88). An important archaeological approach to craft production, which drew extensively on ethnographic evidence, was Peacock's (1982) study of Roman potteries, in which he devised a hierarchy of production models, contrasting the social organisation and social relations of each, and suggesting the extent to which contrasting forms of organisation are likely to be archaeologically detectable. For instance, where the mode of production is at the level of a simple household, practised by a member of a family working part-time, with a single kiln, and located in an isolated area with poor agricultural value, then the pattern of production is likely to be archaeologically almost invisible. In contrast, the pattern is more likely to be archaeologically visible where there are household industries or nucleated workshops comprising clusters of workshops and kilns, ceramic output, though seasonal, is the major economic activity, the production site is mainly in the hands of men, and the distribution patterns and the marketing systems are managed through mutual cooperation (Peacock 1982, 9, 31). At such 'visible' production sites the standards of production are reasonably constant and an explicit sex-based division of

Figure 5.1. Medieval tile from Tring (Hertfordshire), depicting the child Jesus (with halo) instructing his peers in worship and (right) at the well head to draw water, where the children are waiting with earthenware jugs, in an orderly manner to draw water (© Victoria and Albert Museum, London).

labour may be in place, with varying levels of skills. It is apparent, thus, from the analysis undertaken by Peacock that the contributions of children are likely to have occurred in medieval contexts that had invested considerable technical investment, both in urban and rural workplaces (McCarthy and Brooks 1988, 59–60, 68–81). One skilled potter might be serviced by young assistants who prepared the clay, turned the wheel, finished the pottery vessels, mixed the glazes, carried the pots to the drying area and collected firewood (Rice 1987, 184). Peacock's framework has been adapted and interpreted for prehistoric communities by other ethno-archaeological and anthropological researchers (Arnold 1985; Rice 1987), and provides a theoretical basis across a wide chronological spectrum, for observing the technology of traditional pottery and social relations within the work place of craft production, that on occasions embraced children.

Anthropologists often focus on the relationships that children have with adults, with other children and with their environment, seeing the child as a 'cultural actor' (Baxter 2006a, 1, 6). There is material culture evidence, albeit limited, that permits us to take such an approach to the medieval period. For example, a fourteenth-century perspective of childhood between the ages of five and twelve years is afforded by the 'Tring' tiles, which also offers tantalising evidence for the specific role of children within the medieval pottery industry (Eames 1980, 56–61; Casey 2007, 1–53; Graves 2002, figs 1.16, 20) (Figure 5.1). The cartoon images on these tiles are based on an illuminated manuscript illustrating the narrative of the second-century Apocryphal Gospels of the childhood of Christ (Bodleian Library MS Selden supra 38). The context is a village in the countryside illustrating the work and play activities of the child Jesus, his playmates and the bullies he engages with. The images stress the physicality of these medieval children. Jesus is portrayed as a precocious child, who feels misunderstood and is in conflict with his parents and teachers. He is initially trained and 'socialised' by his mother (although with his father present), but both parents are then persuaded to send the five-year-old to school to correct his behaviour, to teach him to respect others and

Figure 5.2. Medieval jug with bridge spout and bearded face mask made at Grimston, near the port of King's Lynn (Norfolk). The decoration may have benefitted from a child's nimble fingers (© Norwich Castle Museum and Art Gallery. Height: 240cm). I am grateful to Drs Andrew Rogerson and Tim Pestell and to Emma Brough for their help.

Figure 5.3. Drawing taken from an illumination illustrating a medieval tile workshop, with one child shovelling clay, and another putting tiles on a shelf to dry (originally published in Der mittlealterliche Baubtrieb in zeitgenössischen Abbildungen (2001), translated into Medieval Building Techniques (2004)). I am grateful to Professor Günther Binding, University of Bonn, for permission to use this illustration.

to learn to read. In the manuscript narrative Jesus is shown modelling sparrows out of clay, implying that this was a child's activity (His flew away of course!). Moulded face masks, some with beards, are a feature of many potteries in Britain (McCarthy and Brooks 1988, 127, 228–9) (Figure 5.2) and in the light of the illustrated manuscript and the Tring tiles it is worth considering whether some of these decorative additions to vessels, some of which are by any measure crude, represent the work of children; the process of learning to work with clay by a child could easily take place within a tilery (Figure 5.3) or potting family's household (Smith 2006, 71). On the Tring tiles Jesus also enjoys ordinary boyish activities – throwing stones into the river – a game enjoyed by less precocious children (Hanawalt 1986, 26). Jesus' social behaviour improves and he is depicted queuing behind a female, waiting to draw water from a well, accompanied by his peers. Here, in sum, the child Jesus, as a 'cultural actor' (see also Smith this volume), is shown capable of making significant contributions to the everyday life of his family and the community (Figure 5.1).

Sources of inspiration for learning have been studied by ethnographers in other cultures and several modes of learning for children of craft workers have been identified, including examples of learning that occurred in the context of relationships between mother/daughter, mother-in-law/daughter-in-law, aunt/niece and neighbour/neighbour. The workshop may be family-centric (nuclear family) or corporate (kin-extensive), it may be minimally structured, or there may be a more formal schooling (Rice 1987, 255, 270; Greenfield 2000, 75–85). The potential insights of such research have scarcely been addressed by medieval archaeologists, although some researchers of the archaeology of childhood have focused on craft production and the acquisition of technological competence (Smith 2006, 68), with children seen as potential economic contributors, as servants or apprentices, tied to the craftsmen (Langdon 2011, 34), learning to perform adult tasks. These studies reveal traits that are most likely the work of children at different stages of learning or apprenticeship. The process of teaching and learning between adults and children is an essential component of the development of social categories such as gender (Hanawalt 1986, 161; Baxter 2006a; 2006b). Yet, the archaeological visibility of the workspace in Britain is variable, and craft workshops have not been a central focus of archaeological enquiry (Grenville 2004, 29). Potting tenements varied in scale, mirroring demographic changes, but the success of a particular enterprise depends on the human agency and management of the production cycle. Kilns, kiln debris, pottery scatters, waste dumps, workshop buildings and associated structures hint at some 700 medieval potting craft production sites across England, but understanding of the physical nature of production centres is hampered by the lack of fully excavated sites (Marter 2005, 2). However, as we shall see, by re-visiting some of the better published sites we can discern evidence for the relationships between production, space and social organisation, which reveal the diversity of the medieval potter's craft environment, with temporal and regional variations, and this will allow us to place the learning about craftworking by medieval children in context.

The medieval child prepared for work in the household: toys and tools

By combining evidence from the historical and archaeological record, we can discern something of the processes by which children were initiated into the workplace. In medieval England, childhood was conceived as a distinct stage in human development, which ended at age seven. In elite households girls between seven and twelve years of age had to be become equipped for their future lifestyles (Howell 2001, 3–4), while in the medieval peasant economy children were an asset by the age of seven and their contribution was essential to the smooth running of the household economy (Dyer 1989, 114, 116–17). In other craft apprenticeships a child might also leave home at this age, but was not legally responsible for criminal acts until twelve years of age (Hanawalt 1986, 270; Crawford 1999, 172). Barbara Hanawalt's research on the coroners' rolls of the fourteenth and fifteenth centuries in England indicates that the pattern of fatal accidents of peasant children who had grown up in a family environment tended to imitate that of their parent's from an early age (Hanawalt 1986, 146; see also McAlister 2013; Smith 2006). Thus, 'little girls are already becoming involved in accidents that paralleled their mother's routine working with earthenware pots, gathering food, and drawing water', whereas boys, in contrast, were more involved in observing and copying men's activities (Hanawalt 1986, 157–8, 168; Smith this volume).

Archaeological investigations in north-west Europe, particularly in towns, have recovered evidence for children's toys made from a variety of materials (Egan 1998, 10–11). While some of these seem to have been intended to be used purely for amusement – such as the pottery whistles made at a production site at Stanion (Northamptonshire) (Blinkhorn 1991, 21–2) or a horse figurine made at a major pottery industry in Tudor Hampshire (Pearce 2007, fig. 33, 62–3) – others were in the form of miniature tools or weapons that seem intended to introduce children to the adult roles that they would be expected to adopt in due course. For example, waterlogged remains in Dublin have yielded a number of wooden toys, including miniature boats, and a single example each of a miniature wooden sword and horse, and these artefacts are of types found widely across the Viking diaspora between the tenth and twelfth centuries (McAlister 2013). Miniature quernstones and millstones from Shetland have been interpreted as demonstrating both the importance of agriculture in a region that was at the edge of Europe's grain growing zone, and also the importance placed on socialising children into the roles that they would eventually play. Moreover, it is even thought possible that these implements were used by children to make contributions to household production (Ågotnes 2008; McAlister 2013).

In the late medieval period, children between the ages of eight and twelve began to undertake real chores around the house. Girls contributed to the household economy by picking fruit, nuts, herbs and gathering wood. Boys likewise gathered a variety of foodstuffs but were also engaged in guarding geese, watching lambs, and watering horses (Hanawalt 1986, 29, 158, 168, 183). The pattern of work began to change from thirteen to nineteen years of age, with more agricultural activities for boys, but the accidental death pattern studied by Hanawalt suggests that they still did not play as full a role as their fathers in agriculture, crafts and building construction. Learning the skills of household work, agriculture and crafts took place largely during adolescence, under the family guidance, when boys began to plough, to use the scythe and the reaping hook, and to load and drive carts. The coroners' rolls indicate that the children in the medieval household 'went through distinct biological stages of development recognisable to us today' (Hanawalt 1986, 184).

Ceramic production:
the medieval child and social practices in the workshop

Each pottery had its own methods for preparing clay, forming the vessels and packing the kiln, which then developed into different regional and local traditions (Fishley

Holland 1958, 31). The traditional processes involved in pottery making can be understood by enhancing what can be deduced from available medieval documentation (Le Patourel 1968, 101–22) with the insights to be gained from analysis of recent practices of country potters (Fishley Holland 1958; Draper and Copland-Griffiths 2002). Potters are one of the most archaeologically visible members of the town and its immediate hinterland through the ubiquity of their pottery products in the archaeological record, and through personalised finishing, their products can be informative about past social practices and can offer an insight into the lives of individual potters (Moorhouse 1981, 96), from which we can begin to explore the roles and experiences of children within the pottery industry.

Although domestic pottery and tile manufacture required a relatively modest outlay for equipment and raw materials necessary to set up in business, working space, both undercover and outside, was a necessity, and often required assistance for the potter from his workshop, family or wider community. A workshop may be divided into special activity areas for mixing clays, storing and drying clays and gathering fuel such as brushwood or peat. Forming vessels, decorating the pots and storing the finished product may take place in different spaces. Building or refurbishing kilns is a specialist task and may necessitate calling upon a more experienced potter to help fire the kiln. Indeed, the potter may be assisted in his work by several other people including children. For example, a successful workshop is likely to be integrated into the regional economy and hawking the pots from settlement to settlement or selling the wares at market would be required, and are likely to be activities undertaken by an adult. The move to rural locations, that began in the eleventh century (see above), enabled potters to scale up to meet the increasing number of markets in the twelfth and thirteenth centuries (Mellor 2005, 150–1). At some places there is evidence of mutual co-operation between potters, with potters carting for each other, occupying market stalls adjoining allied craft workers (*e.g.* charcoal makers) and possibly, therefore, sharing transport from the forest settlements to market (Mellor 1994, 34). On occasions, both men and women helped to collect fuel for kilns, while dealers helped to sell their products (Le Patourel 1968, 119).

The technological advance provided by the potter's wheel (Freestone 1997, 16) was irrelevant to child labour as it would take at least two years of practice before the child could consistently make pots to a standard size and produce sufficient pots per day to sell (Jim Keeling, pers. comm.). From there the aspiring potter would gradually build up a repertoire of pots of different shapes and sizes, working up to very large storage jars. When William Fishley Holland began his apprenticeship at the age of fourteen in 1903, the traditional potter still used a kick wheel, and it took him four years to move from making flower pots 3¼ inch (8.25 cm) in diameter to making 12 inch (30.48 cm) diameter pots (Fishley Holland 1958, 7, 31). Within the various tasks required in the making of pottery vessels there was room for a range of competencies some of which might be appropriate to a child, and these tasks are now considered with a view to assessing the likelihood of children having been involved in them. In most cases, there is admittedly no specific medieval evidence to prove that children undertook these various tasks, but then there is no direct evidence as to the specific roles played by any individual – whether child or adult – in many of the tasks required of the medieval potter. There is, nonetheless, analogous evidence from other periods to suggest the potential roles that children played in medieval potting.

The technologies employed at a pottery production centre

Preparing the clay

Fishley Holland (1958, 19) recounts how clay was prepared in the nineteenth century, by working it with bare feet, which were sensitive to foreign bodies (stone, chalk nodules and marl); *'nu pied'* was a practice also adopted by French potters in the sixteenth century (Ravoire 2011, 115). Young children could assist with picking out the stones and carrying them away from the workshop. In the Netherlands at Bergen op Zoom, the potters' guild of the fifteenth century gives details of the craft down to the sizes of clay balls required to make specific shapes (McCarthy and Brooks 1988, 17), and the making of the various sized balls for different sized vessels is a task that a child of six or older might undertake.

Simple vessel construction

Pots can be formed in a number of ways, and medieval children may have been involved in pinching out a piece of clay to the desired shape, such as occurred on the hand-made crucibles from Lincoln (Young and Vince 2005, 65), or preparing coils of clay to be laid one on top of the other and then joining them together (Newell 2008). They could also have assisted with pressing sheets of clay into a mould for pot and tile making, or they may have helped by using a paddle to form the clay into the body of the pot.

Decorating pottery vessels or ridge tiles

Decoration of ceramic vessels can be undertaken with finger or thumb impressions (Spoerry 2008, 30, figs 21–3), coloured slip, or hand-moulded clay representing face masks, and all of these decorative styles might benefit from smaller nimble fingers (Leah 1994, 89, fig. 59, 33–7, 73; see fig. 5.2 above).

Ancillary activities

Medieval evidence is most informative about the role of children in those ancillary tasks that supported the work of the potter. Documents occasionally mention boys in the collecting of fuel for pottery making, as was the case among the forest potters at Brill, who had 'their boys and others collect loppings for their kilns' in 1255 (Le Patourel 1968, 116). Large quantities of fuel were needed to fire kilns, and this sometimes led to those involved in the pottery industry engaging in illegal means of acquiring wood. Trespassing against the *vert*, the unlawful taking of wood from the royal forest or lord's land, was frequently recorded in documents, and the personal names of the accused, such as Nicholas le Potter and Richard le Potter of Leafield in the Wychwood forest (Oxfordshire), suggest that this trespassing was sometimes related to potting (Stebbing *et al.* 1980, 4, 21). It is notable that boys are amongst the trespassers and manorial court rolls show that children were also fined for collecting dry wood (Hanawalt 1986, 156, 158). Other activities that would have been essential to potting, and that may have been carried out by children, included the fetching and carrying water to the workshop (Lewis 1987, 3–14), and the carrying of the finished vessels or tiles to drying sheds (Figure 5.3). Indeed, the identification of children's fingerprints on the surface of Siegburg stoneware from north Germany, dating from the thirteenth to fifteenth centuries, has confirmed the employment of children (perhaps family members) in the unskilled task of transporting freshly thrown vessels from the wheel to the drying area (Gaimster 1997, 127; for the identification of the involvement of children in the production of fired clay vessels in prehistoric contexts from fingerprints, see Králik *et al*. 2008, 7–11). Packing the pots and tiles, with bracken, heather or straw for delivery to the consumer or market were all roles that could have been undertaken by children. There are no known specific references to girls associated with pottery production, but women did become pottery owners and probably master craft workers in the fourteenth and fifteenth century (Le Patourel 1968, 109, 114, 116; McCarthy and Brooks 1988, 79), and a widow in England could enter into capital investments of land contracts on her own (Hanawalt 1986, 71, 220) and so be enabled to grow a business and plan the future of her dependants.

These suppositions about the proposed role of children in ancillary roles for the pottery industry are supported by evidence from other medieval crafts. For example, in the construction industry women collected moss for the bedding of roof tiles and were involved in the collection of bracken, a task that children may also have helped with (Langdon 2011, 36, 40–3). Four sisters are mentioned as helping a mason at Rockingham Castle (Northamptonshire) in 1278–88 (Langdon 2010, 115–26), girls at Durham in 1532 carried mud for a wall, and the following year 'eight girls carrying stones' at 2d a day are cited (Salzman 1992, 71). The collecting of wood from the forest floor, gorse, dung, straw, reed and chaff or sea coal from the coast along the eastern seaboard of the north-east of England would all have been tasks with which the wider family group, including children, could assist. Pottery manufacture was often only a part-time undertaking during the annual agricultural cycle (Dyer 1989, 132–3; Jennings 1992, 5). The presence of children in the vicinity of rural clay industries has been identified on a mid-fifteenth-century brick from Brno (Czech Republic) from the footprint of a child, along with the paw print of a dog and the hoof prints of a small cow, which have been interpreted as evidence for the involvement of children in associated activities, tending to animals or crops, while occasionally venturing into the workshop (Králik *et al*. 2008, 5–7). In such rural communities there may have been more opportunities for children to look after grazing sheep or pigs in the forest, raising chickens, and collecting their eggs (Woolgar *et al*. 2006, 276), releasing adults for heavier work in agriculture or in the potting tenements and workshops. After all, the potter's busy season coincided with the busiest months in the agricultural cycle, from Lady Day (25th March) to Michaelmas (29th September), and there must, on occasions, have been a tension between the demands of the agricultural cycle and pottery production, but equally it would afford another opportunity for children to assist with potting events. In these rural communities, where the family was the basic economic unit for working the land and socialising the children, there was also more opportunity for children to observe a variety of craft industries undertaken by their immediate families, kinsmen and neighbours and to undertake simple tasks themselves related to craft production and to experience hand-building with clay.

The role of medieval children around the pottery workshop

The presence of children in the medieval clay workshop is most evident in accounts of apprenticeships. In medieval crafts, generally, apprenticeships were not taught, but achieved through watching the master at work. By the sixteenth century, apprenticeships in Norwich (Norfolk) began at fourteen years of age (Ayres 2012), but in some earlier regulations of guilds for craft workers, in London and other towns, a child of seven or eight might enter an apprenticeship agreement (Hanawalt 1986, 157) or workplace without an apprenticeship (Dyer 1989, 232; Ayres 2012). The making of roof tiles was well established by the beginning of the thirteenth century, as may be seen from the evidence of the London building by-laws of 1212 (Salzman 1992, 140). Apprentices in the building trade were taken on for seven years, and they had to be 'born free, legitimate and sound in body and limb'. They were not to tell tales nor report the gossip of their master and fellows, nor were they to reveal what is done in 'the logge' – the lodge (Salzman 1992, 72, 41).The importance of the tile-makers to the building trade probably helped them gain guild status in 1468, a privilege not afforded to English medieval potters, but apprentices, in all but name, existed at some of the larger pottery production centres, particularly towards the end of the medieval period as the scale of production at individual sites increased (Gaimster and Nenk 1997, 177–7; Grenville 2004, 37; Pearce 2007).

Pottery guilds did, however, exist on the continent, where they are well documented, and it is useful to consider the evidence from the surviving guild records of the stoneware industry at Siegburg (Germany), studied by Gaimster (1997), in order to understand something of the way in which the medieval English pottery industry may have been organised. The organisation and working practices of its members during the sixteenth and seventeenth century were based around the family unit. Each main production centre comprised a number of families, each with several master-potters operating their own kilns. The Siegburg guild of the Rhenish potters controlled standards of manufacture, the levels of productivity and trading rights. There were three classes of craftsmen: masters, workmen and apprentices. A seven year apprenticeship was required in order to become a workman in the guild, and only legitimate or adoptive sons of masters, who had to be native of Siegburg, were entitled to become apprentices. It was expressly forbidden for masters to employ foreign craftsmen lest the secrets of their craft be copied outside the region. The status and role of women in the stoneware industry is recorded in 1516 and again in 1531 and this reveals that if a master fell ill or died his spouse would be permitted to continue running the workshop with assistance from the workmen and apprentices for the duration of the sickness or widowhood; on remarriage, however, the woman had to relinquish the ownership of the workshop to her new husband. The hierarchy of master and apprentices associated with workshops in the centre of Paris is recorded in sixteenth-century wills and inventories, where access to the profession was again highly regulated (Ravoire 2011, 108).

Similar evidence from England is not forthcoming, and the potting industry may not have been as well regulated. Nonetheless, at Harlow (Essex), wills suggest a system of nucleated workshops run by families related by marriage (Davey and Walker 2009, 165–6), and this is paralleled in Tudor Hampshire (Pearce 2007). Although there are no references to medieval apprentices – largely as a result of the lack of guild regulation – the comparative continental evidence and the evidence from English guilds of comparable industries suggests that it is reasonable to conclude that an occupation in the clay industries could begin with an apprenticeship from as young as seven years, but often older, and while formal training may have been minimal, the apprentice child potter would pick up skills from their parents.

While the written evidence for the roles of children in the medieval pottery workshop is limited, then, it can be supplemented with circumstantial evidence from archaeological investigations. Carenza Lewis has recently argued that in addition to seeking out evidence for toys and functional miniatures (of the types discussed above), archaeologists may be able to identify the presence and behaviours of children in more subtle ways: 'It is conceivable that small items, or badly drawn or sculpted figures in the archaeological record, were used and created by children' (Lewis 2009, 9). Similarly, in a study of the material culture from Viking-Age Dublin, Deirdre McAlister (2013) has recently suggested that craft trial pieces, poorly executed decoration on a wooden horse, and the 'untidy' runic inscription on a cattle scapula may all be evidence of the actions of children. In light of these studies, some of the archaeological evidence from excavated pottery production sites is, at the very least, suggestive of the roles of children. For example, archaeological evidence from an excavated pottery and tile multi-kiln production centre at Chilvers Coton, Nuneaton (Warwickshire), shows that 'small crudely shaped pots about the size and shape of a modern plant pot' were used as kiln furniture (Moorhouse 1981, 99) and were clearly made by unskilled labour. Could these have been the products of children, learning the processes of pottery manufacture? The decoration of some of the products from the Harlow potteries was of such poor quality that it has recently been suggested that it could have been done by a child (Davey and Walker 2009, 149).

Among medieval craftworkers, it is the potters above all that leave their fingerprints, quite literally, on their products. The most direct evidence for the role of children in the clay industries comes in the form of children's hand prints and fingerprints left on the clay products (Willemsen 2009, 26; Mynard 1984). Different clays will shrink at different rates on drying to the leather hard state, and again on firing in the kiln, but even allowing for a shrinkage rate of 15% in the local clay, finger impressions evident on the base of cup handles at Wrenthorpe (West Yorkshire) must belong to children (Moorhouse 1992, 97, 109). At the deserted medieval settlement and a production centre at Olney Hyde excavation revealed a house/workshop, clay pit and kiln, while an adjacent kiln was excavated later. The pottery from this kiln was sorted manually with the help of modern school children and three finishing treatments which were both functional and decorative were noted: stabbing; thumbing at the junction of the handle and body; and decoration where thumb impressions ran down the sides of the handle or finger and thumb impressions around the rims of bowls, on the bodies of storage jar or firecovers (Figure 5.4). Common to all jug rims were four finger impressions on the inside of the vessel at the upper junction of the handle, and analysis led to the deduction that 'the two leading fingers created a deeper impression, from which it can be seen whether left or right hand had been used' (Mynard 1984, 74). The likelihood that these impressions were made by medieval children was confirmed in an experiment by the modern girls processing the pottery, aged nine to eleven, who had fingers of the same size as those that made the finger marks. It would seem, then, that medieval children were engaged at least in attaching the handles to the jugs. Children's finger prints are sometimes recognised and noted by archaeological ceramic specialists, but these observations rarely progress to a printed report (Julie Edwards, pers. comm.), and this means that establishing the scale of children's involvement in the decoration of medieval ceramics is currently not possible. No systematic study or forensic examination has been carried

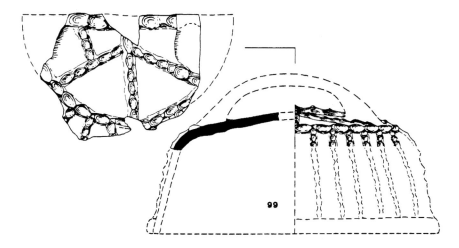

Figure 5.4. A medieval firecover decorated with applied thumb pressed strips from Olney Hyde (Buckinghamshire). Finger/thumb impressions may give an insight into the labour force.

out on medieval fired clay in the British Isles, but recent research on Neolithic pottery from London has shown the potential: a scanning electron microscope was used to identify that a small thin-fingered individual with fingernails had left an imprint on the pottery vessel and further investigation on another vessel from Heathrow revealed a 'still more slender little finger' (Cotton 2004, 128–47; see also Králik *et al.* 2008).

Contact with unfired lead glazed pottery might be expected to leave a physiological 'fingerprint' in a child's body. Stephen Moorhouse (1987, 29; 1992, 87) has noted a gradual change in quality of an individual potter's products over time, which he suggested might be due to the effect of lead poisoning, rather than a variety of competencies within a potting tenement or workshop, and this leads on to a different approach to identifying the working child. At a later date, Fishley Holland (1958, 24) recounted that the grinding of lead in the nineteenth century used to give men 'bellyache', and Fishley Holland's grandfather called it colic which was probably due to the dust from the lead. Stomach cramps in children in new Europe have been the subject of medical investigation in the twenty-first century, tracing annual pottery fairs moving across the countryside selling their lead-glazed wares. When apples or soft acidic fruit are baked in these earthenware dishes with internal glaze, lead acetate is released, resulting in children suffering from stomach cramps (Tony Waldron pers. comm.). Poorly glazed earthenware vessels exposed potters and consumers to lead poisoning, and it could cause death in children, or at least interfere with normal growth of the skeleton (Budd *et al.* 2004; Lessler 1988). Waldron (2006, 265–6) has suggested that a radiological survey of the long bones of children from a medieval assemblage would prove instructive in determining the extent to which children had been exposed to lead. A side effect of atmospheric pollution from smoke-producing industries such as pottery production and tile-making may result in sinusitis (Roberts and Cox 2003, 233) and can be deduced from the skeletal evidence of children (Lewis 2002). A cemetery of a potting community might be expected to reveal a higher percentage of lead poisoning and of sinusitis; at the very least, the study of occupational health of children's skeletons from such a community would prove instructive.

The range of competencies within a pottery workshop: reassessing the evidence from a child-centred perspective

In addition to extrapolating back from an early twentieth-century craft industry, and drawing on occasional insights from medieval written records, the spectrum of tasks open to a child can be speculated from archaeological study. Such an approach requires a reassessment of familiar evidence, and in the following discussion the pottery industries of eastern England in the later Anglo-Saxon period are examined with a view to identifying the involvement of children in these industries.

Lincolnshire has a long tradition of pottery making (Symonds 2003), and, indeed, it has been argued that urbanisation within the so-called Danelaw (*i.e.* the regions of Scandinavian settlement from the late ninth century) was accelerated through investment in such craft and related trade (Schofield and Vince 1994, 113–15). This may, in turn, explain the emergence of wheel thrown hard-fired pottery within the Danelaw towns during the late ninth century, perhaps conferring an urban identity different from that of the surrounding rural settlements (Leahy 2007). The sudden appearance of these competently made wheel-thrown wares in both Lincoln and Stamford towards the end of the ninth century argues for the immigration of potters versed in the continental craft traditions (Symonds 2003, 68). Stamford ware represents one of the finest of the East Midlands pottery traditions, producing pots from the late ninth to the thirteenth century, while Lincoln appears to have fostered a number of pottery industries, all serving the community at about the same period (Symonds 2003, 68, 90). At Stamford, the initial vessels were made on a fast kick wheel resulting in thin-walled vessels. The vessel forms appear to have been standardised and some rims may have been produced with the aid of a template (Kilmurry 1980, 45–6). Handles were formed by throwing on a wheel, which was a Carolingian trait. Potters within these towns favoured a narrower base and more globular form than was typical of the vessels found in Wessex. One workshop in Stamford appears to have produced a wider range of vessels than the other workshops in the town, suggesting perhaps a master potter or potters with more experience than was available in another nearby workshop in the town. However, in the early tenth century, the bases changed from flat wire-cut bases to concave sagging bases, a characteristic noted at Torksey and Lincoln (Lincolnshire) (Young and Vince 2005, 47, 88–90). There was also a shift from wheel-thrown thin-walled vessels to more irregular, thicker pots, which were not well centred.

Was the change within the workshop due to an inexperienced second or third generation; the result of pressure of work and the need to produce quantity over quality; or could it be evidence of lowering the age range of the helpers, *i.e.* using child labour? Handles and applied strips that had previously been cut from wheel thrown cylinders, were now slab-cut – a technique that children could master. During the tenth century it is possible to trace some of the changes in one pottery industry in Lincoln that was producing what is known to ceramic specialists as Lincoln Kiln-Type (LKT). As at Stamford, in the early to mid-tenth century the quality of production began to decline and LKT bases were coil-made and pressed onto the body which was thrown as a hollow cylinder (Miles *et al.* 1989, 205), again a task that a child could at least help with. Here we see evidence of possible division of labour with the coil-made bases being made by less skilled and potentially younger helpers. The wall thickness also began to vary and the vessels became irregularly centred, additional evidence of unskilled labour trying to master the wheel. If the pioneers of these industries were trained journeymen from a continental industry, a slow erosion of their status, their brand and their market might see parallels with the nineteenth-century Staffordshire industry as set out at the beginning of this paper. This is not conclusive of child labour, but presents a pattern for future study taking a child-centred perspective.

Conclusions

Until industrialisation in the nineteenth century, children as agents for production are not clearly 'visible' in the archaeological record, and cannot therefore be demonstrated to have suffered real stress. But we have reviewed the difficulty of demonstrating their presence throughout the medieval period, and we have at least demonstrated that the economic expansion of England's tenth-century Danelaw created the conditions for urban exploitation of child labour. Rural family craft environments are, in contrast, likely to have been more nurturing to the child, whether a future master potter or future labourer. And whatever their abilities, employment opportunities are likely to have fluctuated inversely with the availability of adult male labour on a minimum wage. To corroborate this labour pattern for the medieval period would need a programme of scanning electron microscope analysis of fingerprints in parallel with skeletal and dental analysis for occupational poisoning and stress related trauma across the age spectrum of an urban and a rural potting cemetery population. It is apparent that a hierarchy of tasks was available with the growing strength and skill of the medieval child, from fetching and carrying, trampling the clay, preparing clay balls, and making slab-bases, coil bases, and simple pots, both small and large. Direct evidence of this emerges from fingerprints, and a recommendation is made to encourage the capture of this type of information in future pottery studies.

Acknowledgements

I am grateful to Brian Ayres for allowing me to read his manuscript prior to publication and to Christopher Dyer for bringing my attention to John Langdon's recent published work and to Dawn Hadley for introducing me to literature from across the pond and central Europe.

Bibliography

Ågotnes, A. 2008. *The Story Behind: archaeological finds from the Middle Ages in Bergen*. Bergen: Bryggens Museum.

Arnold, D. 1985. *Ceramic Theory and Cultural Process*. Cambridge: Cambridge University Press.

Ayres, B. 2012. Infancy and adolescence, education and recreation in medieval and post-medieval Norwich, pp. 25–38 in Gläser, M. (ed.), *Lübecker Kolloquium zur Stadtarchäologie im Hanseraum VIII: Kindheit und Jugend, Ausbildung und Freizeit*. Lübeck: Verlag Schmidt-Romhild.

Baker, D. 1991. *Potworks: industrial architecture of the Staffordshire potteries*. London: Royal Commission on the Historical Monuments of England.

Baxter, J. E. 2006a. Introduction: the archaeology of childhood in context, pp. 1–9 in Baxter, J. E. (ed.), *Children in Action: perspectives on the archaeology of childhood* (Archaeological Papers of the American Anthropological Association 15). Berkeley: University of California Press.

Baxter, J. E. 2006b. Making space for children in archaeological interpretations, pp. 77–88 in Baxter, J. E. (ed.), *Children in Action: perspectives on the archaeology of childhood* (Archaeological Papers of the American Anthropological Association 15). Berkeley: University of California Press.

Binding, G. (ed.) 2001. *Der mittlealterliche Baubtrieb in zeitgenössischen Abbildungen*. Darmstadt: WBG Literarium (translated in 2004 by A. Cameron as *Medieval Building Techniques*. Oxford: Oxbow).

Birkbeck, V. 2000. *Archaeological Investigations on the A34 Newbury By-Pass, Berkshire/Hampshire 1991–7*. Salisbury: The Trust for Wessex Archaeology, on behalf of the Highways Agency.

Blackmore, L. and Pearce, J. 2010. *A Dated Type Series of London Medieval Pottery: part 5, shelly-sandy ware and the greyware industries*. London: MOLAS.

Blinkhorn, P. 1991. Three pottery bird whistles from Stanion, Northamptonshire. *Medieval Archaeology* 15, 21–2.

Brown, L. and Mepham, L. 2007. The Broughton to Timsbury pipeline, Part 1: a late Saxon pottery kiln and the production centre at Michelmersh, Hampshire. *Proceedings of the Hampshire Field Club and Archaeological Society* 62, 35–68.

Bryant, G. F. and Steane, J. M. 1969. Excavations at the deserted medieval settlement at Lyveden: a second interim report. *Journal of the Northampton Museum and Art Gallery* 5, 3–15.

Bryant, G. F. and Steane, J. M. 1971. Excavations at the deserted medieval settlement at Lyveden. *Journal of the Northampton Museum and Art Gallery* 9, 7–47.

Budd, P., Montgomery, J., Evans, J. and Trickett, M. 2004. Human lead exposure in England from approximately 5500 BP to the 16th century AD. *The Science of the Total Environment* 318, 45–58.

Casey, M. F. 2007. The fourteenth-century *Tring Tiles*: a fresh look at their origin and the Hebraic aspects of the child Jesus' actions. *Peregrinations – International Society for the Study of Pilgrimage Art*, pp. 1–53 (available at: http://peregrinations.kenyon.edu/vol2–2/FeaturedSection/Tring Tiles.pdf).

Cole, A. 2010. Place-name patterns, pp. 22–5 in Darkes, G. and Tiller, K. (eds), *An Historical Atlas of Oxfordshire*. Chipping Norton: Oxfordshire Record Society.

Cotter, J. A. 1997. *Twelfth-Century Pottery Kiln at Pound Lane, Canterbury: evidence for an immigrant potter in the late Norman period* (Canterbury Archaeological Trust Occasional Paper 1). Canterbury: Canterbury Archaeological Trust.

Cotter, J. A. 2009. More late Saxon Stafford-type ware kilns discovered at Stafford. *Medieval Pottery Research Group Newsletter* 65, 1–4.

Cotton, J. with Johnson, R. 2004. Two decorated Peterborough bowls from the Thames at Mortlake and their London context, pp. 128–47 in Cotton, J. and Field, D. (eds), *Towards a New Stone Age: aspects of the Neolithic in south-east England* (Council for British Archaeology Research Report 137). York: Council for British Archaeology.

Crawford, S. 1999. *Childhood in Anglo-Saxon England.* Stroud: Sutton.

Davey, W. W. and Walker, H. 2009. *The Harlow Pottery Industries* (Medieval Pottery Research Group Occasional Paper 3). London: Medieval Pottery Research Group.

Draper, J. and Copland-Griffiths, P. 2002. *Dorset Country Pottery: the kilns of the Verwood district.* Marlborough: The Crowood Press.

Dyer, C. 1989. *Standards of Living in the Later Middle Ages.* Cambridge: Cambridge University Press.

Dyer, C. 1997. Peasants and farmers: rural settlements and landscapes in an age of transition, pp. 61–76 in Gaimster, D. and Stamper, P. (eds), *The Age of Transition: the archaeology of English culture, 1400–1600.* Oxford: Oxbow.

Eames, E. S. 1980. *Catalogue of Medieval Lead Glazed Tiles in the Department of Medieval and Later Antiquities of the British Museum.* London: British Museum Press.

Egan, G. 1998. Miniature toys of medieval childhood. *British Archaeology* 35, 10–11.

Farley, M. E. 1982. A medieval pottery industry at Boarstall, Buckinghamshire. *Records of Buckinghamshire* 24, 107–17.

Fishley Holland, W. 1958. *Fifty Years a Potter.* Fremington: Pottery Quarterly.

Foard, G. 1991. The medieval pottery industry of Rockinghamshire Forest, Northamptonshire. *Medieval Ceramics* 15, 13–20.

Ford, D. 1998/9. A late Saxon pottery industry in Staffordshire: a review. *Medieval Ceramics* 22/3, 11–35.

Freestone, I. 1997. *Pottery in the Making: world ceramic traditions.* London: British Museum Press.

Gaimster, D. 1997. Stoneware production in medieval and early modern Germany, pp. 122–7 in Freestone, I. (ed.), *Pottery in the Making: world ceramic traditions.* London: British Museum Press.

Gaimster, D. and Nenk, B. 1997. English households in transition c. 1450–1550: the ceramic evidence, pp. 172–95 in Gaimster, D. and Stamper, P. (eds), *The Age of Transition: the archaeology of English culture 1400–1600* (Society for Medieval Archaeology Monograph 15). Oxford: Oxbow.

Graves, A. 2002. *Tiles and Tilework.* Hong Kong: V&A Publications.

Greenfield, P. 2000. Children, material culture and weaving: historical change and developmental change, pp. 72–86 in Sofaer-Derevenski, J. (ed.), *Children and Material Culture.* London: Routledge.

Grenville, J. 2004. The archaeology of the late and post-medieval workshop – a review and proposal for a research agenda, pp. 28–37 in Barnwell, P., Palmer, M. and Airs, M. (eds), *The Vernacular Workshop: from craft to industry, 1400–1900* (Council for British Archaeology Research Reports 140). York: Council for British Archaeology.

Hanawalt, B. A. 1986. *The Ties That Bound: peasant families in medieval England.* Oxford and New York: Oxford University Press.

Howell, M. 2001. *Eleanor of Provence.* Oxford: Blackwell Publishers Ltd.

Ivens, R. J. 1982. Medieval pottery from the 1978 excavations at Temple Farm, Brill. *Records of Buckinghamshire* 24, 144–70.

Jennings, S. 1992. *Medieval Pottery in the Yorkshire Museum.* York: The Yorkshire Museum.

Johnston, G., Foster, P. J. and Bellamy, B. 1997. The excavation of two late medieval kilns with associated buildings at Glapthorne, near Oundle, Northamptonshire. *Medieval Ceramics* 21, 13–42.

Jones, R. and Page, M. 2006. *Medieval Villages in an English Landscape: beginnings and ends*. Macclesfield: Windgather Press.

Králik, M., Urbanová, P. and Hložek, M. 2008. Finger, hand and foot imprints: the evidence of children on archaeological artefacts, pp. 1–15 in Dommasnes, L. H. and Wrigglesworth, M. (eds), *Children, Identity and the Past*. Cambridge: Cambridge Scholars Publishing.

Kilmurry, K. 1980. *The Pottery Industry of Stamford, Lincolnshire, c. A.D. 850–1250: its manufacture, trade and relationship with continental wares, with a classification and chronology* (British Archaeological Reports British Series 84). Oxford: British Archaeological Reports.

Langdon, J. 2010. Waged building employment in medieval England: subsistence safety net or demographic trampoline?, pp. 109–26 in Goddard, R., Langdon, J. and Müller, M. (eds), *Survival and Discord in Medieval Society: essays in honour of Christopher Dyer*. Turnhout: Brepols.

Langdon, J. 2011. Minimum wages and unemployment rates in medieval England, pp. 25–44 in Dodds, B. and Liddy, C. (eds), *Commercial Activity, Markets and Entrepreneurs in the Middle Ages: essays in honour of Richard Britnell*. Woodbridge: Boydell.

Le Patourel, H. E. J. 1968. Documentary evidence and the medieval pottery industry. *Medieval Archaeology* 12, 101–22.

Leah, M. 1994. *The Late Saxon and Medieval Pottery Industry of Grimston Norfolk: excavations 1962–92*. Dereham: Field Archaeology Division Norfolk Museums Service.

Leahy, K. 2007. *'Interrupting the Pots': the excavation of Cleatham Anglo-Saxon cemetery, North Lincolnshire* (Council for British Archaeology Research Report 155). York: Council for British Archaeology.

Lessler, M. A. 1988. Lead and lead poisoning from antiquity to modern times. *The Ohio Journal of Science* 88 (3), 78–84.

Lewis, C. 2009. Children's play in the later medieval countryside. *Childhood in the Past* 2, 86–108.

Lewis, J. M. 1987. Roof tiles: some observations and questions. *Medieval Ceramics* 11, 3–14.

Lewis, M. 2002. *Urbanisation and Child Health in Medieval and Post-Medieval England: an assessment of the morbidity and mortality of non-adult skeletons from the cemeteries of two urban and two rural sites (AD 850–1859)* (British Archaeological Reports British Series 339). Oxford: Archaeopress.

McAlister, D. 2013. Childhood in Viking and Hiberno-Scandinavian Dublin, 800–1100, pp. 86–102 in Hadley, D. M. and Ten Harkel, A. (eds), *Everyday Life in Viking-Age Towns: social approaches to towns in England and Ireland, c. 800–1100*. Oxford: Oxbow.

McCarthy, M. and Brooks, M. 1988. *Medieval Pottery in Britain AD 900–1600*. Leicester: Leicester University Press.

Marter, P. 2005. *Medieval Pottery Production Centres in England AD 850–1600*. Unpublished Ph.D. thesis, University of Winchester.

Meddens, F., Sabel, K., Akeroyd, A., Egan, G., Horsley, T., Keys, L., Linford, P., Mackley, R., Payne, A., Walsh, N., White, M., Williams, D. and Wilson, P. 2002/3. The excavation of a medieval ceramic production site and tile kiln at Weald View, Noak Hill, Essex. *Medieval Ceramics* 26/7, 3–43.

Mellor, M. 1994. A synthesis of middle and late Saxon, medieval and early post-medieval pottery in the Oxford region. *Oxoniensia* LIX, 17–217.

Mellor, M. 2005. Making and using pottery in town and country, pp.149–64 in Giles, K. and Dyer,

C. (eds), *Town and Country in the Middle Ages* (Society for Medieval Archaeology Monograph 22). Leeds: Maney.

Mellor, M. 2010. *Pottery and Potters*, pp. 64–5 in Darkes, G. and Tiller, K. (eds), *An Historical Atlas of Oxfordshire*. Chipping Norton: Oxfordshire Record Society.

Miles, P., Young, J. and Wacher, J. S. 1989. *A Late Saxon Kiln Site at Silver Street, Lincoln* (The Archaeology of Lincoln 17). London: Council for British Archaeology for City of Lincoln Archaeological Unit.

Moorhouse, S. A. 1981. The medieval pottery industry and its markets, pp. 96–125 in Crossley, D. W. (ed.), *Medieval Industry* (Council for British Archaeology Research Report 40). London: Council for British Archaeology.

Moorhouse, S. A. 1987. A note on the terminology of pottery making sites. *Medieval Ceramics* 11, 25–30.

Moorhouse, S. A. 1992. *Wrenthorpe Potteries: excavations of 16th- and 17th-century potting tenements near Wakefield, 1983–86*. Wakefield: West Yorkshire Archaeology Service.

Mynard, D. C. 1984. A medieval pottery industry at Olney Hyde. *Records of Buckinghamshire* 26, 56–85.

Newell, R. W. 2008. Medieval pottery construction (available online at: http://www.campots.co.uk).

Page, W. (ed.) 1907. *The Victoria History of the County of Sussex, Vol. 2*. London: Archibald Constable.

Peacock, D. P. S. 1982. *Pottery in the Roman world: an ethnoarchaeological approach*. London: Longman.

Pearce, J. 2007. *Pots and Potters in Tudor Hampshire: excavations at Farnborough Hill convent, 1968–72*. Guildford: Guildford Museum and Guildford Borough Council.

Ravoire, F. 2011. La production de poterie de terre à Paris au Moyen Âge (XIIIe–XVIe siècle) à travers les source écrites, pp. 107–21 in Bocquet-Lienard, A. and Fajal, B. (eds), *À propo[t]s de l'usage, de la production et de la circulation des terres cuites dans l'Europe du Nord-Ouest autour des XIVe–XVIe siècles*. Caen: CRAHM.

Rice, P. M. 1987. *Pottery Analysis: a sourcebook*. London: University of Chicago Press.

Roberts, C. and Cox, M. 2003. *Health and Disease in Britain: from prehistory to the present day*. Stroud: Sutton.

Salzman, L. F. 1992. *Building in England down to 1540: a documentary history*. Oxford: Oxford University Press.

Schofield, J. and Vince, A. 1994. *Medieval Towns*. London: Leicester University Press.

Smith, P. E. 2006. Children and ceramic innovation: a study in the archaeology of children, pp. 65–76 in Baxter, J. E. (ed.), *Children in Action: perspectives on the archaeology of childhood* (Archaeological Papers of the American Anthropological Association 15). Berkeley: University of California Press.

Spoerry, P. 2008. *Ely Wares* (East Anglian Archaeology 122). Cambridge: Cambridge County Council.

Stebbing, N., Rhodes, J. and Mellor, M. 1980. *The Clay Industries of Oxfordshire: Oxfordshire potters*. Oxford: Oxfordshire Museums Service Publication.

Stopford, J. 2005. *Medieval Floor Tiles of Northern England. Pattern and Purpose: production between the 13th and 16th centuries*. Oxford: Oxbow.

Symonds, L. 2003. *Landscape and Social Practice: the production and consumption of pottery in tenth-century Lincolnshire* (British Archaeological Reports British Series 345). Oxford: Archaeopress.

Waldron, T. 2006. Nutrition and the skeleton, pp. 254–66 in Woolgar, C., Serjeantson, D. and Waldron, T. (eds), *Food in Medieval England: diet and nutrition*. Oxford: Oxford University Press.

Willemsen, A. 2009. *Dorestad*. Zutphens: Walburg Pers.

Wood, P. N., Bradley, J. and Miller, I. 2006/8. A pottery production site at Samlesbury, near Preston, Lancashire. *Medieval Ceramics* 30, 21–48.

Woolgar, C., Serjeantson, D. and Waldron, T. 2006. Conclusion, pp. 267–80 in Woolgar, C., Serjeantson, D. and Waldron, T. (eds), *Food in Medieval England: diet and nutrition*. Oxford: Oxford University Press.

Young, J. and Vince, A. with Nailor, V. 2005. *A Corpus of Anglo-Saxon and Medieval Pottery from Lincoln* (Lincoln Archaeological Studies 7). Oxford: Oxbow.

6. Eavesdropping on Short Lives: Eaves-drip burial and the differential treatment of children one year of age and under in early Christian cemeteries

Elizabeth Craig-Atkins

Throughout the Anglo-Saxon period, funerary rites were utilised in a variety of ways to express aspects of the identity of the deceased (*e.g.* Stoodley 1999; Buckberry 2007). This chapter deals exclusively with one pattern identified in previous studies concerning the funerary treatment of the youngest individuals: the clustering of the burials of babies and young children in proximity to churches in some early Christian cemeteries. The following discussion draws together the evidence for this funerary rite, utilising published examples and also presenting examples from unpublished sites, in order to characterise this practice in detail, provide a critical evaluation of the theories concerning its meaning and explore the reasons why it was deemed necessary to differentiate the youngest individuals in death in this way. The presence of a small number of graves of adult females, some of whom were buried with foetuses or new born babies, amongst eaves-drip burials is also highlighted and evaluated, and it is hypothesised that these women were those who died during pregnancy, childbirth and early motherhood, at a time when their identities were inextricably linked to those of infants.

The practice of burying young children in close proximity to buildings was first identified and described in detail at Raunds Furnells (Northamptonshire) (Boddington 1996, 53–5). At this tenth- and eleventh- century churchyard cemetery, the small graves of infants cluster close to the foundations of the church (Boddington 1996, 54). Here, and at other early Christian sites, the practice of interring babies close to churches has become known as 'eaves-drip' burial (Boddington 1996, 55; Crawford 1999, 85–9; Hadley 2010, 109). The substantial cemetery at Raunds comprised 363 inhumations surrounding a two-celled stone church on all four sides (Boddington 1996, 28). Originally constructed as a single cell in the mid-tenth century, the church at Raunds became a focus for burials after the addition of a chancel in the later tenth century, with burial ceasing towards the end of the eleventh and beginning of the twelfth century, when a new, larger church was constructed (Boddington 1996, 7). A burial zone within 1.5 m of the church walls is particularly notable for its concentration of densely packed small graves which housed the remains of neonates (from forty weeks post-conception to one month) and infants (from two months to one year) (Figure 6.1). Of the thirty interments within 1.5 m of the walls, twenty-five were assigned an age at death and could be located on the published

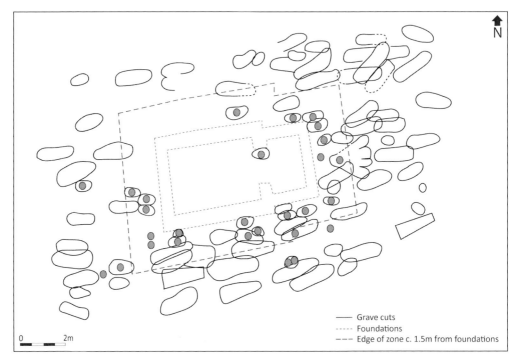

Figure 6.1. Section of the cemetery at Raunds Furnells (Northamptonshire) showing interments of individuals aged one year or under at death (grey dots) (illustration by E. Craig-Atkins and I. Atkins).

site plan by the present author: fifteen were under one month at death and five were aged between one month and one year, thus 80% (20/25) of individuals assigned an age at death in this zone were neonates or infants (Boddington 1996, 55; Craig 2005). The remainder comprised three older children (two aged under three years and one aged three to four years) and two adults, one male and one of indeterminate sex. There is also one intramural burial of an infant at the crossing between the nave and chancel. Across the entire cemetery at Raunds, children under two years comprise only 18.1% (66/363) of the total population (Boddington 1996, 30), indicating a strong bias towards younger individuals in the demographic profile of the so-called 'eaves-drip' zone. By no means are all neonates and infants interred in closest proximity to the church at Raunds, in fact those within 1.5 m of the walls comprise only 30.3% (20/66) of the total population under one year at death. Andy Boddington (1996, 54) considered the burials in the eaves-drip zone to have occupied an area of ground intentionally left empty of graves during the earliest phases of burial, therefore, it seems that neonates and infants were only spatially segregated towards the end of the burial sequence at Raunds, probably from the latter half of the eleventh century.

A cluster of neonate and infant burials has also been identified at Tanners Row, Pontefract (West Yorkshire) (Wilmott in prep.). The excavators divide activity in this part of the cemetery at Pontefract into three distinct phases. The burials in phases one and

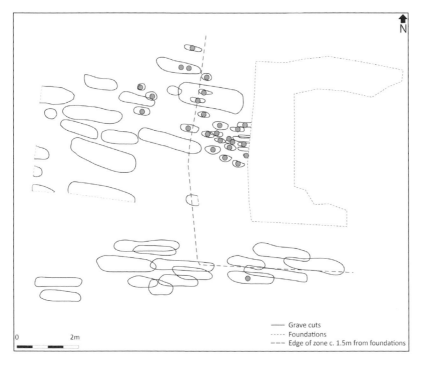

Figure 6.2. Section of the cemetery at Pontefract (West Yorkshire) showing interments of individuals aged one year or under at death (grey dots) (illustration by E. Craig-Atkins and I. Atkins).

two produced radiocarbon dates spanning the sixth to eighth and ninth to thirteenth centuries respectively (phase one: sk. 267 – AD 591–771 and sk. 519 – AD 550–710; phase two: sk. 548 – AD 830–1220 all to two sigma) (Wilmott in prep.). The last phase of burial (phase three) stratigraphically post-dated phase two and is argued by the excavators to pre-date alterations made to Pontefract castle defences in the twelfth and thirteenth centuries, but has not been subject to radiocarbon dating (Wilmott in prep.). This final phase of interment is characterised by a distinct cluster of neonates and infants located along the westernmost wall of a newly-constructed stone building, thought to have been a church (Figure 6.2). As at Raunds, the majority of these interments are within 1.5 m of the wall. The cluster of juveniles comprises eleven neonates and seven infants under two years, and there were also two individuals that were not assigned age at death and only two adults. Thus, 81.8% (18/22) of the interments in this zone are individuals under two years at death, and two thirds (18/27) of the excavated remains of children under two years from phase 3 are buried in this zone. The high prevalence of young children extends up to 2 m from the church at Pontefract, but predominantly in the area to the west of the church. There is, however, also a mixed cluster of an infant, a young child, an adolescent and two adults within 2 m of the southern wall. At Pontefract, children over two years are more widely spread throughout the cemetery, serving to emphasise further that burial close to the church was afforded primarily to the youngest. The

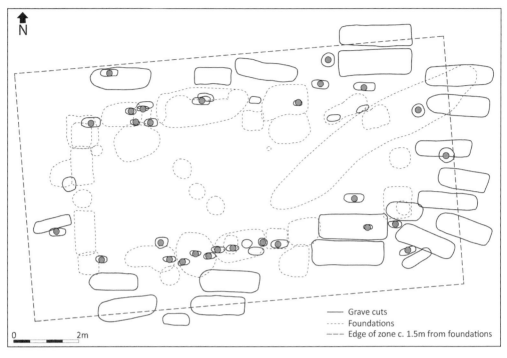

Figure 6.3. Section of the cemetery at Cherry Hinton (Cambridgeshire) showing interments of individuals aged one year or under at death (grey dots) (illustration by E. Craig-Atkins and I. Atkins).

absence of any clustering of children in phases one and two, prior to construction of the building in the cemetery, also supports the hypothesis developed at Raunds, that the presence of a building played a significant part in the decision to locate the burials of neonates and infants in specific places.

At Cherry Hinton (Cambridgeshire) burials were associated with a wooden building which is considered to have represented the first and second phases of a Saxo-Norman church dating from, potentially, the eighth to the twelfth century (McDonald and Doel 2000). Although no radiocarbon dates were obtained, stratigraphic relationships suggest that a substantial number of burials are contemporary with the second phase of this building, including a reported thirty-three neonates and infants buried 'beneath the church eaves', cutting structural features associated with the earliest church building (McDonald and Doel 2000, 5.5.26). Concordance of skeletal records and site plans from the unpublished Cherry Hinton report confirms that at least twenty-eight children under the age of two years were interred in close proximity to the relatively ephemeral remains of the church's foundations (Figure 6.3). A further seven small graves are represented on the site plan, but an age at death is not recorded for these individuals in the osteological report. If, once again, we designate the eaves-drip zone as 1.5 m from the church walls, a strong pattern emerges at Cherry Hinton: fifty-four burials lie within this zone, of which 51.9% (28/54) were under the age of two years at death. This contrasts with an overall proportion of neonates and infants in the population of

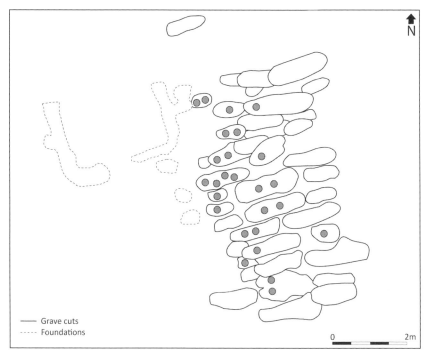

Figure 6.4. Section of the cemetery at Thwing (East Yorkshire) showing interments of individuals aged one year or under at death (grey dots) (illustration by E. Craig-Atkins and I. Atkins).

only 6.3% (43/683) (di Ruffano and Waldron 2000, table 5). Put another way, at least 65.1% (28/43) of all children under two years buried at Cherry Hinton were interred within 1.5 m of the church. Young children were also particularly predominant in some areas of this eaves-drip zone. A string of graves abutting short end to short end containing at least nine individuals, all of whom are neonates and infants, ran directly alongside the southern-most foundation of the building. One further neonate to the west (sk. 3077) was also on the same alignment, but separated from the other graves by just under 2 m. In fact it appears that the eaves-drip zone at Cherry Hinton was more circumscribed than at Pontefract or Raunds, particularly on the north and south sides of the western end of the church, where the majority of infant interments were positioned directly alongside the foundation trenches of the building, with adults and older children slightly further away.

Clustering of the burials of neonates and infants was also encountered at Thwing (East Yorkshire). An Anglo-Saxon cemetery on Paddock Hill, Thwing sits within an extensive multi-period earthwork complex with a long occupation sequence including late Neolithic, Bronze Age and early medieval phases (Harding and Lee 1987, 171; Manby 1980, 231–2). The cemetery comprised the interments of 132 individuals in sixty-eight distinct grave cuts (Manby n.d.). The post-in-trench footings of a small, single-celled building 3 m by 4 m in plan were located in the northwest corner of the cemetery and a series of five substantial post holes, *c.* 50 cm in diameter, were also located to the west of the main burial zone: two were positioned at the west and east sides of the building, and three ran north to south along the western boundary of burial (Figure 6.4). As at Raunds, Pontefract and Cherry Hinton, at Thwing a large proportion of neonates and infants were preferentially buried in proximity to the building. However, unlike these other sites, where a single focal point was used, at Thwing the line of post holes also formed a focus for the burial of young children. Amongst the western-most row of graves 70.0% (16/23) of individuals were under two years, including seven neonates and nine infants. If the next row to the east is included, the population comprises twenty-five individuals one year and under, which in total represents 83.3% (25/30) of the neonates and infants in the entire population. The use of multiple foci for the burial of neonates and infants seen at Thwing has yet to be identified at any other site where eaves-drip burials have been reported. The individuals buried close to the building and along the line of post holes are distinct: infants dominated the area alongside the building while neonates were more numerous by the posts. Only five children under two years were buried outside these two western-most rows, four of which were interred in the same grave group. That the vast majority of the neonates and infants at Thwing were buried in a cluster indicates that the practice of selective burial was adopted throughout the cemetery's usage. Eight radiocarbon dates were obtained soon after excavation of this site in the late 1980s. The majority of these dates centre around the seventh to ninth centuries, however it is possible that burial began in the sixth century or earlier, suggested by two extremely broad dates of AD 228–880 and AD 376–680 obtained from skeletons 89 and 54 respectively (Manby n.d.). Thus, Thwing may represent one of the earliest examples of the eaves-drip form of burial.

Another site at which the eaves-drip phenomenon has been identified, but which has yet to be discussed in print, is Spofforth (North Yorkshire) (Craig 2008; 2010; Northern Archaeological Associates 2002). This seventh- to ninth-century burial ground had a substantial structure – again likely a church – which was located towards the north and west of the burial zone. Disturbance to the site makes interpretation of the size of the church difficult, and there were various features identified in excavation that may represent further structures on the site contemporary with the burials. Here, there were only eleven neonates in the entire cemetery population, and nine of those were buried along the line of the building's southern wall with one more located close to the north of the building (Figure 6.5). Children over one month at death are few, but appear to have been buried more widely across the cemetery. Unfortunately, there were too few young individuals and too much post-depositional disturbance at Spofforth to provide more detailed interpretation of the clustering of neonates and infants.

The differential burial of neonates and infants in spatial zones in proximity to buildings has been described at a range of other early Christian cemetery sites, hinting that eaves-drip burial was a widespread practice. Excavations on Castle Green, Hereford conducted in 1960 and 1973 identified a cluster of largely children's burials to the north of the walls of a contemporary stone church, which is thought to predate the mid-twelfth century (Shoesmith 1980, 17). These burials comprised thirteen children under two years, three children aged between five and ten years, and seven children under the age of seven years as well as seven adults (groups 5c, 6 and 7) (Shoesmith 1980, 30, 46, 51). Unfortunately, there is only a published plan provided for the 1973 excavations, but importantly this reveals that the youngest individuals (four neonates

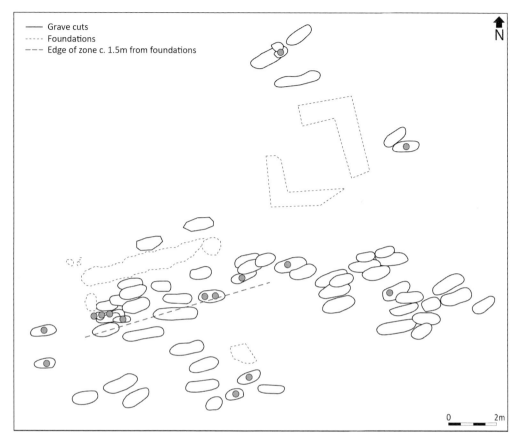

Figure 6.5. Section of the cemetery at Spofforth (North Yorkshire) showing interments of individuals aged one year or under at death (grey dots) (illustration by E. Craig-Atkins and I. Atkins).

and two infants under nine months) had been afforded burial locations closest to the building, within approximately one metre of its foundations (Shoesmith 1980, 20). At the site of Whithorn (Dumfries and Galloway), a cluster of children were buried to the east of a stone-footed building located to the north of the Northumbrian minster complex (Hill 1997, 134–82). Detailed analysis of site phasing indicates that the earliest phase of this 'children's cemetery', lasted for a period of maybe only ten to fifteen years during the second quarter of the eighth century (Hill 1997, 136, 171). During this time nine children under two years and one four- to seven-year-old were interred just beyond a boundary wall located *c.* 1 m east of the stone-footed building (Hill 1997, 145, 170; Cardy 1997, 558). This area of the site continued in use as a children's cemetery for a period of approximately forty years, but in later phases children of all ages up to twelve years were interred here. Peter Hill (1997, 171) argues that the infant cluster are likely to have formed part of a larger cemetery, but also that the infants at the minster site might reflect the presence of a transient workforce and their more dependant younger children in the area at that time. Whilst this theory may explain the presence of a significant number of children at an ecclesiastical site, it does not provide any reasons for the spatial zoning of children's burials.

An unusually high proportion of interments of foetuses was encountered at Norwich castle (Norfolk) (n=13; 11.6%). The excavators note that these pre-term babies were associated with two phases of a building dating to the eleventh century, and were interred both within and directly north of the structure (Ayers 1985, 58). Five of these foetal skeletons can be clearly associated with distinct graves on the published site plan, all of which are within 1 m of the remains of the building and, thus, consistent with other eaves-drip burials discussed here. The site report for Winwick (Cheshire) notes that the cemetery included an area with 'a higher proportion of child burials in the north' in close proximity to a structure *c.* 4 m by 8 m in plan (Freke and Thacker 1987/8, 33). The site is characteristic of an early medieval western British cemetery, in that interments are unfurnished inhumations arranged in rows, but the interments were not dated any more accurately. Nor is there any more detail provided to elucidate whether these so-called child burials represent infants, as is the case in the other examples highlighted here.

In some cases the presence of eaves-drip burials is suggested, but a paucity of archaeological evidence makes their evaluation problematic. At Nunnaminster, Winchester (Hampshire) a cluster of four infants was located directly north of a stone church of tenth- to eleventh-century date. Only two further burials were excavated, both located to the west of the minster – an adult and an eight- to ten-year-old child (Annia Cherryson pers. comm.; Scobie and Qualman 1993). Only three burials in total, all infants, were excavated in Compton Bassett (Wiltshire) alongside the eleventh- to thirteenth-century church of St Swithun (Hawkes and Adam 2001). In both these cases the lack of information concerning the rest of the burial community means that it cannot be determined whether the identified burials represent part of distinct clusters of neonates and infants. In sum, despite the variability in the detail and extent of evidence available in some cases, it is now possible to identify the clustering of infant burials in proximity to churches at a number of early medieval cemeteries in addition to the well-known example at Raunds Furnells.

Interpretations of eaves-drip burial

The most consistently favoured explanation for eaves-drip burial is that rain falling onto the church roof would have become sanctified by contact with a holy building, and then have fallen directly onto the zones of neonate and infant burials providing some form of posthumous reinforcement of the baptismal ritual (Boddington 1996, 55; Crawford 1999, 85–9; Hadley 2010, 109). This interpretation draws upon a folk myth of unknown antiquity, recorded during the nineteenth century, whereby the remains of an unbaptised infant were secreted away under the eaves of a church sanctuary roof in the hope that water running from the building's eaves, over the body, would afford posthumous baptism (Wilson 2000, 216). It has been argued, therefore, that eaves-drip burial reflects uncertainty within early Christian communities over the efficacy of baptism (Boddington 1996, 55; Crawford 1999, 85–9; Hadley 2010, 109) and that ameliorative funerary practices were sought to ease this fear. The unbaptised infant can be seen to occupy an ambivalent role and, for example, there appears to have been a long-held fear throughout European history that children who died before baptism could be performed were never at rest and could easily return as a revenant to haunt their family (Barber 1988; Wilson 2000, 216).

This eaves-drip model suggests an explanation for differential burial of infants relating to the role of baptismal ritual in Christian communities. However, the relevance of baptism amongst the general population prior to the ninth century is debated (Morris 1991). At the beginning of the fifth century, St Augustine argued that a child who died unbaptised would be condemned to Hell (Crawford 1999, 85), thus beginning a period of Christian doctrine that placed the unbaptised in a precarious position. Yet evaluating the extent to which Augustinian attitudes influenced Christian communities from the seventh century is problematic, and, moreover, there is a notable absence from any of the sources of any reference to specific burial rites as an ameliorative practice for the unbaptised. Documentary evidence does suggest that baptism was growing in popularity during the seventh century. For example, Bede's *Historia Ecclesiastica* of *c.* 730 recounts mass baptisms by Gregorian missionary Paulinus in the north of England at York, Yeavering (Northumberland) and along the River Swale in 627, but even if, to cite Bede, 'crowds ... flocked from every village and district' these events could not have affected more than a small minority of the populace (*Historia Ecclesiastica* ii, 14; Colgrave and Mynors 1969, 97–8). The first reference to baptism in lawcodes also appears at about the same time. For example, the laws of Ine of Wessex, dated to *c.* 694, stated that an infant must be baptised within thirty days of birth or a fine – albeit a relatively small one – was imposed on its parents (*Ine* 2; Crawford 1999, 85; Whitelock 1955, 364). The extent to which these directives permeated everyday life is unknown, nor can we be sure that similar prescriptions to those enumerated in Ine's code were in place beyond Wessex at this early date. Indeed, in his review of evidence for places of baptism in Anglo-Saxon England, Richard Morris (1991, 16) has argued that, in the centuries directly after the conversion, particularly during the seventh and eighth centuries, the need to find someone to perform the rite and the requirement to travel to an appropriate location on a suitable holy day could combine to dissuade parents from seeking baptism for their infants at all.

A further issue with the applicability of the eaves-drip model is raised by the pattern of burial at Thwing, where, aside from the burials of infants clustered around what is thought to have been a church, neonates were interred in close proximity to a line of three post holes. The post holes have been reconstructed by the excavator as a line of three free-standing posts (Manby n.d.), but could also potentially have been some form of screen or barrier. Either way, a literal interpretation of the eaves-drip effect does not fit here – there could not have been water washing from the eaves of a series of posts – but the pattern of infant burial at Thwing shares many features with more stereotypical eaves-drip sites: the demographic pattern of the infants is the same, and a group of young children at this site was, indeed, buried around a small building in a similar way to all other examples of eaves-drip burial. The cemetery at Thwing is one of the earliest eaves-drip burial sites, with burial commencing in the seventh century, if not earlier. It is plausible that variation might be seen in the rite amongst its early adopters, but as with the issue of the relevance of baptism discussed previously, this also has implications for the interpretation of other seventh- to eighth-century examples of the eaves-drip burial phenomenon.

The uncertainty surrounding the significance of baptism in the earliest Christian cemeteries, combined with the apparent use of structures that could not create 'eaves-drip' as foci for infant burial clusters, suggests that we should be cautious in our interpretations of seventh- to eighth-century clusters of infant burials as directly comparable to the eaves-drip burial phenomenon more clearly identified in later centuries. Whilst it might be entirely valid to use groups of infant burials to infer the position of a church, even where there is no supporting structural evidence, in examples of confirmed ninth-century date and later (Buckberry 2007, 125), such an approach is clearly problematic for earlier cemeteries. Thus, the suggestion that a cluster of infant burials in the south-east corner of the Church Walk cemetery (Hartlepool), which may date to as early as the mid-seventh century, indicates a contemporary church lay just outside the area of archaeological investigation (Daniels 1999, 112; Daniels and Loveluck 2007, 82–93) and that these infants were 'probably unbaptised' may not be entirely secure.

It is possible to reflect on alternative explanations for the patterns of infant clustering identified in early Christian cemeteries. Broader cultural distinctions between the very young child, who could not speak and was completely dependant on others, and older children are implicit in the vocabulary of Old English written sources (Crawford 1999, 54; 2007, 84). This suggests an inherent and enduring difference in the conceptualisation of infancy in Anglo-Saxon society that goes beyond whether or not baptism had taken place. This may have been a long-lived distinction, as the burial of infants in the eaves is mentioned in various Roman texts, but in these cases it is not explicitly linked to baptism. In her review of funerary practices afforded to infants in Romano-British Christian contexts, Dorothy Watts (1989, 372) cites several sources that suggest infants' burials were made in the eaves (*in subgrundariis*). Roman polymath Pliny's *Naturalis Historia*, published around AD 77–79, specifically notes the exclusion of infants who died before teething from the cremation rite, and their burial under the eaves. Fulgentius, a fifth-century Carthaginian bishop, develops this some 400 years later with the suggestion that infants who had not lived forty days would receive this form of burial (Watts 1989, 372). As with the undated folk myth highlighted above, the practice described here links the burials of the very young with the eaves of buildings, but implies that chronological age or rites of passage, such as teething, might have defined the age groups to which it was afforded.

Simon Mays (2007, 93–4) has tentatively linked another rite of passage – weaning age – with differential burial treatment. At Wharram Percy (North Yorkshire), infants under the age of one year, whose nitrogen isotope ratios indicated that they were still being breast-fed, tended to be buried immediately north of the church in the later medieval period. It is not clear, however, whether cessation of breast feeding was the stimulus for the provision of more normative burial, or whether it was another rite of passage which coincided with weaning, such as speech development, walking, teething, or, indeed, even baptism.

There is also evidence for the differential treatment of children immediately prior to the conversion to Christianity. Some clustering of individuals aged under twelve years has been noted at Westgarth Gardens (Suffolk), Sewerby (East Yorkshire) and West Heslerton (North Yorkshire) (Crawford 2013; Lucy 1998, 69–70, 74), although the age groups represented in these clusters are much wider than amongst the later cemeteries described above and there was no apparent differential treatment of infants as a group. In fact, it has been widely acknowledged that infants and children are generally underrepresented in early Anglo-Saxon cemeteries across England (Buckberry 2000; Crawford 1993, 84; Evison 1987, 146; Lucy 1994, 26–7; Molleson and Cox 1993, 16). Unlikely to be purely the result of differential decomposition, recovery bias or shallow burial, this paucity of interments of the youngest individuals appears to reflect active exclusion of children from community cemeteries (Buckberry 2000; Crawford 1993, 84–5; see also Squires this volume). The discovery of infant burials in several early and middle Anglo-Saxon settlement contexts, particularly in sunken-featured buildings at sites such as West Stow (Suffolk) and Wharram Percy, confirms that the youngest individuals could, indeed, receive burial away from the main cemetery focus (Crawford 1999; 2008; Hamerow 2006, 13–14; Milne and Richards 1992, 84; West 1985). The differential treatment of infants seems, then, to be a consistent, but far from universal, feature of funerary practices during the Anglo-Saxon period, albeit with some significant differences between pre- and post-Christian periods in the means by which the youngest members of the burial community were distinguished (Crawford 1999; 2008).

A series of pragmatic hypotheses have also been offered to explain the spatial clustering of groups of infants in Anglo-Saxon cemeteries, and these, therefore, require exploration as potential explanations for eaves-drip burial. It has, for example, been suggested that proximity to church foundations would have prevented the digging of deep graves, such as would be required for adult burials, and, thus, this location became most appropriate for the smaller, shallower graves of infants (Anderson 2007, 98). However, there is no intrinsic reason why the foundations of some of the small buildings from the cemeteries highlighted here should have interfered with the depth of burial. Indeed, a few adult graves are interspersed with the infants in several cases, suggesting that there was no physical barrier to the digging of adult graves in those areas dominated by infant burials. Alternatively, it has been hypothesised that an epidemic illness or famine might necessitate the rapid, successive burial of abnormally large numbers of young children, and that this might reasonably manifest in the archaeological record as spatially distinct clusters of juveniles (Wilmott in prep.). Whilst this remains an entirely viable reason for the presence of large numbers of young children in single phases of burial, it is not an entirely convincing explanation for eaves-drip burial for several reasons. It fails to explain satisfactorily the spatial patterning seen in the placement of neonate and infant burials without also drawing on the other arguments presented above. It is also problematic for this interpretation that the intercutting of distinct juvenile burials is seen frequently, making it unlikely that clusters of infant burials represent either a single catastrophic event, or even a relatively short period of high infant mortality. It is also unclear why the victims of such epidemics would be interred separately in distinct graves rather than multiple or communal graves as is seen in other examples of mass fatality in the archaeological record (*e.g.* Antoine and Hillson 2004/5, 26–8). Evidence from palaeopathological analysis is unable to make a useful contribution to this debate, as many of the causes of infant mortality do not leave evidence on the bones and, in particular, epidemic illnesses that lead to rapid death in children do not effect the body for long enough for bone tissue to develop characteristic indications of disease.

A hypothesis to explain the occurrence and distribution of eaves-drip burials

It must be emphasised that eaves-drip burial is not universally encountered in early Christian cemeteries, and some sites contemporary with those described above provide convincing evidence that neonates and infants were not interred in spatially distinct zones. At St Nicholas Shambles, in London, where it is suggested that burials were made from the date of construction of a church in the eleventh century until about the mid-thirteenth century, density of interments varied across the site (White 1988, 9–10). Infants were present in small numbers in all clusters of burial, as were older children. Nor was there any apparent relationship between the age at death of an individual and proximity to the church walls. At Wearmouth (County Durham), Anglo-Saxon burials were located to the south of the minster, which was constructed *c.* 673 (Cramp 2005). Seventeen infants were widely spread throughout the cemetery area, with no evidence of age-specific zoning (Cramp 2005, 84, 89). Not only are there some sites where neonates and infants are not afforded differential treatment, but it has been noted above that at some sites – such as Raunds and Pontefract – eaves-drip burials are only found in one phase of burial, with the burials of young children being more widely spread during other phases. This emphasises that the practice of eaves-drip burial was not adopted in all early Christian cemeteries, nor was it always a consistent feature of funerary practices across the lifetime of cemeteries where it is found. Several potential reasons for the adoption of eaves-drip burial that draw on the desire to afford special protection to those who died in infancy have already been highlighted, but why should some communities adopt this practice, others not adopt it at all, and others adopt it for a specific period only? The answer may lie at the root of the debate over the relevance of baptism presented by Morris (1991), in that our understanding of how directives concerning new doctrine and new burial rites disseminated within the early Christian milieu is extremely limited (Geake 2003). Whilst we know something of funerary doctrine and law that is documented from the seventh century, we are much less clear of its direct impact on local practice. If eaves-drip burial were to have been one of a range of funerary practices that could be adopted on a local level, the patterns observed in its appearance might be rationalised. The extent to which baptism was accepted and desired, developing concepts of sacred space, the degree to which use of burial grounds (and the practices permitted within them) were controlled and the strength of belief in the potential for funerary rites to affect post-mortem fate would all serve to increase or decrease the attractiveness of eaves-drip burial at different times and in different locations.

It is apparent that the early Christian period saw an increasing emphasis on the active exclusion of certain individuals from consecrated ground (Gittos 2002, 202–4; Hadley 2007, 196; Halsall 1995, 246–7; Reynolds 2009, 96–179). Yet if baptism were a pre-requisite for burial in consecrated ground, where were those who had not received it interred? Andrew Reynolds (2009) has provided a detailed review of those cemeteries that he argues were provided for those prohibited burial in churchyards, but this has revealed only a single example of a very young child – a foetus or infant interred at Bran Ditch (Cambridgeshire) (Reynolds 2009, 108). Nevertheless, the denial of burial in churchyard cemeteries to the unbaptised may help to explain the appearance of eaves-drip burials in the final phases of interment at Rounds, Pontefract and Hereford, where it is suggested that infants were buried after the remainder of the community had moved its burial ground elsewhere (Shoesmith 1980, 30, 51). If people were forced to find alternative places for the burial of infants, an old cemetery would no doubt have seemed an acceptable, if not preferable, alternative to those sites Reynolds has highlighted. The eaves-drip pattern of burial may, thus, reflect the increasing regulation of cemetery space and enforcement of doctrine regarding the denial of burial in consecrated ground to certain people. A similar development has recently been identified in early medieval Wales, where it has been argued that clusters of infant burials in the later stages of the cemeteries at Caer (Pembrokeshire), Capel Eithin (Gwynedd) and Llandough (Glamorgan) may reflect the use of cemeteries that had been abandoned or were going out of use for the burial of infants, perhaps those who were unbaptised (Page 2011, 108). In discussing the evidence of the cluster of infant and child burials from Whithorn, Sally Crawford (2008, 202) has seen in the emergence of eaves-drip burial at churches that were in decline or had been abandoned a practice similar to that reflected by the *cillíní* of Ireland, which were burial places for stillborn and unbaptised infants who were excluded from burial in consecrated ground as a consequence. The present chapter suggests that this practice of using churchyards that had been abandoned or were going out of use may have been a wider practice than has previously been recognised.

Adult burials in eaves-drip zones

Eaves-drip burial zones were not exclusively occupied by the graves of neonates and infants. Adult graves were encountered intermittently amongst juvenile clusters at the majority of sites. In some cases, as at Rounds, it appears that adult graves in eaves-drip zones derive from earlier phases of burial, and are therefore consistent with the use of a completely segregated area for the burial of infants for only a certain period of the cemetery's duration. However, at other sites, adult burials amongst clusters of neonates and infants appear to be roughly contemporary with them, and tend to be females more frequently than males. At Pontefract, the two adult graves incorporated with the infant cluster during phase three/four were both for thirty-five- to forty-five-year-old females, one of whom was buried in a chest with a lock (skeletons 567a and 589). At Thwing, there was a concentration of female graves in the western-most row of graves where the highest numbers of neonate and infant burials are located. These individuals comprise three females aged between twenty-five and thirty-five (skeletons 26a, 39a, 48c) and another aged between thirty-five and forty-five (sk. 28). At Cherry Hinton, two graves of adults from within the eaves-drip zone are particularly notable. Skeleton 3747, a female aged over fifty, was buried with neonate 3729 in the same grave, and an unsexed adult skeleton (sk. 4214) was interred with a pre-term baby (sk. 4202) between their legs. Both examples have been argued to represent cases of death during or soon after childbirth, and in the case of the former, advanced maternal age is hypothesised to have been a contributing factor (McDonald and Doel 2000, 15). Archaeologically identifiable examples of peripartum mortalities are not common, however two further examples have been proposed at Norwich castle and St Nicholas

Shambles. At the former, a burial of another adult female (sk. 120) and a pre-term baby was encountered directly north of the church walls, in a zone dominated by the burials of children (Ayers 1985, 18–19). Again, it is argued that these were a mother and baby who both died in childbirth (Ayers 1985, 58). At St Nicholas Shambles the remains of a full-term foetus were encountered in the abdomen of a female with masculine pelvic characteristics that may have contributed to difficulties during childbirth (White 1988, 71–3). This grave is not located notably close to the church, however there is also no evidence for eaves-drip burial at St Nicholas Shambles. Perhaps the use of a special cemetery zone for infants is a prerequisite for the differential treatment of women who may have died in childbirth?

An alternative suggestion for the association of the burials of adult females with those of children is presented by Christina Lee (2008, 31), who has drawn attention to examples of proximity between clusters of children's graves and the burials of adults with skeletal evidence of physical impairment. She focuses predominantly on evidence pre-dating the seventh century, and only two examples cited are from Christian cemeteries: a leper close to the eaves-drip zone at Raunds and the burial of a child and a woman with 'terminal illness' at Flixborough (North Lincolnshire), dating to the eighth century. In the case of the former, the diagnosis of leprosy in the adult male in question (sk. 5256) remains debatable and, in fact, a more securely diagnosed case of leprosy at Raunds exists (sk. 5046), but is interred at the furthest south-east edge of the cemetery, nowhere near the eaves-drip zone (Craig 2005, 77, 83). Moreover, if we follow Boddington's site stratigraphy, the adult burial (and indeed many other adult interments without osteologically identifiable diseases in the same area) substantially pre-dates any of the eaves-drip interments, making it unlikely that the location of the potentially leprous adult affected the placement of the child burials, and visa versa. In the case of the example from Flixborough, the 'terminal illness' in question is possible tuberculosis (identified on the basis of a possible calcified lymph node, but no further skeletal changes) (Geake *et al.* 2007, 114). This disease could have resulted in the death of the female, but it is also plausible that the proximity of her grave to that of an infant may indicate another case of obstetric fatality where a mother is interred in a 'children's zone', similar to those examples highlighted in this chapter.

Thus, it appears that the suggestion that females, some of whom were buried with neonates, and therefore may have died in childbirth, were the group most frequently afforded burial amongst clusters of neonates and infants is better suited to the evidence than that presented by Lee (2008). It is not possible to clarify whether all of the females associated with eaves-drip clusters, including those not buried with babies, were those who died in childbirth, although it must be noted that the available evidence does not rule out this hypothesis. The placement of women who may have died in childbirth in eaves-drip zones does suggest that they held some form of shared identity with the babies. Women who died during the early stages of pregnancy, or had experienced miscarriages with fatal complications, may also be included in this group. Female and infant deaths during pregnancy and birth must have occurred but there would be little osteological evidence for death in this manner. Indeed, the remains of younger foetuses would be scant given that bones begin early embryonic development as cartilaginous templates that would not survive in the soil (Scheuer and Black 2004, 23).

Anglo-Saxon sources tell us very little about childbirth, however pre-Christian Irish sources (including the *Colloquy of Ancients*, thought to have been compiled from oral accounts around 1200) indicate that women who died in childbirth could be afforded special status and honour in their burials (Crawford 2013; Leigh Fry 1999, 182–3). In England, it is not until the thirteenth century that Christian sources begin to link childbirth with contamination, some time after the eaves-drip burial practice had disappeared. The Irish model seems to fit the scenario presented here better than the much later Christian ideals (Gilchrist 2008, 43). Indeed, the burial close to churches of females who may have died as a result of pregnancy and childbirth, and their proximity to the burials of infants and neonates, serves to emphasise they were given special treatment. If infants who died young needed some special help provided by burial in proximity to buildings, it follows that their mothers, and unborn children still in the womb, might need similar protection. Alternatively, although the large groups of neonates and infants accompanied by only small numbers of female burials are unlikely to be conventional family units, it might have been hoped that a small number of adult female 'mother figures' could have protected large groups of children after death. The gendered role of women as care-givers including mothers, midwifes and undertakers has recently been reviewed in later medieval contexts (Gilchrist 2008) and it seems that a similar identity may be traced amongst the women considered here.

Conclusions

Infants around the age of one year or younger were preferentially interred in graves positioned in close proximity to standing structures at a number of early medieval Christian cemeteries. The suggestion that water running from the eaves of church buildings onto the graves of babies might provide posthumous baptism has its origins in folk myth, but provides a compelling explanation for much of the evidence. The eaves-drip hypothesis itself, however, does not always fit the available evidence: whilst the majority of clusters of young children are found under the eaves of buildings, in one case, at Thwing, interments of neonates clustered around a post arrangement. The evidence from Thwing serves to caution researchers from assuming that groups of infant burials can be used to infer the position of a church, particularly amongst seventh- and eighth-century sites. Moreover, there remains debate about the ubiquity of baptism in the seventh and eighth century that could undermine the widespread applicability of the eaves-drip model.

Eaves-drip burials are not encountered at all early Christian cemeteries, and where they do occur, the rite does not necessarily persist for the entire period of burial. In several cases eaves-drip burials are only found in the final phases of cemetery use. This raises the possibility that, in these cases, infants were buried in old, disused cemeteries after a newer site had been adopted by the remainder of the population. Broadly, it seems that decisions as to whether babies should be buried interspersed with older children and adults, or even in the same cemetery, were being made inconsistently across the country and across time. The existence of local level interpretations of baptismal ritual and the ameliorative power of burial rites for the unbaptised helps to explain the variations observed in the form of the eaves-drip rite over time and space. It is also notable that some adult burials are found in eaves-drip zones. These comprise adult females of child-bearing age and three apparent examples of death in childbirth, where it appears mother and child are interred together. It has been hypothesised that a few adult females might be afforded a funerary rite otherwise reserved for newborn babies where they died during pregnancy, childbirth or early motherhood, thus reflecting the linked identities of mother and child.

Acknowledgements

Thanks are particularly due to those who provided access to unpublished data and draft manuscripts for this research: Terry Manby and East Riding Archaeological Trust; and Tony Wilmott and Ian Roberts of Archaeological Services WYAS. Grateful thanks are due to Jo Buckberry and Annia Cherryson for discussion of information from Yorkshire and Compton Bassett respectively. Comments on earlier drafts by Dawn Hadley and the anonymous peer reviewers, and on the original research from which this paper was derived by Andrew Reynolds and John Moreland, were gratefully received. Assistance with illustrations was kindly provided by Ian Atkins. The original research this paper was developed from was funded by the Arts and Humanities Research Council Doctoral Award scheme, grant no. 2006/127490 awarded to the author at the University of Sheffield.

Bibliography

Anderson, S. 2007. The human population, pp. 97–102 in Daniels, R. (ed.), *Anglo-Saxon Hartlepool and the Foundations of English Christianity*. Hartlepool: Tees Archaeology.

Antoine, D. and Hillson, S. 2004/5. Famine, Black Death and health in fourteenth-century London. Archaeology International 8, 26–8.

Ayers, B. 1985. *Excavations within the North East Bailey of Norwich Castle, 1979* (East Anglian Archaeology Report 28). Norfolk: Norfolk Museums Service and Norfolk Archaeological Unit.

Barber, P. 1988. *Vampires, Burial and Death: folklore and reality*. New Haven: Yale University Press.

Boddington, A. 1996. *Raunds Furnells: the Anglo-Saxon church and churchyard*. London: English Heritage.

Buckberry, J. L. 2000. Missing, presumed buried? Bone diagenesis and the under-representation of Anglo-Saxon children. *Assemblage* 5 (available at http://ads.ahds.ac.uk/catalogue/adsdata/assemblage/html/5/buckberr.html).

Buckberry, J. L. 2007. On sacred ground: social identity and churchyard burial in Lincolnshire and Yorkshire, *c.* 700–1100 A.D., pp. 120–32 in Williams, H. and Semple, S. (eds), *Early Medieval Mortuary Practices* (Anglo-Saxon Studies in Archaeology and History 14). Oxford: Oxford University School of Archaeology.

Cardy, A. 1997. The human bones, pp. 519–92 in Hill, P. (ed.), *Whithorn and St Ninian: the excavation of a monastic town 1984–91*. Stroud: Sutton.

Colgrave, B. (ed. and trans.) and Mynors, R. A. B. (ed.) 1969. *Bede's Ecclesiastical History of the English People*. Oxford: Oxford University Press.

Craig, E. 2005. *An Osteological and Palaeopathological Assessment of Stress Indicators and Social Status at Raunds Furnells, Northamptonshire*. Unpublished M.Sc. thesis, University of Bradford.

Craig, E. 2008. *Village Farm, Spofforth Osteological Report*. Unpublished report for Northern Archaeological Associates.

Craig, E. 2010. *Burial Practices in Northern England c. AD 650–850: a bio-cultural approach*. Unpublished Ph.D. thesis, University of Sheffield.

Cramp, R. 2005. *Wearmouth and Jarrow Monastic Sites*. Swindon: English Heritage.

Crawford, S. 1993. Children, death and the afterlife in Anglo-Saxon England, pp. 83–91 in Filmer-Sankey, W. (ed.), *Anglo-Saxon Studies in Archaeology and History 6*. Oxford: Oxford University Committee for Archaeology.

Crawford, S. 1999. *Childhood in Anglo-Saxon England*. Stroud: Sutton.

Crawford, S. 2007. Companions, co-incidences or chattels? Children and their role in early Anglo-Saxon multiple burials, pp. 83–92 in Crawford, S. and Shepherd, G. (eds), *Children, Childhood and Society* (British Archaeological Reports International Series 1696). Oxford: Archaeopress.

Crawford, S. 2008. Special burials, special buildings? An Anglo-Saxon perspective on the interpretation of infant burials in association with rural settlement structures, pp. 197–204 in Bacvarov, K. (ed.), *Babies Reborn: infant/child burials in pre- and protohistory. Proceedings of the XV UISPP World Congress (Lisbon, 4–9 September 2006)/Actes du XV Congrès Mondial (Lisbonne, 4–9 Septembre 2006) Vol. 24, Session WS26* (British Archaeological Reports International Series 1832). Oxford: Archaeopress.

Crawford, S. 2013. Baptism and infant burial in Anglo-Saxon England, pp. 55–80, in Cochelin, I. and Smyth, K. (eds), *Medieval Lifecycles: continuities and change* (International Medieval Research 18). Turnhout: Brepols.

Daniels, R. 1999. The Anglo-Saxon monastery at Hartlepool, England, pp. 105–12 in Hawkes, J. and Mills, S. (eds), *Northumbria's Golden Age*. Stroud: Alan Sutton.

Daniels, R. and Loveluck, C. 2007. *Anglo-Saxon Hartlepool and the Foundations of English Christianity*. Hartlepool: Tees Archaeology/English Heritage.

di Ruffano, L. F. and Waldron, T. 2000. *The Skeletal Analysis of an Anglo-Saxon Population from Cherry Hinton, Cambridgeshire*. Unpublished report for Archaeological Solutions Ltd.

Evison, V. I. 1987. *Dover: the Buckland Anglo-Saxon cemetery*. London: Historic Buildings and Monuments Commission for England.

Freke, D. and Thacker, A. 1987/8. The inhumation cemetery at Southworth Hall Farm, Winwick. *Journal of the Chester Archaeological Society* 70, 31–8.

Geake, H. 2003. The control of burial in middle Anglo-Saxon England, pp. 259–70 in Carver, M. O. H. (ed.), *The Cross Goes North*. Woodbridge: Boydell.

Geake, H., Mays, S. and Ottaway, P. 2007. The inhabitants, pp. 113–24 in Loveluck, C. and Atkinson, D. (eds), *The Early Medieval Settlement Remains from Flixborough, Lincolnshire. Volume 1: the occupation sequence c. AD600–1000*. Oxford: Oxbow.

Gilchrist, R. 2008. Magic for the dead? The archaeology of magic in later medieval burials. *Medieval Archaeology* 52, 119–60.

Gittos, H. 2002. Creating the sacred: Anglo-Saxon rites for consecrating cemeteries, pp. 195–208 in Lucy, S. and Reynolds, A. (eds), *Burial in Early Medieval England and Wales* (Society for Medieval Archaeology Monograph 17). Leeds: Maney.

Hadley, D. M. 2007. The garden gives up its secrets: the developing relationship between rural settlements and cemeteries, c. 800–1100, pp. 194–203 in Williams, H. and Semple, S. (eds), *Early Medieval Mortuary Practices* (Anglo-Saxon Studies in Archaeology and History 14). Oxford: Oxford University School of Archaeology.

Hadley, D. M. 2010. Burying the socially and physically distinctive in and beyond the Anglo-Saxon churchyard, pp. 101–13 in Buckberry, J. L. and Cherryson, A. (eds), *Burial in Later Anglo-Saxon England, c. 650–1100 A.D.* Oxford: Oxbow.

Halsall, G. 1995. *Early Medieval Cemeteries: an introduction to burial archaeology of the post-Roman West.* Glasgow: Cruithne Press.

Hamerow, H. 2006. 'Special deposits' in Anglo-Saxon settlements. *Medieval Archaeology* 50, 1–30.

Harding, A. F. and Lee, G. E. 1987. *Henge Monuments and Related Sites of Great Britain.* (British Archaeological Reports British Series 175). Oxford: British Archaeological Reports.

Hawkes, J. and Adam, N. J. 2001. *Archaeological Investigations at St. Swithin's Church, Compton Bassett, Wiltshire.* Unpublished report from Wiltshire SMR.

Hill, P. (ed.) 1997. *Whithorn and St Ninian: the excavation of a monastic town 1984–91.* Stroud: Sutton.

Lee, C. 2008. Forever young: child burial in Anglo-Saxon England, pp. 17–36 in Lewis-Simpson, S. (ed.), *Viking Age Perspectives on Youth and Age in the Medieval North.* Leiden: Brill.

Leigh Fry, S. 1999. *Burial in Medieval Ireland, 900–1500.* Dublin: Four Courts Press.

Lucy, S. 1994. Children in early medieval cemeteries. *Archaeological Review from Cambridge* 13 (2), 21–34.

Lucy, S. 1998. *Early Anglo-Saxon Cemeteries of East Yorkshire* (British Archaeological Reports British Series 272). Oxford: J. & E. Hedges.

McDonald, T. and Doel, P. 2000. *Land at 69–115 Church End, Cherry Hinton, Cambridgeshire.* Unpublished report for Hertfordshire Archaeological Trust no. 722.

Manby, T. 1980. Settlement in eastern Yorkshire, pp. 307–70 in Barrett, J. and Bradley, R. (eds), *The British Later Iron Age, Part 2* (British Archaeological Reports British Series 83 (ii)). Oxford: British Archaeological Reports.

Manby, T. no date. *Thwing.* Unpublished report from the Thwing archive.

Mays, S. 2007. The human remains, pp. 77–192 in Mays, S., Harding, C. and Heighway, C. (eds), *Wharram XI: the churchyard.* York: English Heritage.

Milne, G. and Richards, J. D. 1992. *Wharram. A study of settlement on the Yorkshire Wolds: two Anglo-Saxon buildings and associated finds.* York: York University Archaeological Publications.

Molleson, T. and Cox, M. 1993. *The Spitalfields Project. Volume 2. Anthropology: the middling sort* (Council for British Archaeology Research Report 86). York: Council for British Archaeology.

Morris, R. 1991. Baptismal places: 600–800, pp. 15–24 in Wood, I. and Lund, N. (eds), *People and Places in Northern Europe 500–1600.* Woodbridge: Boydell.

Northern Archaeological Associates 2002. *Cemetery Excavations at Village Farm, Spofforth, North Yorkshire. Archaeological post-excavation assessment.* Unpublished report for Northern Archaeological Associates.

Page, M. R. 2011. Ble mae'r babanod? (Where are the babies?): infant burial in early medieval Wales, pp. 100–9 in Lally, M. and Moore, A. (eds), *(Re)Thinking the Little Ancestor: new perspectives on the archaeology of infancy and childhood* (British Archaeological Reports International Series 2271). Oxford: Archaeopress.

Reynolds, A. 2009. Anglo-Saxon Deviant Burial Customs. Oxford: Oxford University Press.

Scheuer, L. and Black, S. 2004. *The Juvenile Skeleton.* London: Elsevier.

Scobie, G. and Qualmann, K. 1993. *Nunnaminster. A Saxon and medieval community of nuns.* Winchester: Winchester Museums Service.

Shoesmith, R. 1980. *Hereford City Excavations, Volume 1. Excavations at Castle Green* (Council for

British Archaeology Research Report 36). London: Council for British Archaeology.

Stoodley, N. 1999. *The Spindle and the Spear: a critical enquiry into the construction and meaning of gender in the early Anglo-Saxon burial rite* (British Archaeological Reports British Series 228). Oxford: British Archaeological Reports.

Watts, D. 1989. Infant burials and Romano-British Christianity. *Archaeological Journal* 146, 372–83.

West, S. E. 1985. *West Stow. The Anglo-Saxon village.* Ipswich: Suffolk County Planning Department.

White, W. 1988. *Skeletal Remains from the Cemetery of St Nicholas Shambles, City of London.* London: English Heritage.

Whitelock, D. 1955. *English Historical Documents, Vol. 1, c. 500–1042.* Cambridge: Cambridge University Press.

Wilmott, T. in prep. *An Anglo-Saxon Church and its Cemetery: excavations in The Booths, 1985–86.* West Yorkshire Archaeological Services.

Wilson, S. 2000. *The Magical Universe: everyday ritual and magic in pre-modern Europe.* London: Hambledon Press.

7. Through the Flames of the Pyre: The continuing search for Anglo-Saxon infants and children

Kirsty E. Squires

Over the last thirty years many studies have explored the ways in which gender, the lifecycle and social hierarchy were expressed through Anglo-Saxon funerary rites. Such studies have mainly examined the relationship between the age and sex of individuals and the material culture with which they were buried, the form of their grave and its location within the cemetery. However, this research has focused overwhelmingly upon inhumation burials (*e.g.* Lucy 1998; Stoodley 2000), while contemporary sites where cremation was the predominant funerary rite have been relatively understudied and largely excluded from social archaeologies of the period (for exceptions, see Richards 1987; Lucy 2000; Ravn 2003). It is no surprise, therefore, that within the context of studies of Anglo-Saxon childhood it has been the evidence of inhumation cemeteries that has principally informed interpretations. For example, in her analysis of the treatment of children in the Anglo-Saxon funerary rite, Sally Crawford (1999, 16) mainly drew on the evidence from inhumation cemeteries, stating that '[c]remation cemeteries … may yield some information about early Anglo-Saxon society, but their interpretation is much more difficult than inhumation sites, so inhumations are the major source of archaeological evidence for childhood in the earlier Anglo-Saxon period'. However, given the considerable amount of information extracted from cremated bone from a number of large early Anglo-Saxon cemeteries, including Sancton I (East Yorkshire) (McKinley 1993), Spong Hill (Norfolk) (McKinley 1994), Cleatham and Elsham (both North Lincolnshire) (Squires 2011), an understanding of this funerary rite can, in fact, now be achieved, along with the ways in which the youngest members of society were treated in this funerary context. This chapter sets out to redress the balance in studies of Anglo-Saxon childhood, and to provide a detailed analysis of the ways in which infants (birth to four years) and children (five to twelve years) were treated and disposed of in the cremation ritual of early Anglo-Saxon England through an examination of demographic profiles and accompanying grave assemblages. It will be argued that infants and children were treated in a similar manner in death regardless of the funerary rites that were practiced by the communities in which they lived.

Children in the Anglo-Saxon funerary ritual: where are they?

The examination of age organisation by funerary archaeologists primarily deals with the differential treatment of individuals belonging to different stages of the lifecycle, with respect to the burial conditions and deposition of age-specific objects (Parker Pearson 1999, 74). The main aim of such analyses among Anglo-Saxon archaeologists interested in childhood has been to provide an insight into attitudes towards, and special treatment afforded to, the youngest members of early Anglo-Saxon communities in life and death (Crawford 1999, 19–32; Lucy 2000, 87–90, 111; Stoodley 2000, 105–18). A recurrent issue among such studies is the significant deficiency of infants and children from early Anglo-Saxon cemeteries where inhumation is the predominant rite. The cemetery at Great Chesterford (Essex), which is dominated by the inhumation rite, appears to be exceptional in that 49% of the cemetery population is comprised of non-adults, and Vera Evison (1994, 31) has concluded that all individuals of the Great Chesterford community were buried in this graveyard regardless of age. In contrast, infant and child mortality rates from most contemporary cemeteries have long been recognised as being considerably lower than at Great Chesterford (Crawford 1993, 84; Stoodley 1999, 106). For example, 27% of the cemetery population from Worthy Park (Hampshire) were below thirteen years of age (12% infants; 15% children) (Wells *et al.* 2003, 154–57), and a similar percentage was noted at Butler's Field, Lechlade (Gloucestershire) (19% infants; 8% children) (Harman 1998, 48–52). This mortality profile is not what should be expected among pre-modern populations, when infant (less than one year old) mortality should be as high as 40 to 50% (Weiss and Wobst 1973; Coale and Demeny 1983). A number of suggestions have been put forward as to the whereabouts of these missing individuals from early Anglo-Saxon cemeteries, and each of these hypotheses will be briefly explored as a context for the results presented in this chapter.

First, it has been suggested that due to the fragility of infant bones these skeletal remains are more prone to taphonomic decomposition than the remains of older individuals, especially at sites with acidic soils (Crawford 1993, 84; Scott 1999, 121). However, Jo Buckberry (2000) has disputed this notion as a plausible explanation since under favourable burial conditions the bones of infants and young children can survive just as well as their adult counterparts. Buckberry (2000) also points out that acidic, gravely or sandy soil not only destroys the skeletal remains of the youngest members of society but can cause the loss of entire adult skeletons. The inhumation graves at Snape and Sutton Hoo (both Suffolk), for example, show evidence for this type of taphonomic process. The sandy soil destroyed a significant proportion of bone from these cemeteries, and, in many cases, the presence of human-shaped soil stains provided the only evidence for inhumation burials (Carver 1992, 352; Filmer-Sankey and Pestell 2001, 248). In sum, the skeletal remains of infants and children survive as well or as poorly as those of adults.

Secondly, it has been argued that interment in shallow graves, which consequently led to post-depositional disturbance, plays a significant role in the poor preservation of infant and child burials from early Anglo-Saxon cemeteries (Crawford 1993, 84; Crawford 1999, 76; Scott 1999, 121). This is exemplified at the cemetery at Butler's Field, Lechlade, which was excavated in 1985 (Boyle and Palmer 1998, 1). Shallow graves were recorded on two occasions at this site, one of which contained a foetus while the second held the remains of a foetus or young infant, and both have been interpreted as a careless approach to the burial of very young individuals (Crawford 1999, 76). The burial of a cadaver, regardless of age, in a shallow grave or in the topsoil faces the risk of disturbance from scavengers and could, indeed, account for the small number of infants and children in the funerary record. However, if this practice was intentionally carried out due to the age of an individual, it was certainly not uniformly undertaken, even within the same cemetery, as is demonstrated by the presence of individuals belonging to the same age thresholds that have survived in the early Anglo-Saxon funerary record (Scott 1999, 121). Thus, it seems more likely that many young individuals from the early Anglo-Saxon period were excluded from burial in community cemeteries as a result of cultural influences and ideological beliefs, rather than taphonomic factors. Indeed, while taphonomic factors could equally have affected infant burials from the late Anglo-Saxon period, infants are found in greater numbers in the funerary record of this period (Lucy 1994, 27), and this may be attributable to the introduction of Christianity and interment within consecrated ground (see Craig-Atkins this volume).

Third, recovery bias is a factor that may contribute to the dearth of infants and children from cemeteries of the early Anglo-Saxon period. It is possible that the identification of skeletal remains belonging to immature individuals is dependent on the research interests of the excavator, the area of excavation and time constraints upon archaeological recovery and post-excavation analysis of skeletal remains (Buckberry 2000). The gracile nature of infant remains has sometimes led to them being overlooked during the excavation process and only recognised during the post-excavation analysis of an assemblage. This is demonstrated by the discovery of foetal remains only during the post-excavation osteological assessment of a female burial from the cemetery at Butler's Field, Lechlade; these foetal remains had not been noted during the excavation itself (Crawford 1999, 76).

Fourth, cultural influences have also been considered as factors that led to the differential burial treatment of infants in the early Anglo-Saxon period. It has recently been suggested, for example, that the low frequency of infants from early Anglo-Saxon cemeteries can, at least partly, be accounted for by their burial within settlements and buildings (Hamerow 2006; Crawford 2008), a practice that has also been identified on the continent (Beilke-Voigt 2008), and in Iron Age and Roman Britain (Armit and Ginn 2007; Moore 2009). Helena Hamerow (2006, 13) has pointed out that one third of the human deposits from early Anglo-Saxon settlement contexts belonged to infants, which is a higher frequency of infants than is usually found in contemporary cemeteries. Despite the fact that the sample used in Hamerow's (2006, 4–7) study is rather small, the percentage of infants from settlements is closer to the expected rates of infant mortality compared to cemetery sites of the same period (see above, p. 115). The discovery of infants interred in domestic contexts has been linked to both fertility ideology and infanticide (Scott 1999, 122; Hamerow 2006, 28). It has been proposed that the presence of infants within the domestic sphere may represent an offering to ensure future fertility of the community and protect stored grain (Hamerow 2006, 28). A similar practice has been observed among Hindu-practicing communities in Nepal, where children are buried close to non-arable land in the vicinity of the home (Oestigaard 2000, 24). In this ethnographic study, Terje Oestigaard (2000, 24) suggests that the community believed that the spirit and soul of the deceased infant or child should stay close to the family home as it would have a positive influence on the mother's fertility.

Sally Crawford (1999, 66–7) has suggested that while there is a good chance that infanticide would have been frowned upon during the Anglo-Saxon period it may have been a means of controlling the size of a family unit or disguising the conception of an illegitimate child, and this may have been another factor accounting for burial of infants away from communal cemeteries. It has been argued that similar practices were employed to control the size of family groups in early Anglo-Saxon England. Based on the work of Hansueli Etter and Jürg Schneider (1982, 53), which deals in part with the funerary treatment of infants and children on the continent in the early medieval period, Theya Molleson (1991, 118) has suggested that the Saxons introduced the custom of so-called 'fitness testing' upon their arrival in Britain. This practice involved subjecting babies to cold water, which was most likely to have been a stream or river. If the infant survived it is thought that the baby was kept, but if not, the infant was left in the body of water. This procedure may have been perpetuated to control population numbers for social or economic reasons or may have been used to ensure that only the strongest individuals survived (Molleson 1991, 120). However, there is no direct evidence for this practice in early Anglo-Saxon England, whether documentary or archaeological.

Finally, and of most direct relevance to the present chapter, cremation has been suggested as a mortuary rite disproportionately afforded to the youngest members of society, which might explain the small number of burials of infants and children among early Anglo-Saxon communities practicing inhumation (Crawford 1999, 76; Leahy 2007, 60). For example, in seeking to explain the low numbers of infants in inhumation cemeteries, Crawford (1999, 76) has suggested that '[o]ther methods may have been used to dispose of infants, such as cremation without subsequent burial', while Kevin Leahy (2007, 60) has proposed that the low frequency of infants and children among the inhumation burials at the Cleatham cemetery 'may be due ... to a tendency to cremate children's bodies'. At the time of Leahy's (2007) publication, the idea that infants and children were cremated, as opposed to receiving an inhumation rite, was a plausible explanation given that cremation was the prevalent funerary rite at the Cleatham cemetery, although his report appeared without an analysis of the cremated remains, which had not, at that point, been studied (see Squires 2011). A major problem with this theory is that a detailed assessment of infants and children from a range of cremation cemeteries has never been carried out. This is necessary, and long overdue, to determine whether the small number of infants and children from inhumation cemeteries really is accounted for by high numbers among cremation deposits.

In this chapter, an examination of the demographic profile of Anglo-Saxon cremated bone assemblages aims to establish whether the 'missing' infants and children from inhumation cemeteries were afforded cremation rites. Osteological data that have been obtained through the analysis of cremated bone from infant and child burials will be examined in conjunction with an assessment of associated grave assemblages, including artefacts, cinerary urns and animal bone. Subsequently, these results will be compared with the provision of grave furnishings that were offered to infants and children from contemporary inhumation burials. Based on funerary evidence, this chapter aims to provide an insight into the perceptions and attitudes that were displayed towards the youngest members of early Anglo-Saxon society.

Demography

Before commencing the analysis of early Anglo-Saxon cremation cemeteries, the methodologies for determining age from cremated remains need to be established. As a result of modern cremation methods, there has long been a false impression that the resultant material from the cremation process is fine ash (Murad 1998, 94). However, before the bones are removed from modern cremation hearths, the skeletal remains are still identifiable in their anatomical position, and are subsequently crushed until the cremated material is no longer recognisable (McKinley 1994, 75; Murad 1998, 94–5; Warren and Schultz 2002, 657; Warren *et al.* 2002, 38). This practice was not carried out in Anglo-Saxon England, and, therefore, fragments of bone and teeth can be identified to provide evidence for the number of individuals within a burial, the age and sex of the deceased and the presence of any palaeopathological conditions. Unfused epiphyseal surfaces and tooth development, including the presence of unerupted dentition, are the most valuable diagnostic skeletal elements required for detecting the presence of infants and children within a cremation burial (Moorrees *et al.* 1963; Scheuer and Black 2000) (Figures 7.1 and 7.2). As an individual grows older, the number of these useful age markers decreases and, as a result, establishing the age of an individual becomes more difficult. Thus, the identification of infants and children among cremation assemblages is, to an extent, easier than establishing explicit age categories for adults. In contrast, it is worth stating that, as with unburnt, inhumed bone, the determination of the sex of infants and children cannot be reliably undertaken. The primary reason why traditional osteological methods that are used to ascertain the sex of adults cannot be used in the analysis of infants and children is because sexual dimorphism does not commence until adolescence in both males and females (Scheuer and Black 2004, 14). It should be noted that the age groupings used in this study follow those employed by Jacqueline McKinley (1993; 1994) in her reports on Sancton I and Spong Hill. The aim of employing these age groupings during the analysis of the Elsham and Cleatham assemblages by the present author (Squires 2011) was to facilitate comparisons with the Sancton I and Spong Hill cemeteries, as the latter two cemeteries produced a significant quantity of cremated skeletal material and, consequently, a large body of demographic data.

The findings outlined in this chapter are based on the analysis of nine cemeteries where cremation was the dominant or sole funerary rite: Snape (Suffolk); Rayleigh and Mucking (both Essex); Spong Hill and Caistor-by-Norwich (both Norfolk); Sancton I (East Yorkshire); Newark (Nottinghamshire); and Elsham and Cleatham (both North Lincolnshire). Evidence was also included from thirteen sites where the inhumation rite was practiced, either as the sole mortuary tradition or alongside cremation: Great Chesterford and Mucking (both Essex); Butler's Field, Lechlade (Gloucestershire); Berinsfield (Oxfordshire); Worthy Park (Hampshire); Beckford A and B (Worcestershire); Buckland (Kent); Edix Hill (Cambridgeshire); Spong Hill (Norfolk); Sewerby (East Yorkshire); Castledyke South and Cleatham (both North Lincolnshire). The percentages of infants and children at the cemeteries examined in this chapter were determined in light of the total number of individuals that could be assigned to a biological age category. Among the assemblages considered in this chapter, an average of 11% of individuals were afforded the cremation rite (Figure 7.3) and 8% of individuals that were buried following the inhumation tradition (Figure 7.4) belonged to the infant age

Figure 7.1. Unerupted tooth crowns from burial MT84FX (burial 230) at Cleatham (North Lincolnshire) (photograph author, with permission of North Lincolnshire Museum).

Figure 7.2. Unfused femur diaphysis from burial MT84DM (burial 260) at Cleatham (North Lincolnshire) (photograph author, with permission of North Lincolnshire Museum).

grouping (0 to four years). Thus, it is clear that infants are under-represented among both inhumation *and* cremation practicing populations. A similar picture emerged when examining children (five to twelve years) from these sites. In total, 14% of individuals from the cremation burials and 12% of individuals from the inhumations were assigned to the child category (Figures 7.3 and 7.4). Among all cemeteries where cremation was the dominant mortuary rite the number of foetuses, infants and children was very similar, with the exception of Caistor-by-Norwich (Figure 7.3). This cemetery produced an unusually high frequency of children (39%), and this may illustrate that a wider selection of individuals of the Caistor-by-Norwich population were afforded the cremation rite and subsequently buried in the cemetery than was the case elsewhere. Calvin Wells (1973, 120) notes that the excavator of this site – F. R. Mann – showed a clear preference for the collection of skeletal remains of children, particularly teeth, over those of adults, and this may account for the demographic profile of this cemetery. Nonetheless, the percentage of infants at this site is still low, at just 7%.

Some of the sites examined in this study have provided evidence for the use of both inhumation and cremation, for example Spong Hill (Hills *et al.* 1984; McKinley 1994), Cleatham (Jakob 1999; Leahy 2007; Squires 2011) and Mucking (Mays 2009). The demographic profile of infants and children from these mixed-rite cemeteries is striking: expressed as a percentage of the total number of aged burials, the cremation burials produce at least twice the number of infants and children compared to the inhumations (Figure 7.5). These results can be, perhaps, partly attributed to the fact that cremation was the dominant rite at these three sites and consequently a higher proportion of the cemetery population was afforded this funerary rite. Furthermore, it may also be the case that a select group of individuals, mainly adult, were afforded inhumation at such sites; it is notable, for example, that the percentages of foetuses, infants and children were even lower among the inhumation burials at these mixed-rite cemeteries than in other inhumation cemeteries (Figures 7.4 and 7.5). More broadly, it does appear to be the case that infants and children are more likely to be interred in

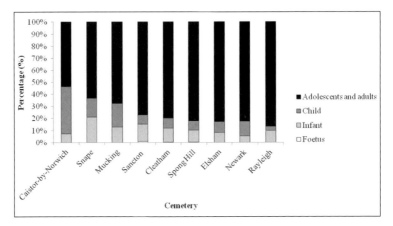

Figure 7.3. Percentage of foetuses, infants and children from the total number of cremation burials from nine early Anglo-Saxon cemeteries.

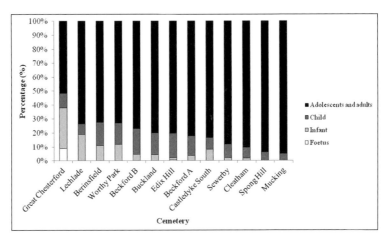

Figure 7.4. Percentage of foetuses, infants and children from the total number of inhumation burials from thirteen early Anglo-Saxon cemeteries.

the community cemetery among groups practicing cremation. In contrast, inhumation practicing groups appear to have more frequently excluded the youngest members of society from large burial sites. Yet, despite the fact that the cremation cemeteries have produced a larger number of infants and children than contemporary inhumation cemeteries, the total number of these individuals cannot, on their own, account for the low number of immature inhumation burials.

The results outlined in this chapter reveal that the average numbers of infants and children from Anglo-Saxon cremation burials are almost as low as those recorded from contemporary inhumation cemeteries. Thus, it is clear that there was not, in general, a preferential tendency for infants and children to be cremated rather than buried, and

Site	Burial type	Foetus	Infant	Child	Total number of aged burials	% of foetuses, infants and children
Cleatham	Inhumations	0	1	5	62	10
Cleatham	Cremations	3	99	71	856	20
Spong Hill	Inhumations	0	0	2	32	6
Spong Hill	Cremations	2	219	168	2196	18
Mucking	Inhumations	0	0	5	98	5
Mucking	Cremations	0	37	56	288	32

Figure 7.5. Number and frequency of foetuses, infants and children observed from three early Anglo-Saxon mixed-rite cemeteries.

this cannot, contrary to previous suggestions, account for the 'missing' infants and children of inhumation practicing groups. There is certainly variation in demographic profiles between cemeteries, but this variation is similar among both cremation and inhumation cemeteries. In sum, infants and children were treated in a similar manner among communities that performed both inhumation and cremation rites.

Grave assemblages

The following section of this chapter will examine the artefacts that were interred with infants and children that were afforded the cremation rite. These grave provisions will be compared with those provided for individuals allocated to the same age categories in inhumation cemeteries. It begins, however, by contrasting the grave (and pyre) goods found in inhumation and cremation burials more generally, in order to highlight what appear to have been the ideological differences between communities that practiced the different mortuary rites. As we will see, these contrasts make the similar treatment of infants and children in death even more striking. In addition, an interesting relationship that was identified between biological age and cinerary urn height will also be addressed in this section. Of course, the association between age and vessel height cannot be compared with contemporary inhumation burials, since the dead were not interred within such receptacles. Yet this discussion aims to highlight that age played an important role in the selection of grave provisions among cremation practicing groups.

The use of both the cremation and inhumation rites at different sites, or indeed within the same cemetery, has been suggested to represent groups holding distinctive ideological beliefs (Williams 2002, 66). This is particularly notable given the differential grave assemblages and actual funerary ceremonies afforded to individuals that belonged to groups that followed divergent mortuary customs. It has been widely recognised that early Anglo-Saxon inhumations display clear gender divisions (Härke 1990; Stoodley 1999; Lucy 2000). Jewellery and dress-accessories, for example brooches and wrist clasps, along with weaving-related items, are strongly associated with females, while military accoutrements, such as swords, shields, and spears, are closely connected with males. Artefacts that occurred with both sexes, often referred to as 'gender neutral', comprised knives, buckles and pottery vessels (Lucy 2000, 87). In stark contrast, cremation burials do not show such clearly defined sex or gender specific divisions based on grave provision (Squires 2011), though some discrete associations do occur and will be discussed later in this chapter.

Howard Williams (2005, 269) has suggested that weapons were infrequently employed in the cremation rite as they acted as mnemonic agents, which represented personhood in an idealised form and were accordingly more suited to the inhumation rite. In contrast, the utilisation of combs and toilet articles in the cremation ritual generated select memories through the display and transformation, fragmentation and redistribution of bodies and artefacts (Williams 2005, 269). This has significant implications and points to ideological differences between communities that practiced different funerary rituals. Combs, in particular, appear to have been an intrinsic part of the cremation rite, though are much rarer in contemporary inhumation burials (Williams 2003, 113). These items were made of bone or antler and were interred with cremated individuals regardless of age or sex. Interestingly, combs were rarely placed on the cremation pyre and were most frequently placed in the cinerary urn in an unburnt state along with the cremated bone after the funerary ritual. Williams (2003, 116–17) has proposed that combs were important items for rituals surrounding personal grooming, and despite being a common item they appear to have been significant personal objects. Complete combs are extremely rare in early Anglo-Saxon cremation burials, and, based on the fact that the recovery of half-combs or even smaller fragments is more common, it appears that these objects were intentionally damaged before deposition (Williams 2003, 107–8). Williams (2010, 74) has suggested that the deliberate breakage of combs would have prevented other individuals from using these artefacts, while the possible distribution of comb fragments between the living and dead would have prompted an ongoing connection between the deceased and living kin. The miniature toilet sets and combs that have been recovered would have been impractical for use in life, suggesting that they were produced solely for funerary purposes (Williams 2010, 74). Williams (2010, 75) has suggested that miniature combs and toilet articles held amuletic and regenerative properties, which were possibly thought to protect the dead and aid the deceased's transformation into a new form in the afterlife. Overall, it appears that various elements of an individual's identity were represented in the cremation rite through the combination of different objects in the grave repertoire. However, these associations are not as clear cut as those identified from contemporary inhumation burials. Instead of displaying the idealised form of an individual in the mortuary rite, cremation practicing groups seem to have been more selective in remembering the dead and emphasising the transformation of the deceased into a new form. Moreover, the frequent use and deposition of combs and toilet sets, which included both full-sized and miniature tweezers, earscoops, razors, shears and blades, in the cremation rite, but scarcely at all in the inhumation rite, illustrates further differences in the ideological beliefs of groups practicing cremation and inhumation.

The remaining section of this chapter will explore grave provisions from infant and child cremation burials from early Anglo-Saxon England, which will, in turn, be compared with grave assemblages from contemporary inhumation burials. To begin, an examination between age and the height of cinerary urns will be provided. Evidence from Sancton I (McKinley 1993, 314), Spong Hill (McKinley 1994, 102) and the results presented in Julian Richards' (1987, 137) multi-site study, which incorporated 18 cemeteries, illustrated that infants and children were typically buried in shorter urns than adults. In addition, as part of the present study, statistical analyses were carried out on the evidence from the Elsham and Cleatham cemeteries, and these tests produced results that were highly statistically significant, confirming the hypothesis that infants and children were buried in shorter urns than adults at these cemeteries. There are practical reasons that, perhaps, account for cinerary urn selection. For example, based on analyses from the Elsham and Cleatham cemeteries, it is notable that the weight of cremated bone from infants and children was significantly less than that from individuals belonging to older age categories. Adults produced more cremated bone than infants and children and, consequently, taller urns would have been required to accommodate the large amount of skeletal material from older individuals. Nonetheless, cultural factors may have still played an important role in the selection of funerary receptacles. There are apparent gradations in vessel height, which relate to each age category from the Elsham and Cleatham cemeteries (Squires 2013, 164). These results support the notion that practical reasons were not the only factors that were considered when selecting cinerary urns. It is possible that adults were interred in taller vessels as these may have indicated the status and position an individual had achieved in life (Richards 1987, 136). These positions were likely to have been ascribed to individuals as they passed through the various age thresholds and, as such, represented important stages of an individual's life, for example the transition to adulthood.

The Elsham and Cleatham evidence was examined by the present author to determine whether there was a relationship between age and the interment of faunal remains (Squires 2011). Animals clearly played an integral part in the early Anglo-Saxon cremation rite. Cremated faunal remains illustrate that animals were placed on the funerary pyre alongside the deceased, either as joints of meat or whole bodies, and their burned bones were deposited in an urn or pit. Statistical analyses revealed that infants and children were less likely to have been afforded animal offerings than adolescents and adults at both Elsham and Cleatham. A similar pattern has been observed at Newark (Harman 1989, 24), Sancton I (McKinley 1993, 310) and Spong Hill (McKinley 1994, 99). In addition, these sites also illustrated that older individuals were afforded a wider range of species than infants and children, who were most commonly afforded joints of meat from small to medium-sized domesticates, particularly sheep/goat (Harman 1989, 24; McKinley 1993, 310; McKinley 1994, 99). In contrast to Anglo-Saxon cremation burials, animals appear to have played a less important role in the contemporary inhumation rite as these types of burials produce a smaller number of faunal remains (Williams 2001, 197; Bond and Worley 2006, 90). This discrepancy appears to show that animals played a more important role in the funerary customs, and possibly the beliefs, of individuals belonging to cremation practicing communities. As a result of the limited number of cemeteries that have produced significant quantities of animal bone from inhumation burials, very little work has been conducted on the lifecycle and provision of faunal offerings in the inhumation rite (Fern 2007; Lee 2007). Based on the inhumation assemblages examined in this chapter, it is notable that all ages and both sexes were afforded animal offerings, though the inhumation burials that did produce animal bone occur in very small numbers (Evison 1994, 35; McKinley 1994, 137; Wilson 1995, 109–11;

Evison and Hill 1996, 1, 77, 88; Leahy 2007, 231–43; Lee 2007, 62). However, faunal remains were found in greater numbers at the cemeteries of Castledyke South, where they were found in 16% of graves, (Nicholson 1998, 236) and Butler's Field, Lechlade, recovered from 30% of graves (Boyle *et al.* 1998, 53–137), which permits some tentative conclusions to be drawn about the deposition of animal remains in inhumations. An examination of these data by the present author revealed that 9% of individuals from the Castledyke South assemblage and 32% of the Lechlade assemblage that were afforded animal offerings were under thirteen years of age. Despite the fact that the amount of animal bone recovered from the inhumations at these two sites was small compared to the amount of faunal remains found in contemporary cremation burials, it is notable that infants and children, regardless of the funerary rite they were afforded, were also less likely than adolescents and adults to have been provided with animal offerings.

Both practical and cultural factors may explain why infants and children were less likely than adolescents and adults to have been provided animal offerings in the mortuary arena. Infants and children would have required a smaller pyre (or grave, when considering the inhumation rite) and the presence of numerous animals, either as joints of meat or whole, would have required additional labour and economic investment, which may not have been deemed viable for individuals belonging to the youngest age thresholds (McKinley 1993, 311). Cultural beliefs may have also influenced the provision and number of animals that were afforded to an individual, which could have applied to both cremation and inhumation practicing groups. The presence of faunal remains in cremation burials seems to reflect the rites of passage that an individual had gone through during their life; for example, animal bone was strongly associated with adolescents compared to infants and children. During adolescence, new roles and responsibilities would have been assigned to individuals. Some of these roles are likely to have involved the management of livestock and participation in economic activities, such as weaving (Richards 1987, 125). Therefore, increased interaction with animals and the contribution to a community's economy may have warranted the endowment of an animal(s) in the cremation rite.

Statistical analyses were also carried out by the author in an attempt to establish whether infants and children were equally as likely to have been afforded pyre and grave goods as adolescents and adults. The results for Elsham illustrated that there was not a significant relationship between age and the presence of grave goods at this site. In contrast, statistically significant results from Cleatham demonstrated that adolescents and adults were more likely to have been buried with pyre and grave goods than the younger members of the cemetery population. The lack of pyre and grave goods associated with infants and children at Cleatham may be explained by their age and position in the community. As a result of the social standing of these individuals, it is possible that they were provided objects fashioned out of organic materials (for example wood). Such artefacts would be invisible in the archaeological record owing to the destructive nature of the cremation process and/or unfavourable burial environment. Items fashioned out of more durable materials, which therefore *perhaps* were deemed to be of greater value, were more commonly found with adolescents and adults and may have reflected their position within society. The fact that infants and children were just as likely to have been afforded pyre and grave goods as adolescents and adults from Elsham may indicate inter-site variation, and that the number of objects provided at an individual's funeral may have been more significant at Elsham. For example, infants and children may have been provided with a smaller number of items, for example a single bead, than adolescents and adults owing to their social role and position within the community. Unfortunately, due to the loss of objects as a result of cremation and the burial environment, it is difficult to confirm that the number of objects afforded to an individual was a means of signifying social position at Elsham. Nonetheless, the information obtained from an examination of the cinerary urns and animal remains at this site illustrates that infants and children were unlikely to have been regarded as 'small adults' or 'low-status adults' (Richards 1987, 130; Crawford 1999, 169). The notion that infants and children were classified as 'small adults' in early Anglo-Saxon England can be dismissed due to its simplicity and the fact that these individuals were buried in shorter urns and less likely to have been afforded animal offerings from all sites examined in this study. This evidence alone is indicative that they were differentiated from older members of society.

When considering artefact types, cluster and correspondence analysis showed that there was no evidence for objects that were solely afforded to infants and children in the cremation rites at Elsham and Cleatham. Some of the most commonly occurring items that were found in the burials of infants and children from these sites included combs, beads and spindle whorls. These objects were found in high numbers in infant and child burials at both sites, although rings and brooches also occurred in relatively high numbers at Cleatham. Spindle whorls are associated with the production of textiles, which are frequently linked to female economic activities, such as weaving and spinning (Gilchrist 2011, 160), while brooches, rings and beads are associated with dress and the social identity of women. It has also been suggested that spindle whorls and beads held healing and protective properties, which indicates that these objects may have been included in grave assemblages for their amuletic significance (Meaney 1981, 206–7). Interestingly, these types of artefacts also occurred in adult deposits at Elsham and Cleatham, particularly among female grave provision. Similarly, McKinley (1994, 90) has noted that the range of artefacts interred with infants at Spong Hill closely reflected the grave assemblage found with females. Comparable with cremation burials, no artefact type has been found exclusively with infants and children from contemporary inhumation graves (Crawford 2000, 171). However, knives, beads, buckles, brooches, containers, pins and coins are frequently recorded from inhumations belonging to individuals under ten years of age (Crawford 2000, 174). Similar to the grave furnishings found with infants and children in cremation burials, objects possessing female and ungendered connotations are associated with infants and children from contemporary inhumation cemeteries. These observations highlight that both inhumation and cremation practicing groups had similar attitudes towards the gendering of infants and children, at least in the context of funerary rites. This may be related to the participation of infants and children, regardless of sex, in basic domestic (feminine) tasks, which suggests that their mothers (or other female carers that belonged to their extended kin group) influenced the social standing of these young individuals (Stoodley 2000, 465). The fact that adolescents and adults were more likely to have been afforded animal offerings may support the notion that as individuals reached adolescence, particularly males, they were ascribed roles and responsibilities that were not solely centred around domestic dwellings.

Artefacts from infant and child burials, both cremations and, to an extent, inhumations, closely reflect the material culture found with young individuals interred in domestic contexts. These burials were often accompanied by animal bone, pottery sherds, spindle whorls, combs and pins (Crawford 2008, 198). Based on the lack of so-called prestige items, such as weapons and jewellery, artefact assemblages found in domestic contexts are thought to have belonged to 'lower status' individuals (Crawford 2000, 173). Two notable examples of such burials are worth pointing out, as they may present a different picture. At Eye Kettleby (Leicestershire), an infant found in a sunken-featured building was accompanied by a complete pottery vessel (Hamerow 2006, 5), while at Yarnton (Oxfordshire) a probable two- to three-year-old was associated with two probable female adults, animal bone and pottery (Hamerow 2006, 7). The notion that these deposits were 'low status' should not be readily accepted. Instead, burials that are located in close proximity to the living, especially areas that would have been frequented by women, appear to have held ideological, or even amuletic, significance. The assemblages found with infants and children in both cemetery and domestic contexts may have been intentionally selected by mourners to demonstrate the close connection between young individuals, their (female) carers in life and the home as a means of protection in the afterlife (Sofaer-Derevenski 1997, 192; Kamp 2001, 3; Hamerow 2006, 19). As mentioned above, it appears that the status of infants and children in their early years was influenced by their mothers. Sally Crawford (2008, 198) has noted that infant burials from settlement sites are often neglected in analyses as they are typically found in areas, for example in the floors of sunken-featured buildings and pits, where material is frequently classified as casual deposits or discarded waste. Yet, as this chapter has illustrated, infants and children that were buried in domestic contexts were accompanied by objects that were carefully chosen by the living and cannot be classed as casual deposits. Overall, based on an examination of grave provision, it appears that attitudes towards infants and children were extremely similar among inhumation and cremation practicing communities, and this similarity of treatment extended into contexts in which such young individuals were buried in settlements.

Conclusion

One of the aims of this chapter was to assess the hypothesis that the missing infants from cemeteries where inhumation was the dominant rite had, instead, been cremated. This can now be dismissed. Instead, perhaps areas outside of community cemeteries, such as woodland and forested areas in addition to settlements and boundaries, should be focused on to gain a greater understanding of the mortuary treatment and social attitudes towards infants and children during the early Anglo-Saxon period. This chapter has also addressed the mortuary rites that were afforded to infants and children from early Anglo-Saxon cremation cemeteries, which, in the past, scholars have neglected in favour of focusing on their contemporaries from inhumation burials. It is apparent that infants and children were treated in a similar manner among groups that practiced the inhumation and cremation rite in early Anglo-Saxon England. This is a significant finding, especially in light of recent work (*e.g.* Williams 2002; 2003; 2005) highlighting the fundamental differences between inhumation and cremation as rites of transition. Despite the ritual differences of the inhumation and cremation rites, and the distinctive treatment of adults in cemeteries characterised by these differing rites, infants and children were treated in a similar manner by communities that practiced these contrasting funerary rites. Associated grave assemblages reveal that infants and children were afforded a less ostentatious grave assemblage than adolescents and adults; for example, they were buried in shorter vessels and were less likely to have been afforded animal offerings. Infants and children were often buried with pyre and grave goods that held female connotations, suggesting that they took on a feminine identity until they reached adolescence among both inhumation and cremation practicing communities. In addition, the strong association between these young individuals, females and the home may hold deeper ideological connotations relating to protection of the deceased in the afterlife and the future fertility of women. The differential funerary treatment of infants and children appears to be the result of their social position and role within society.

Acknowledgements

Special thanks to Professor Dawn Hadley, Dr Nicole Roth, Dr Gareth Perry (all of the University of Sheffield), Dr Toby Martin (University of Oxford), Professor Andrew Chamberlain (University of Manchester), Rose Nicholson (North Lincolnshire Museum) and Ruth Nugent (University of Chester). Many thanks go to the AHRC for financial support of the author's Ph.D. research. The photographs in this chapter were taken by the author, courtesy of North Lincolnshire Museum.

Bibliography

Armit, I. and Ginn, V. 2007. Beyond the grave: human remains from domestic contexts in Iron Age Atlantic Scotland. *Proceedings of the Prehistoric Society* 73, 113–34.

Beilke-Voigt, I. 2008. Burials of children in houses and settlements during the Roman Iron Age and early medieval period in northern Germany and Denmark, pp. 16–35 in Dommasnes, L. H. and Wrigglesworth, M. (eds), *Children, Identity and the Past*. Cambridge: Cambridge Scholars Publishing.

Bond, J. M. and Worley, F. L. 2006. Companions in death: the roles of animals in Anglo-Saxon and Viking cremation rituals in Britain, pp. 89–98 in Gowland, R. and Knüsel, C. (eds), *Social Archaeology of Funerary Remains*. Oxford: Oxbow.

Boyle, A., Jennings, D., Miles, D. and Palmer, S. 1998. *The Anglo-Saxon Cemetery at Butler's Field, Lechlade, Gloucestershire. Volume 1: prehistoric and Roman activity and Anglo-Saxon grave catalogue* (Thames Valley Landscapes Monograph 10). Oxford: Oxford University Committee for Archaeology.

Boyle, A. and Palmer, S. 1998. Chapter 1: introduction, pp. 1–8 in Boyle, A., Jennings, D., Miles, D. and Palmer, S., *The Anglo-Saxon Cemetery at Butler's Field, Lechlade, Gloucestershire. Volume 1: prehistoric and Roman activity and Anglo-Saxon grave catalogue* (Thames Valley Landscapes Monograph 10). Oxford: Oxford University Committee for Archaeology.

Buckberry, J. L. 2000. Missing, presumed buried? Bone diagenesis and the under-representation of Anglo-Saxon children. *Assemblage* 5 (available at: http://www.assemblage.group.shef. ac.uk/5/buckberr.html).

Carver, M. O. H. 1992. The Anglo-Saxon cemetery at Sutton Hoo: an interim report, pp. 343–71 in Carver, M. O. H. (ed.), *The Age of Sutton Hoo: the seventh century in North-Western Europe.* Woodbridge: Boydell.

Coale, A. J. and Demeny, P. 1983. *Regional Model Life Tables and Stable Populations.* Princeton: Princeton University Press.

Crawford, S. 1993. Children, death and the afterlife in Anglo-Saxon England, pp. 83–91 in Filmer-Sankey, W. (ed.), *Anglo-Saxon Studies in Archaeology and History 6.* Oxford: Oxbow.

Crawford, S. 1999. *Childhood in Anglo-Saxon England.* Stroud: Sutton.

Crawford, S. 2000. Children, grave goods and social status in early Anglo-Saxon England, pp. 169–79 in Sofaer-Derevenski, J. (ed.), *Children and Material Culture.* London: Routledge.

Crawford, S. 2008. Special burials, special buildings? An Anglo-Saxon perspective on the interpretation of infant burials in association with rural settlement structures, pp. 197–204 in Bacvarov, K. (ed.), *Babies Reborn: infant/child burials in pre- and protohistory. Proceedings of the XV UISPP World Congress (Lisbon, 4–9 September 2006)/Actes du XV Congrès Mondial (Lisbonne, 4–9 Septembre 2006) Vol. 24, Session WS26* (British Archaeological Reports International Series 1832). Oxford: Archaeopress.

Etter, H. F. and Schneider, J. E. 1982. Zur Stellung von Kind und Frau im Frühmittelalter. *Zeitschrift für Schweizerische Archäologie und Kunstgeschichte* 39, 48–57.

Evison, V. I. 1994. *An Anglo-Saxon Cemetery at Great Chesterford, Essex* (Council for British Archaeology Research Report 91). York: Council for British Archaeology.

Evison, V. I. and Hill, P. 1996. *Two Anglo-Saxon Cemeteries at Beckford, Hereford and Worcester* (Council for British Archaeology Research Report 103). York: Council for British Archaeology.

Fern, C. 2007. Early Anglo-Saxon horse burial of the fifth to seventh centuries AD, pp. 92–109 in Williams, H. and Semple, S. (eds), *Early Medieval Mortuary Practices* (Anglo-Saxon Studies in Archaeology and History 14). Oxford: Oxford University School of Archaeology.

Filmer-Sankey, W. and Pestell, T. 2001. *Snape Anglo-Saxon Cemetery: excavations and surveys 1824–1992* (East Anglian Archaeology Report 95). Ipswich: Suffolk County Council.

Gilchrist, R. 2011. The intimacy of death: interpreting gender and the life course in medieval and early modern burials, pp. 159–73 in Beaudry, M. C. and Symonds, J. (eds), *Interpreting the Early Modern World: transatlantic perspectives.* New York: Springer.

Hamerow, H. 2006. 'Special deposits' in Anglo-Saxon settlements. Medieval Archaeology 50, 1–30.

Härke, H. 1990. 'Warrior graves'? The background of the Anglo-Saxon weapon burial rite. *Past and Present* 126, 22–43.

Harman, M. 1989. Discussion of the finds: cremations, pp. 23–5 in Kinsley, A. G., *The Anglo-Saxon Cemetery at Millgate, Newark-on-Trent, Nottinghamshire* (Nottingham Archaeological Monographs 2). Nottingham: University of Nottingham.

Harman, M. 1998. The human remains, pp. 43–52 in Boyle, A., Jennings, D., Miles, D. and Palmer, S., *The Anglo-Saxon Cemetery at Butler's Field, Lechlade, Gloucestershire. Volume 1: prehistoric and Roman activity and Anglo-Saxon grave catalogue* (Thames Valley Landscapes Monograph 10). Oxford: Oxford University Committee for Archaeology.

Hills, C., Penn, K. and Rickett, R. 1984. The Anglo-Saxon Cemetery at Spong Hill, North Elmham. Part III: catalogue of inhumations (East Anglian Archaeology 21). Norfolk: Norfolk Archaeological Unit.

Jakob, B. 1999. *The Inhumations from the Mixed Rite Anglo-Saxon Cemetery 'Kirton in Lindsey',*

Cleatham, North Lincolnshire. Unpublished M.Sc. dissertation, University of Sheffield.

Kamp, K. A. 2001. Where have all the children gone? The archaeology of childhood. *Journal of Archaeological Method and Theory* 8 (1), 1–34.

Leahy, K. 2007. *'Interrupting the Pots': the excavation of Cleatham Anglo-Saxon cemetery, North Lincolnshire* (Council for British Archaeology Research Report 155). York: Council for British Archaeology.

Lee, C. 2007. *Feasting the Dead: food and drink in Anglo-Saxon burial*. Woodbridge: Boydell.

Lucy, S. 1994. Children in early medieval cemeteries. *Archaeological Review from Cambridge* 13 (2), 21–34.

Lucy, S. 1998. *The Early Anglo-Saxon Cemeteries of East Yorkshire: an analysis and reinterpretation* (British Archaeological Reports British Series 272). Oxford: J. & E. Hedges.

Lucy, S. 2000. *The Anglo-Saxon Way of Death: burial rites in early England*. Stroud: Sutton.

Mays, S. 2009. The human remains, pp. 436–40 in Hirst, S. and Clark, D. (eds), *Excavations at Mucking. Volume 3, part 2, the Anglo-Saxon cemeteries: analysis and discussion*. London: Museum of London Archaeology.

McKinley, J. I. 1993. Cremated bone, pp. 287–316 in Timby, J. (ed.), Sancton I Anglo-Saxon cemetery excavations carried out between 1976 and 1980. *Archaeological Journal* 150, 243–365.

McKinley, J. I. 1994. *The Anglo-Saxon Cemetery at Spong Hill, North Elmham. Part VIII: the cremations* (East Anglian Archaeology Report 69). Norfolk: Essex County Council.

Meaney, A. 1981. *Anglo-Saxon Amulets and Curing Stones* (British Archaeological Reports British Series 96). Oxford: British Archaeological Reports.

Molleson, T. 1991. Demographic implications of the age structure of early English cemetery samples, pp. 113–21 in Buchet, L. (ed.), *Ville et Campagne en Europe occidentale (Ve–XIIIe siècle). Actes des cinquièmes journées anthropologiques de Valbonne, 1990*. Paris: Éditions du CNRS.

Moore, A. 2009. Hearth and home: the burial of infants within Romano-British domestic contexts. *Childhood in the Past* 2 (1), 33–54.

Moorrees, C. F. A., Fanning, E. A. and Hunt, E. E. 1963. Age variation in the formation stages for ten permanent teeth. *Journal of Dental Research* 42, 1490–502.

Murad, T. A. 1998. The growing popularity of cremation versus inhumation: some forensic implications, pp. 86–105 in Reichs, K. J. (ed.), *Forensic Osteology II: advances in the identification of human remains*. Springfield: Charles C. Thomas.

Nicholson, R. 1998. Animal bone from the graves, pp. 236–40 in Drinkall, G. and Foreman, M. A. (eds), *The Anglo-Saxon Cemetery at Castledyke South, Barton-on-Humber* (Sheffield Excavation Reports 6). Sheffield: Sheffield Academic Press.

Oestigaard, T. 2000. *The Deceased's Life Cycle Rituals in Nepal: present cremation burials for the interpretations of the past* (British Archaeological Reports International Series 853). Oxford: J. & E. Hedges.

Parker Pearson, M. 1999. *The Archaeology of Death and Burial*. Stroud: Sutton.

Ravn, M. 2003. *Death Ritual and Germanic Social Structure (c. AD 200–600)* (British Archaeological Reports International Series 1164). Oxford: Archaeopress.

Richards, J. D. 1987. *The Significance of Form and Decoration of Anglo-Saxon Cremation Urns* (British Archaeological Reports British Series 166). Oxford: British Archaeological Reports.

Scheuer, L. and Black, S. 2000. *Developmental Juvenile Osteology*. London: Academic Press.

Scheuer, L. and Black, S. 2004. *The Juvenile Skeleton*. London: Elsevier Academic Press.

Scott, E. 1999. *The Archaeology of Infancy and Infant Death* (British Archaeological Reports International Series 819). Oxford: Archaeopress.

Sofaer-Derevenski, J. 1997. Engendering children, engendering archaeology, pp. 192–202 in Moore, J. and Scott, E. (eds), *Invisible People and Processes: writing gender and childhood into European archaeology*. London: Leicester University Press.

Squires, K. E. 2011. *An Osteological Analysis and Social Investigation of the Cremation Rite at the Cemeteries of Elsham and Cleatham, North Lincolnshire.* Unpublished Ph.D. thesis, University of Sheffield.

Squires, K. E. 2013. Piecing together identity: a social investigation of early Anglo-Saxon cremation practices. *Archaeological Journal* 170, 154–200.

Stoodley, N. 1999. *The Spindle and the Spear: a critical enquiry into the construction and meaning of gender in the early Anglo-Saxon burial rite* (British Archaeological Reports British Series 288). Oxford: British Archaeological Reports.

Stoodley, N. 2000. From the cradle to the grave: age organization and the early Anglo-Saxon burial rite. *World Archaeology* 31 (3), 456–72.

Warren, M. W., Falsetti, A. B., Kravchenko, I. I., Dunnam, F. E., Van Rinsvelt, H. A. and Maples, W. R. 2002. Elemental analysis of bone: proton-induced X-ray emission testing in forensic cases. *Forensic Science International* 125 (1), 37–41.

Warren, M. W. and Schultz, J. J. 2002. Post-cremation taphonomy and artifact preservation. *Journal of Forensic Sciences* 47 (3), 656–9.

Weiss, K. M. and Wobst, H. M. 1973. Demographic models for anthropology. *Memoirs of the Society for American Archaeology* 27, 1–186.

Wells, C. 1973. The cremations, pp. 120–1 in Myres, J. N. L. and Green, B. (eds), *The Anglo-Saxon Cemeteries of Caistor-by-Norwich and Markshall, Norfolk* (Reports of the Research Committee of the Society of Antiquaries of London 30). London: The Society of Antiquaries of London.

Wells, C., Grainger, G., Denston, B. and Chadwick Hawkes, S. 2003. Chapter 3: the inhumations and cremations, pp. 153–89 in Chadwick Hawkes, S. with Grainger, G., *The Anglo-Saxon Cemetery at Worthy Park, Kingsworthy, near Winchester, Hampshire* (Oxford University School of Archaeology Monograph 59). Oxford: Oxford University School of Archaeology.

Williams, H. 2001. An ideology of transformation: cremation rites and animal sacrifice in early Anglo-Saxon England, pp. 193–212 in Price, N. (ed.), *The Archaeology of Shamanism*. London: Routledge.

Williams, H. 2002. Remains of pagan Saxondom? – the study of Anglo-Saxon cremation rites, pp. 47–71 in Lucy, S. and Reynolds, A. (eds), *Burial in Early Medieval England and Wales* (Society of Medieval Archaeology Monograph Series 17). London: Maney.

Williams, H. 2003. Material culture as memory: combs and cremation in early medieval Britain. *Early Medieval Europe* 12 (2), 89–128.

Williams, H. 2005. Keeping the dead at arm's length: memory, weaponry and early medieval mortuary technologies. *Journal of Social Archaeology* 5 (2), 253–75.

Williams, H. 2010. At the funeral, pp. 67–82 in Carver, M. O. H., Sanmark, A. and Semple, S. (eds.), *Signals of Belief in Early England: Anglo-Saxon paganism revisited*. Oxford: Oxbow.

Wilson, B. 1995. The bone and shell remains, pp. 109–11 in Boyle, A., Dodd, A., Miles, D. and Mudd, A. (eds), *Two Oxfordshire Anglo-Saxon Cemeteries: Berinsfield and Didcot* (Thames Valley Landscape Monograph 8). Oxford: Oxford University Committee for Archaeology.

8. Are We Nearly There Yet? Children and migration in early medieval western Britain

K. A. Hemer

The archaeological record from western Britain has long seemed to offer little potential for studying aspects of early medieval social identity, including childhood. This is principally because the poor preservation of skeletal remains in some cemeteries, such as Tandderwen (Clwyd) (Brassil *et al.* 1991), leaves excavators with little more than a handful of crumbling teeth to analyse. Archaeologists interested in childhood in early medieval western Britain have sometimes had to resort purely to the lengths of graves to distinguish the burials of children from those of adults (*e.g.* Page 2011, 101–6). Combined with the general paucity of grave goods in burials, this has prevented archaeologists from undertaking the types of analysis that are now commonplace in studies of the contemporary Anglo-Saxon burial record, in which the relationship between biological age and grave goods has been scrutinised for information about the life cycle and the symbolic significance of related rites of passage (*e.g.* Lucy 1994; Crawford 1999; 2007; Stoodley 2000; Gowland 2006). Perhaps as a consequence, scholars interested in western British funerary practices have focussed primarily on the stone funerary sculpture (Edwards 2001; Petts 2003), although this offers those interested in childhood little material with which to work. Recently, however, the potential of the funerary record from western Britain to elucidate aspects of childhood has been enhanced through analyses based on the investigation of stable isotope evidence (*e.g.* Hemer 2010; Hadley and Hemer 2011), and these can – importantly – be undertaken on even poorly preserved cemetery populations. This chapter discusses the implications of this recent analysis of stable isotope evidence for our understanding of childhood, through discussion of the insights it provides into childhood migration. It then examines the historical record in order to determine the contexts in which children may have been moving across the western British landscape. Finally, the chapter highlights the potential for future investigations using stable isotope evidence to illuminate further aspects of childhood mobility.

Stable isotope analysis and evidence for migration

The analysis of strontium and oxygen isotopes from human tooth enamel is commonly used in the study of past population mobility. Isotopic values – correlating to local geological and climatic factors – shed light on where an individual resided during tooth crown formation; the time when these isotopes were incorporated into the tooth enamel

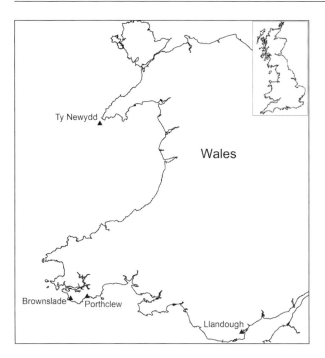

Figure 8.1. Map of Wales illustrating the location of the cemeteries of Ty Newydd (Bardsey Island), Brownslade, Porthclew (both Pembrokeshire) and Llandough (Glamorgan).

from consumed food and water (Budd _et al._ 2004; Montgomery and Evans 2006). Stable isotope analysis is now widely recognised as making a valuable contribution to the study of populations excavated from Anglo-Saxon England (_e.g._ Budd _et al._ 2003; 2004), but only recently has such analysis on populations from Wales and the Isle of Man begun to be undertaken. Nonetheless, this recent research has started to highlight the potential of this evidence, and demonstrate its particular value in light of fragmentary evidence from the burial record (_e.g._ Hemer 2010; Hadley and Hemer 2011, 72–5).

The investigation of past population mobility often involves the isotopic analysis of enamel from the second permanent molars as strontium and oxygen isotope values provide an indication of the individual's place of childhood residence between three and seven years of age, that is, during tooth crown formation (Hillson 1996; Budd _et al._ 2004). When tooth enamel is sampled from the second molar of an adult skeleton, similarities or differences between the enamel isotope values and those expected for the place of burial will indicate whether or not the individual had moved _at some point_ between the formation of the tooth enamel – which occurred by about seven years of age – and the age at death (Hillson 1996, 125; Hadley and Hemer 2011, 72). For example, the isotopic analysis of individuals from the early medieval cemetery of Cronk Keeillane, Isle of Man identified members of the cemetery population who may have travelled to the island from the northwest of England or Scotland (Hemer 2012a, 477–9). Moreover, evidence for long-distance travel comes from the early medieval cemetery of Brownslade (Pembrokeshire), where individuals with enriched oxygen isotope values may have travelled to Wales from warmer climates outside the British Isles (Hemer 2012b; Hemer _et al._ 2013) (Figure 8.1). This type of approach, which analyses the results from a single tooth, can reveal evidence for migration, but it does not have anything to reveal about migration *during* childhood. If, however, the tooth sampled is from the skeleton of a child and the isotopic value is different from that expected for the child's place of burial, then we have direct evidence indicating that the individual migrated as a child. To illustrate this point, we can consider an example from a recent study of the early medieval cemetery of Porthclew (Pembrokeshire) (Schlee 2009; Hemer *et al.* 2013). Strontium and oxygen isotope analysis was undertaken on the remains of a child who died between seven and twelve years of age, and which has produced a radiocarbon date of AD 680–900 (2σ) (Figure 8.2). The child's second permanent molar yielded a significantly enriched phosphate oxygen isotope value (>18.7‰)[1] (Hemer *et al.* 2013), which is beyond the range defined for the British Isles (Eckardt *et al.* 2009, 2822; Chenery *et al.* 2010; Evans *et al.* 2012). As such, it is unlikely that this child was local to Pembrokeshire and it is far more likely that as a young child he/she had lived in a much warmer climate, outside the British Isles. Given the child's age at death, it is likely that the child travelled to south Wales – where he/she was eventually buried – in later childhood, between the completion of the second molar crown (that is by the age of seven years) and

Figure 8.2. Skeleton PC 03 from the early medieval cemetery of Porthclew (Pembrokeshire) (©Dyfed Archaeological Trust).

his/her death by twelve years. This example demonstrates that some children had the opportunity to embark on long-distance travel to western Britain during the early medieval period.

Recently, it has been suggested that childhood migration may also be identifiable through the strontium and oxygen isotope analysis of multiple enamel samples, providing that the movement of the child between different geological and climatic zones coincided with the formation of each permanent molar (Hadley and Hemer 2011, 73–5). Whilst serial sampling is not routinely employed, not least because it relies on the availability of multiple teeth for study, it does have the potential to identify whether a child had moved away from his or her home during childhood, and even whether they moved location on more than one occasion. For example, the isotopic values obtained for the second and third molar teeth of a mature adult male buried in a probable pre-tenth-century phase of the cemetery at Peel Castle on the Isle of Man suggest that this

---

[1] Isotope ratios are expressed in parts per thousand (‰) (Schwarz and Schoeninger 1991, 289).

individual moved at least once, possibly twice, before the age of thirteen, spending time on the continent (Hemer 2010; Hadley and Hemer 2011, 73), whilst similar examples have been identified for the late Anglo-Saxon population of Black Gate, Newcastle-Upon-Tyne (Northumberland) (Macpherson 2006; Hadley and Hemer 2011, 74–5).

While the analysis of stable isotope evidence for migration into and within western Britain has only recently commenced, the initial results are of considerable interest. They go a long way to demonstrating the potential of the burial record from the region both for understanding population movement in general – even where there are poorly preserved skeletons and a lack of grave goods – and also for illuminating the lived experiences of children, in particular. The next sections of this chapter seek to set the evidence from stable isotope analysis in context, by examining the written evidence for childhood and children's experiences of migration.

Children and the family in early medieval western Britain

Stable isotope analysis is undoubtedly an invaluable tool in the study of early medieval migration, although, as yet, there is only a small amount of evidence to suggest that the youngest members of society experienced migration. Furthermore, the routine approach to the sampling of adults – usually the analysis of a single molar crown, often the second molar tooth crown which forms by the age of seven years (Hillson 1996, 125) – means that it is rarely possible to say whether the person had moved as an older child or once they had reached adulthood. In the following section of this chapter the written evidence will be examined to identify the contexts in which children of various ages might have been required or encouraged to leave their home. This discussion is intended to encourage future examination of stable isotope evidence for migration during childhood, by demonstrating that there is considerable contextual evidence within which to interpret scientific data.

Rites of passage

Historical sources reveal much about the family unit and kinship relations. Whilst some concerns, including inheritance, involved the wider kindred group, at the heart of society was the nuclear family (Davies 1982, 73). The historical sources provide insights into the lifecycle, rites of passage, and the transition from childhood to adulthood in early medieval Wales, albeit that there are acknowledged concerns about the reliability of some of the sources. Many of the Welsh lawbooks – both complete, such as *Llyfr Iorwerth*, and incomplete such as *Llyfr Colan* – were compiled in the thirteenth century (Charles-Edwards 1993, 13), and all claim to be versions of *Cyfraith Hywel*, or the Laws of Hywel Dda (Charles-Edwards 1993, 15), who held control over both northwest and southwest Wales during his reign as the king of Gwynedd in the early tenth century (Davies 1982, 106). Whilst Thomas Charles-Edwards (1993) acknowledges the problems – as well as the scepticism of some historians – of using later lawbooks for the purpose of reconstructing early medieval Irish and Welsh kinship systems, he also demonstrates the wealth of information about childhood and rites of passage that can be gained from the study of these texts. For example, according to *Llyfr Iorwerth*, the life cycle had distinct stages, each marked by a rite of passage (William 1960, 65–7). Following birth, an infant held the status of a 'foetus', that is, of an unnamed, unsexed individual, which persisted until the child was named. It was this rite of naming that publically recognised the sex of the child and the child's kinship, since the given name would include either a patronymic or denote the child's bilateral descent (Charles-Edwards 1993, 176). In seeking to understand the age at which an infant underwent the naming process, Thomas Charles-Edwards (1993, 177–80) has drawn attention to the story of Lleu Llaw Gyffess from the Welsh eleventh- to twelfth-century tales known collectively as the Four Branches of the Mabinogi. According to this tale, Arianrhod refuses to acknowledge responsibility for her son, Lleu – possibly due to his incestuous conception by her brother, Gwydion – by attempting to prevent the child's transition through the stages of the lifecycle. To ensure that the child has no recognised kinship or sex in the eyes of society, Arianrhod first refuses to name the boy when he is taken to her by Gwydion, asking 'What is the boy who is following you?'. This question implies that the child is able to walk, indicating that he was clearly not a newborn at this point.

Whilst this account from the Mabinogi is fictive, and not necessarily a true reflection of life in early medieval Wales, it may be deduced that the process of naming a child was not necessarily undertaken immediately after birth, but rather, may have occurred sometime during the child's first few years of life. Albeit a speculative suggestion, this may have been due to the higher risk of mortality in the first five years of life (Weiss and Wobst 1973), and the desire of parents to wait until the infant survived the first critical months of life before accepting legal responsibility for the infant. Alternatively, as Sally Crawford (1993, 88; 1999, 86) has suggested, baptism may have been reserved for sickly children, and parents may have been reluctant to baptise their infants for fear that it would result in premature death. We cannot, in sum, assume that the rite of naming an infant and the associated transition from the status of 'foetus' to 'child' took place immediately after birth.

Following the naming ceremony, the infant passed into childhood, during which time the child would remain 'at his father's plate, with his father as lord over him' (William 1960, 65–7; Charles-Edwards 1993, 176). Two of the most significant rites of passage performed during and at the end of childhood involved the act of hair cutting. The first rite was that of *capillatoria*, the first cutting of a young child's hair. This rite was usually performed by the child's biological father, however, the rite could also be performed by an adoptive father. In such instances, it would seem that the rite created a ritual fatherhood, symbolising the kinship between the adult and the child, regardless of the child's true paternity (Charles-Edwards 1993, 181). For a child who had been fostered or adopted at an early age, this rite may have been the responsibility of the foster-father, and was thus a ritual that reinforced kinship relations between the foster parent and the fosterling. The second rite was *barbatoria*, that is, cutting the beard of an adolescent; a rite also performed by the father. This rite marked the transition from childhood to the status of 'youth' (Charles-Edwards 1993, 180).

According to *Llyfr Iorwerth*, the age of majority differed for male and female children in early medieval Welsh society. After childhood, female children became 'youths' at the age of twelve, and it was at this age that a girl could be betrothed to a man, who must subsequently take responsibility for her care (Charles-Edwards 1993, 176). Male children, on the other hand, transitioned to a period of 'youth' at the age of fourteen.

From this age until the death of his father a youth was known as a *bonheddig canhwynol*, or innate noble. According to the thirteenth-century lawbook, *Llyfr Cyfnerth*, a *bonheddig canhwynol* was 'a Welshman by mother and father, without slave and without alien [blood] and without one-sided-pedigree in him' (Charles-Edwards 1993, 173). A *bonheddig canhwynol* could belong to the lord's household troop by taking up arms, which was also a rite of passage for boys according to *Llyfr Iorwerth* (William 1960, 65; Charles-Edwards 1993, 176).

A male youth would maintain the status of an innate noble until the death of his father, at which point he became an *uchelwr*. At this point, he would have inherited his father's land and would be the head of his *own* household suggesting that by now he was slightly older. On becoming an *uchelwr*, he was fully associated with his paternal lineage and assumed the responsibilities of his father – and perhaps as a father himself – as 'man of the house' (Charles-Edwards 1993, 173). For a man, the stages in the lifecycle and the associated rites of passage focused on his emergence into society and on inheriting responsibilities as head of the family. The situation was different for women who were often married at an early age and assumed a shared kinship – that of their family and their husband. Consequently, women did not have the same legal responsibilities as their male siblings, and Charles-Edwards (1993, 177) argues that the transition through the female lifecycle was determined by a woman's child-bearing responsibilities, with the menopause marking the transition from a status of youth to a status of old age. As Charles-Edwards (1993, 177) notes, 'The main divisions of a woman's life are thus tied up with her sexuality and child-bearing, whereas the man's have to do more with emerging into the public life of his people and with succession to land and headship of a household'. Thus, the ages at which a woman made the transition from one social status to another were biologically determined by the onset of menarche and the menopause, whereas the ages at which a man made the transition through the lifecycle may have varied depending on the age at which the head of the household died, and society acknowledged the son as rightful heir.

The wandering fosterling

In the light of the evidence that has begun to emerge from isotopic studies of migration within early medieval western Britain (Hemer 2010; Hemer *et al.* 2013), it may be significant that the written sources highlight the influence of family practices as prompting the movement of children around the landscape. Fosterage was practiced in both early medieval Ireland and Wales (Charles-Edwards 1993; Davies 1982), although there is far greater evidence from literary sources for Ireland than there is for Wales, and, as a consequence, 'scholars have used Irish evidence to fill in the blanks for Wales in regards to fosterage' (Anderson 2004, 1). Fosterage was a legally defined arrangement by which a boy or a girl was entrusted to the care of foster parents (Charles-Edwards 1993, 79). Children were usually fostered from the age of seven, until adolescence; the exact age varies between fourteen and seventeen depending on which legal text is consulted. For example, according to the seventh- to eighth-century Irish legal text concerning fosterage, *Cáin Íarrath*, a girl completed her fosterage at fourteen, whilst a boy completed his at seventeen (Kelly 1988, 88, 225). In contrast, another Irish legal text, *Bretha Crólige*, dated to the early eighth century, suggests that both boys *and* girls could be fostered up to the age of seventeen (Binchy 1938, 9). According to the Irish sources, the end of fosterage correlated with the age at which the individual assumed legal responsibility (Kelly 1988, 81). Thus, by the age of fourteen a girl was old enough for betrothal or admission to a nunnery, thereby assuming either the legal capacity as a wife or as a nun (Kelly 1988, 82). The legal capacity of a boy, however, varied, between the ages of fourteen to seventeen years, with the youth accepting greater legal responsibility from the age of seventeen years (Kelly 1988, 82). Thus, for a boy's family, it may have been beneficial for them if the boy remained in fosterage until the age of seventeen, because until that point it was the foster father who held responsibility for the fosterling and thus had to pay any fines incurred by the child whilst in his care (Kelly 1988, 88).

There were two forms of fosterage: *altramm serce* or 'fosterage for love' – which was usually undertaken by family friends or close kin – and fosterage whereby the natural parents were legally bound to pay a fosterage fee, the *íarrath* or 'after-gift' (Kelly 1988, 87). The fee was a *sét*, which according to Kelly (1988, 321) translates to mean jewel, treasure, or valuable. According to the seventh- to eighth-century Irish legal texts, *Críth Gablach* and the *Cáin Aicillne*, the value of a *sét* was equivalent to a heifer plus its calf, and was the basic unit of currency in early medieval Ireland (Kelly 1988, 113; Charles-Edwards 1993, 480). The amount of fee paid to the foster parents depended on the sex of the child and the status of the parents. A fee of three *séts* was paid for the fosterage of a boy of freeman status, whilst the fee for a girl of freeman status was four *séts* (Kelly 1988, 87). Various explanations have been given for the difference in fees for boys and girls, including the suggestion that girls were more difficult to raise, and that a girl would offer fewer benefits to the foster parents later in life, presumably because after marriage a 'woman is generally without independent legal capacity' (Kelly 1988, 75). In addition to considering the sex of the child, a higher fee would also be paid for the fosterage of a higher-status child; for example, a fee of thirty *séts* would be paid for fostering the son of a king (Kelly 1988, 87).

The foster parents were obliged to instruct and care for the foster child to a level appropriate to his or her status. For example, the son of a king had to be supplied with a horse for riding, and clothes worth seven *séts*. The child of a noble was also expected to learn marksmanship, swimming, horse riding, and how to play board games such as *fidchell* (a game similar to chess which was played between a king and his companions) (Kelly 1988, 87; Dye 1998/9, 36). The son of a freeman had less time to play, as he was expected to learn how to look after livestock including lambs, calves, and piglets, to dry corn, comb wool and chop firewood. The daughter of a king was expected to learn sewing, embroidery and cloth-cutting, whilst the daughter of a freeman would have learnt to use domestic equipment, including the quern and the sieve (Kelly 1988, 87).

Fosterage fulfilled two functions: the formation of alliances and provision of education (Charles-Edwards 1993, 79). Noble children were reared in another noble household in order to form alliances between families. Certainly the process of fosterage was an investment on behalf of the natural parents, and thus there may have been the expectation that the child would return having gained some skill or learning that they could not provide themselves. Whilst the *Cáin Iarrath* notes that the only learning a noble boy would receive was the ability to play games and undertake sports, this education was clearly important for a child of high status, and therefore the parents invested in having their son prepared for the responsibilities of a noble adult (*e.g.* being able to play board games with the king; for comparable, if later, examples see Hall this volume). Perhaps of even greater importance for the nobility were the relationships that were formed through the process of fosterage. Ties were formed not only between the fosterling and his/her foster parents, but also between the foster father and the natural father and, by extension, between the foster father and the kin of the natural father (Kelly 1988, 90). Relations could also form between the fosterling and the children of the foster parents and between different foster children where more than one fosterling was raised concurrently in the same household (Charles-Edwards 1993, 80). The network of relations could be called upon in times of need, and, thus, fosterage really was important to the formation of alliances between households.

Noble children, particularly boys, could be fostered by a succession of different foster parents (Charles-Edwards 1993, 79). According to the seventh- to eighth-century account of St Patrick's life in Tírechán's *Collectanea*, we hear that as Patrick preached to the daughters of Loegaire, king of Tara – who themselves were fostered by druids – one daughter questioned Patrick about his god, asking 'Is he [God] ever-living, is he beautiful, have many fostered his son...?' (Bieler 1979, 145). There was clearly the expectation that the son of such an almighty individual would have been fostered on multiple occasions. The use of multiple foster parents in Wales may also be deduced from the story of Pwyll Pendefig Dyfed, from the Four Branches of the Mabinogi (Charles-Edwards 1993, 79). In a discussion between Pwyll and Teirnon, the foster father of Pryderi, Pwyll claims 'because you [Teirnon] have reared him [Pryderi] until now, we shall henceforth give him in fosterage to Pendaran Dyfed', indicating that the child had spent an adequate amount of time with Teirnon and was therefore ready to move to another household (Williams 1930 cited in Charles-Edwards 1993, 79). The use of multiple foster parents would ensure that the financial burden associated with rearing an additional child would only exist for a short period of time, whilst on the other hand, multiple foster parents would also extend the network of allegiance to more than one household. For the nobility living in early medieval Wales and Ireland, fosterage, therefore, provided an impetus for childhood mobility as children were sent away by their parents. Moreover, children who were fostered by more than one household may have embarked on a succession of journeys across the landscape of western Britain as they fulfilled the agenda of their parents through mediating alliances between families.

Whilst some children of noble birth were fostered for the purpose of forming alliances between households, other children were sent away and fostered for purely educational purposes in order to receive specialised training from a master in a craft, medicine or poetry (Kelly 1988, 91). Whilst a child may have pursued the same craft as his father, the opportunity to train elsewhere allowed the child to learn methods that were perhaps unknown to the father (Kelly 1988, 91). The natural parents would have paid a fee to the master for the education of the child, and, in some instances, the master may have had more than one pupil (and, thus, quite a lucrative business) (Kelly 1988, 91).

In other instances, a child may have been fostered by a priest or placed in the care of a monastery in order to train as a young cleric or nun (Kelly 1988, 91; Charles-Edwards 1993, 80). By the sixth century in Wales, important monastic houses were established at Llancarfan, Llantwit-Major and St David's in the south, and Bangor and Bangor-is-coed in the north (Davies 1978, 130). Writing in the early sixth century, the

British cleric Gildas paints a picture of the Welsh Church in his *De Excidio Britonnum*, referring to bishops, priests, abbots, monks and communities called *monasteria* (Pryce 1992, 47). Whilst some children were sent away to join Christian communities, in other cases, the child themselves may have had the impetus to leave his or her family for that purpose. For example, in the late fifth century, as a child of five years old, St Samson asked permission from his parents 'to go to the school of Christ', and was entrusted to the care of St Illtud, abbot of Llantwit Major (Taylor 1991, 12). Similarly, in the early sixth century, the young St Cadog requested the permission of his parents to leave his family to join the Irish hermit Meuthi at his monastery in Caerwent (Rees 1853, 317; Davies 1982, 74, 208).

Once entrusted to the care of a cleric, children may have embarked on journeys along with their carer. For example, in *Collectanea*, Tírechán recalls how 'first he [St Patrick] came to the valley of Sescnán and built his first church there and took along with him the son (of Sescnán), the bishop named Sesceneus, and left two foreign boys there' (Bieler 1979, 127). It is possible that Sesceneus and perhaps also the 'two foreign boys' had been taken into the care of St Patrick, and as a consequence they accompanied him whilst on his mission to convert the pagan people of Ireland.

The travelling family

For many families, fosterage would not have been an option, and those parents for whom it was necessary to travel to find work, would, in all likelihood, have taken their children with them. For example, we hear in the *Life of St Cadog* that Llywri, who became the master builder of St Cadog, was poor, and had to move around the land with his children in order to find work. It is thought that Llywri was originally from Ireland (Davies 1982, 73; Henken 1991, 57), suggesting that he – and perhaps also his family – travelled across the Irish Sea out of the necessity to find work. Some children may have been born en-route whilst their parents were moving around the land. Indeed, in Tírechán's *Collectanea*, we hear that St Patrick met and baptised a man and his young son: 'his father had bundled him in linen (and carried him) round his neck, because he was born on the way, coming with his father from the mountain' (Bieler 1979, 161). Such an account, therefore, suggests that not only was it necessary for some pregnant women to travel, but also that some parents had no option but to travel with their children. Journeying and long-distance travel was by no means an easy task, and one example that recalls the effort involved comes from the *Life of Saint Samson*. Initially, Samson's mother Anna was barren, and consequently she and her husband, Amon, embarked on a journey to 'a remote land to the north' to seek divine assistance – in return for a small fee – from the master, Librarius. The journey 'to the north' was particularly long, and the account informs the reader of the fatigue experienced by Amon and Anna, as Librarius asks, 'Oh my children, tell me the reason of your toil in such a long journey' (Taylor 1991, 10). Clearly, travel was an arduous task, and there were inherent hazards such as unknown terrain and the threat from thieves, amongst others (Davies 1982, 15). Nonetheless, in certain circumstances it was clearly necessary for adults and children alike to travel both short and long distances across the early medieval landscape.

That even the youngest members of society embarked on long-distance journeys has been illustrated in a recent study by Mark Handley (2011). Through the analysis of fourth- to eighth-century funerary inscriptions from Britain, Gaul, Spain, Italy, North Africa and the Balkans, Handley (2011) identified individuals – both adults and children – who had migrated from their homeland and had subsequently died elsewhere. Whilst only twenty-two recorded individuals – from a total of 623 – were below the age of fifteen years (Handley 2011, 117–38), the epigraphic evidence, albeit scant, offers a unique insight into the migration of early medieval children and their parents. Details including the age and names – and by virtue the biological sex – of the young migrants is particularly insightful, whilst information about where these individuals were travelling to and from demonstrates that even the youngest members of society were able to travel abroad. For example, an inscription dated to AD 562 from Salteras (southern Spain), records the death of Anna Gaudiosa, aged seven, who was originally from North Africa (Handley 2011, 121). Examples also show that even infants were taken on long journeys; for example, a sixth-century inscription from Salakta (Tunisia), records the death of nine month old Iohannes who had travelled from *Surie Apamia* (Apamea) in northern Syria (Handley 2011, 131), a distance of approximately 1424 miles. Given the young age of Iohannes, it is likely that he travelled with his mother, or alternatively, he may have been born en-route, and the recorded place of origin was in fact his mother's homeland. Epigraphic evidence such as that collated by Handley (2011) offers those investigating early medieval migration in the West a unique and valuable source of evidence which lends support to isotopic data indicating the migration of people – including children – over very long distances during the early medieval period.

Archaeological approaches to childhood in western Britain: the potential

Despite the aforementioned limitations of the early medieval burial record from western Britain, it is clear from the studies undertaken to date (*e.g.* Hemer 2010), that the examination of stable isotope evidence has the potential for the furtherance of our understanding of childhood in this region. It is nonetheless important that isotopic evidence for migration is interpreted within the context of the written record, such as the aforementioned inscribed stone monuments, lawbooks, and accounts noted in the saints' *Lives*, which can provide a useful historical framework within which to interpret the isotopic evidence for migration. Certainly, written accounts concerning children and the lives of children can go some way to explaining why individuals may have moved around the early medieval landscape during childhood. In the final part of this chapter, one example of the potential of employing this approach to explore both childhood and migration is considered, in the context of multiple burials.

Examples of contemporary multiple burials, comprising the interment of two or more individuals, have typically been interpreted as evidence of a shared 'death event', that is where more than one individual died at the same time or close together. As a consequence, the mourners made a deliberate decision to bury the individuals together, and in doing so deviated from the predominant funerary rite of individual burial (Crawford 2007, 84). Yet the possibility that these multiple burials might find their origins in the context of migration is suggested by two forms of evidence. First, some of the aforementioned inscriptions collated by Handley (2011) reveal that members of families that had migrated were sometimes buried together. For example, an undated inscription from Savaria (in modern-day Hungary) records that fifty-year-old Aurelius Iodorus was buried with his children, Aurelius Frontonus (two years) and Aurelia Ceslina (eight months). They were commemorated by the wife and mother, Aurelia Domnica, and it appears that they had migrated as a family from their home in Syria (Handley 2011, 136). Inscriptions like that of Aurelius Iodorus and his children suggest that related individuals who died simultaneously were buried together. This may have implications for funerary archaeologists investigating multiple burials because, as the epigraphic evidence suggests, some multiple burials may belong to related individuals who travelled together from their place of origin to their final resting place. Such individuals may have been perceived as outsiders and were thus afforded a multiple burial to reflect their non-local status, and to symbolise that they had travelled – and subsequently died – together.

Second, stable isotope analysis has recently revealed that at least one individual from a multiple burial at the early medieval cemetery at Llandough (Glamorgan) (Holbrook and Thomas 2005) was a migrant to the area (Figure 8.2). This middle-aged adult male (B10) had been interred in a contemporary double burial, alongside another male of similar age. The oxygen isotope values for skeleton B10's second molar crown suggest that he had spent between three and seven years of age in a much warmer climate outside the British Isles, with one possible place of residence being the Mediterranean Sea region (Hemer 2010, 142–3; Hemer *et al.* 2013). This is the only adult-only multiple burial at Llandough (Holbrook and Thomas 2005, 10, 13), and it was notably located in Area I where sherds of imported B*ii* amphorae from the Mediterranean have been recovered. These sherds are thought to have been deliberately introduced into the grave fill of five burials during a high-status burial ritual, and the excavators draw parallels with the discovery of similar B*ii* amphorae sherds from a group of sixth-century mound burials at the churchyard of St Materiana, Tintagel (Cornwall) (Morris *et al.* 1990, 845–8; Holbrook and Thomas 2005, 31). Morris *et al.* (1990, 845) suggest that the cist graves beneath the low mounds at St Materiana belonged to *special* individuals of high status whose burials were visible within the landscape, whilst the amphorae sherds and a burnt area nearby are thought to represent the remains of a 'graveside picnic or cultic meal at the time of burial' (Morris *et al.* 1990, 848). In this context, the presence of imported amphorae in Area I at Llandough may indicate that this part of the cemetery was designated for the burial of high-status individuals (Holbrook and Thomas 2005, 88), at least one of whom it is now thought to have migrated to Wales (Hemer 2010, 260; Hemer *et al.* 2013). Why skeleton B10 received a double burial alongside another adult male cannot be determined for certain, and, as skeleton B11 has not yet been sampled for stable isotope evidence, we cannot say whether his grave companion was also of non-British origin. Nonetheless, the burial offers an intriguing new perspective on the significance of migration as a potential explanation for multiple burials, and provides a potential context for exploring other multiple burials. Among these are a number that include children. For example, at Llandough two children (B206/B212) aged ten and eleven years were buried together (Holbrook and Thomas 2005, 10), two child-only multiple burials were identified at the site of Brownslade – burial 515/527 included two infants, while burial 510 consisted of a juvenile and an infant (Groom *et al.* 2012) – and a large multiple burial was excavated at Ty Newydd on Bardsey Island, containing the remains of five children including a ten- to twelve-year-old and four six- to eight-year-olds (Arnold 1998) (Figure 8.1). The possibility that some non-local individuals were afforded multiple burials should be born in mind by those investigating population mobility through stable isotope analysis, and the opportunity to sample both skeletons – where possible – should be considered. Of course, confirmation of whether the individuals interred in a multiple burial were genetically related could only be confirmed through DNA testing (Brown and Brown 2011, 169), but nonetheless such scientific methods have the potential to transform our understanding of migration, the relationships between those who were migrating, and to provide scientific evidence to corroborate the written record.

Conclusion

Until recently, there has been little study of the osteological material from early medieval western Britain, and consequently our understanding of society's youngest members from this region is limited. This chapter aimed to highlight various aspects of childhood in western British society, and, in particular, sought to illustrate that migration and travel were experienced by children and adults alike. The discussion highlights the value of a multidisciplinary approach to the study of populations from early medieval western Britain, and the importance of contextualising scientific data within a historical and archaeological context. It is hoped that by continuing with such an approach our appreciation and understanding of early medieval western British society will soon be comparable to that of Anglo-Saxon England. The funerary record from this region is, contrary to long-held assumptions, a potentially rich resource, and therefore it is hoped that future studies employing stable isotope analysis will also consider what they can reveal about the lives and experiences of children in early medieval western Britain.

Bibliography

Anderson, K. 2004. Urth Noe e Tat: the question of fosterage in high medieval Wales. *North American Journal of Welsh Studies* 4 (1), 2–11.

Arnold, C. J. 1998. Excavation of Ty Newydd, Ynys Enlli (Bardsey Island), Gwynedd. *Archaeologia Cambrensis* 147, 96–132.

Bieler, L. 1979. *The Patrician Texts in the Book of Armagh*. Oxford: Oxford University Press.

Binchy, D. A. 1938. Bretha Crólige. *Ériu* 12, 1–77.

Brassil, K. S., Owen, W. G. and Britnell, W. J. 1991. Prehistoric and early medieval cemeteries at Tandderwen, near Denbigh, Clwyd. *Archaeological Journal* 148, 46–97.

Brown, T. A. and Brown, K. A. 2011. *Biomolecular Archaeology: an introduction*. Chichester: Wiley-Blackwell.

Budd, P., Chenery, C., Montgomery, J., Evans, J. A. and Powlesland, D. 2003. Anglo-Saxon residential mobility at West Heslerton, North Yorkshire, UK from combined O- and Sr-isotope analysis, pp. 195–208 in Holland, J. G. and Tanner, S. D. (eds), *Plasma Source Mass Spectrometry: theory and applications*. Cambridge: Royal Society of Chemistry.

Budd, P., Millard, A., Chenery, C., Lucy, S. and Roberts, C. 2004. Investigating population movement by stable isotope analysis: a report from Britain. *Antiquity* 78 (299), 127–41.

Charles-Edwards, T. 1993. *Early Irish and Welsh kinship*. Oxford: Clarendon Press.

Charles-Edwards, T. 2000. *Early Christian Ireland*. Cambridge: Cambridge University Press.

Chenery, C., Müldner, G., Evans, J. A., Eckardt, H. and Lewis, M. 2010. Strontium and stable isotope evidence for diet and mobility in Roman Gloucester, UK. *Journal of Archaeological Science* 37 (1), 150–63.

Crawford, S. 1993. Children, death and the afterlife in Anglo-Saxon England, pp. 83–91 in Filmer-Sankey, W. (ed.), *Anglo-Saxon Studies in Archaeology and History 6*. Oxford: Oxford University Committee for Archaeology.

Crawford, S. 1999. *Childhood in Anglo-Saxon England*. Stroud: Sutton.

Crawford, S. 2007. Companions, co-incidences or chattels? Children and their role in early Anglo-Saxon multiple burials, pp. 83–92 in Crawford, S. and Shepherd, G. (eds), *Children, Childhood and Society* (British Archaeological Reports International Series 1696). Oxford: Archaeopress.

Davies, W. 1978. *An Early Welsh Microcosm. Studies in the Llandaff charters* (Royal Historical Society Studies in History Series 9). London: Swift Printers.

Davies, W. 1982. *Wales in the Early Middle Ages*. Leicester: Leicester University Press.

Dye, L. 1998/9. The game of sovereignty. *Proceedings of the Harvard Celtic Colloquium* 18/19, 34–41.

Eckardt, H., Chenery, C., Booth, P., Evans, J. A., Lamb, A. and Müldner, G. 2009. Oxygen and strontium isotope evidence for mobility in Roman Winchester. *Journal of Archaeological Science* 36 (12), 2816–25.

Edwards, N. 2001. Early medieval inscribed stones and stone sculpture in Wales: context and function. *Medieval Archaeology* 45, 15–39.

Evans, J. A., Chenery, C. A. and Montgomery, J. 2012. A summary of strontium and oxygen isotope variation in archaeological human tooth enamel excavated from Britain. *Journal of Analytical Atomic Spectrometry* 27 (5), 754–64.

Gowland, R. 2006. Ageing the past: examining age identity from funerary evidence, pp. 143–54 in Gowland, R. and Knüsel, C. (eds), *Social Archaeology of Funerary Remains*. Oxford: Oxbow.

Groom, P., Schlee, D., Hughes, G., Crane, P., Ludlow, N. and Murphy, K. (eds) 2012. Two early medieval cemeteries in Pembrokeshire: Brownslade Barrow and West Angle Bay. *Archaeologia Cambrensis* 160, 133–203.

Hadley, D. M. and Hemer, K. A. 2011. Microcosms of migration: children and early medieval population movement. *Childhood in the Past* 4, 63–78.

Handley, M. 2011. Dying on foreign shores. Travel and mobility in the Late-Antique West. *Journal of Roman Archaeology Supplementary Series* 86, 1–167.

Hemer, K. A. 2010. *In the Realm of Saints. A reconstruction of life and death in early medieval Wales and the Isle of Man*. Unpublished Ph.D. thesis, University of Sheffield.

Hemer, K. A. 2012a. A bioarchaeological study of the human remains from the early medieval cemetery of Cronk Keeillane, Isle of Man. *Proceedings of the Isle of Man Natural History and Antiquarian Society* XII (3), 469–86.

Hemer, K. A. 2012b. Stable isotope analysis of human remains: Brownslade and West Angle Bay, pp. 182–7 in Groom, P., Schlee, D., Hughes, G., Crane, P., Ludlow, N. and Murphy, K. (eds), *Two early medieval cemeteries in Pembrokeshire: Brownslade Barrow and West Angle Bay. Archaeologia Cambrensis* 160, 133–203.

Hemer, K. A., Evans, J. A., Chenery, C. A., and Lamb, A. L. 2013. Evidence of early medieval trade and migration between Wales and the Mediterranean Sea region. *Journal of Archaeological Science* 40 (5), 2352–9.

Henken, E. R. 1991. *The Welsh Saints. A study in patterned lives.* Cambridge: D. S. Brewer.

Hillson, S. 1996. *Dental Anthropology.* Cambridge: Cambridge University Press.

Holbrook, N. and Thomas, A. 2005. An early medieval monastic cemetery at Llandough, Glamorgan: excavations in 1994. *Medieval Archaeology* 49, 1–92.

Kelly, F. 1988. *A Guide to Early Irish Law.* Dublin: Mount Salus Press Ltd.

Lucy, S. 1994. Children in early medieval cemeteries. *Archaeological Review from Cambridge* 13 (2), 21–34.

Macpherson, P. M. 2006. *Tracing Change: an isotopic investigation into Anglo-Saxon childhood diet.* Unpublished Ph.D. thesis, University of Sheffield.

Morris, C. D., Nowakowski, J. and Thomas, C. 1990. Tintagel, Cornwall: the 1990 excavations. *Antiquity* 64 (245), 843–9.

Montgomery, J. and Evans, J. A. 2006. Immigrants on the Isle of Lewis – combining traditional funerary and modern isotope evidence to investigate social differentiation, migration and dietary change in the Outer Hebrides of Scotland, pp. 122–42 in Gowland, R. and Knüsel, C. (eds), *Social Archaeology of Funerary Remains.* Oxford: Oxbow.

Page, M. R. 2011. Ble mae'r babanod? (Where are the babies?): infant burial in early medieval Wales, pp. 100–9 in Lally, M. and Moore, A. (eds), *(Re)Thinking the Little Ancestor: new perspectives on the archaeology of infancy and childhood* (British Archaeological Reports International Series 2271). Oxford: Archaeopress.

Petts, D. 2003. Memories in stone. Changing strategies and contexts of remembrance in early medieval Wales, pp. 193–214 in Williams, H. (ed.), *Archaeologies of Remembrance. Death and memory in past societies.* New York: Kluwer Academic/Plenum Press.

Pryce, H. 1992. Ecclesiastical wealth in early medieval Wales, pp. 22–32 in Edwards, N. and Lane, A. (eds), *The Early Church in Wales and the West.* Oxford: Oxbow.

Rees, W. J. 1853. *Lives of the Cambro British Saints.* London: Longman & Co.

Schlee, D. 2009. *The Pembrokeshire Cemeteries Project: excavations at Porthclew chapel, Freshwater East, Pembrokeshire* (Interim Report 2008). Llandeilo: Dyfed Archaeological Trust Ltd.

Schwarz, H. P. and Schoeninger, M. J. 1991. Stable isotope analysis in human nutritional ecology. *Yearbook of Physical Anthropology* 34, 288–321.

Stoodley, N. 2000. From the cradle to the grave: age organisation and the early Anglo-Saxon burial rite. *World Archaeology* 31 (3), 456–72.

Taylor, T. 1991. *The Life of St. Samson of Dol* (reprint of 1925 edition). Somerset: Llanerch Press Ltd.

Weiss, K. M. and Wobst, H. M. 1973. Demographic models for anthropology. *Memoirs of the Society for American Archaeology* 27, 1–186.

William, A. R. 1960. *Llyfr Iorwerth.* Cardiff: University of Wales Press.

9. Interdisciplinarity, Archaeology and the Study of Medieval Childhood

Carenza Lewis

Children's lives are important, both in their own right because childhood is a universally experienced stage of life, and because the perception and treatment of children both reflects and impacts on society more widely. However, children's lives are elusive to the archaeologist, as children leave less physical trace than adults in the material record (*e.g.* Lillehammer 1989; Chamberlain 1997, 249). In order to find archaeological evidence for childhood we need to know what it looks like; but in order to know what it looks like, we need to find it: the ultimate taphonomic conundrum. One way of attempting to resolve this is to consider the contribution other sources of evidence can make. This chapter explores a selection of analyses pertaining to medieval children carried out within four non-archaeological disciplines – History; Art History; Literature; and Folklore Studies – in the hope that it may inform, inspire and encourage greater interdisciplinary familiarity and exploration.[1] Considering approaches from these disciplines is not intended to suggest that there are (or should be) rigid distinctions separating material of interest to different disciplines: this is simply not the case – an illustrated parchment account of a medieval saint's life, for example, is simultaneously text, art and artefact. But different disciplines do use different techniques and approaches, and so the aim in this chapter is to look at the potential that different analytical approaches have to illuminate and expand our knowledge and understanding of medieval children and childhood, and how this can complement archaeological approaches. We will also see that the prevailing theoretical framework within which research is conducted is crucial to the capacity of scholars, in any discipline, to engage with the evidence for childhood.

---

[1] These disciplines inevitably touch on material from other disciplines such as Philosophy, Theology and Historical Geography which will not be discussed separately for reasons of space. These are of course not the only disciplines from which archaeologists of medieval childhood can potentially learn: Social Anthropology, Sociology, Psychology, Education and Social Geography have all contributed useful information and ideas while Medicine, Pathology, Forensics, Physics, Chemistry and Biology provide many invaluable investigative techniques. But these disciplines are not generally concerned with medieval material as such, so will not be included here.

History

History is defined here as study of the past constructed through (purportedly) factual written texts. Historical sources for the medieval period include a wide range of texts mostly created for the purposes of observation, administration and/or instruction, such as chronicles, letters, financial and legal records and medical texts. History is perhaps the most obvious discipline to consider in this chapter, as written sources can record people's personal experiences and attitudes in ways that no other source can. Medieval textual records are partial in what they record, but of equal significance to realising the potential of written sources for illuminating the lives of medieval children have been the attitudes of historians.

Significant changes can be discerned in the practice of historical research over the last 150 years. As E. H. Carr (1961, 3) commented, by the nineteenth century, the optimistic belief of 'clear-eyed self-confident' British historians was that texts could be used to reconstruct narrative accounts of the past tracing sequential chains of cause and effect using an empiricist positivist approach, in which the historian should 'first ascertain the facts, then draw your conclusions from them' (Carr 1961, 5). Thus, the historian would be able 'simply to show how it really was' (Carr 1961, 5), ideals epitomised in the 'national narratives and admiring biographies' of historians such as George Trevelyan, the 'Grand Old Man of British History' (Cannadine 2002, viii). But by the 1950s this imperious confidence had been replaced by a 'distracted scepticism' (Carr 1961, 5), which recognised that historical 'facts' are rarely simply factual and that historical explanations are not final or immutable, but profoundly mutable, influenced by the time and circumstances within which the historian is working. Under the influence of social science, scholars such as Carr (1961) in his influential *What is History?* urged historians to focus on understanding long-term economic and social processes, rather than the roles of individual events or people. The so-called 'New History' dominated historical scholarship in the 1970s and 1980s, dividing the discipline between advocates of Carr and those who preferred more traditional approaches (*e.g.* Elton 1967). When David Cannadine revisited Carr's 'What is History?' question in 2002, the contents page alone showed how History as a discipline had developed, with chapters on Social History, Political History, Religious History, Cultural History, Gender History, Intellectual History and Imperial History, each written by different authors (Cannadine 2002). History now is broader but also more specialised with 'a more modest, more realistic and thus more helpful agenda – not the history of society as a whole, but the history of various aspects of society' (Cannadine 2002, x).

Reading this, we might reasonably hope that children would loom large in recent historical research. Certainly, children are of more interest to post-modern historians interested in minorities and focussed on multi-vocal narratives and on understanding the past rather than explaining it. Indeed, as Carr penned his final words, Philippe Ariès' (1960) seminal publication broke the silence surrounding children in the past: although seriously flawed and much-criticised, Ariès deserves credit for opening up the subject. Since then there has been a blizzard of historical research on children (deMause 1974; Stone 1977; MacFarlane 1985; Hanawalt 1986; Shahar 1990; Postman 1995; Jenks 1996; Heywood 2001; Orme 2003; Cunningham 2005; Rosenthal 2007). Much early interest focussed on ways in which information about children could advance understanding of other subjects, such as Gender History (*e.g.* Labarge 1986; Bennett 1987; Goldberg 1992; Leyser 1995), Medical History (*e.g.* Porter 1997; Rawcliffe 1995) and Family History (Hanawalt 1986; 1993). Now, however, there is growing interest in children's lives for their own sake. By 2007, Margaret King was able to summarise the achievements of the previous forty years of research into the early modern period as follows:

> historians have uncovered the traces of attitudes toward children – were they neglected, exploited, abused, cherished? – and patterns of child-rearing. They have explored such issues, among others, as the varieties of European household structure; definitions of the stages of life; childbirth, wetnursing, and the role of the midwife; child abandonment and the foundling home; infanticide and its prosecution; apprenticeship, servitude, and fostering; the evolution of schooling; the consequences of religious diversification; and the impact of gender
>
> *King 2007, 371*

However, despite some notable publications (*e.g.* Shahar 1990; Orme 2003), the medieval period has been given less attention, with interest focussed mainly on medical and didactic sources, where children are most visible (*e.g.* Orme 1973; 1989). Part of the reason for this neglect is that the conventional sources for a history of medieval childhood have scant material of obvious use. The narratives of contemporary chroniclers, for example, form the backbone of our understanding of the political history of the medieval period and provide the closest equivalent we have to individual biographies. Many medieval writers knew the people they wrote about well enough to record intimate details, such as William of Malmesbury (*c.* 1095–1143), who records, for example, that Henry I was a heavy sleeper with a tendency to snore (Giles 1847, 446–7) – but they tell us hardly anything about his childhood. On this period of life, the medieval chroniclers are mostly frustratingly silent.

Legal and administrative sources have – perhaps unexpectedly – proved more fruitful, as Barbara Hanawalt (1986; 1993) has demonstrated, meticulously combing through thousands of coroners' records to explore medieval family life. These legal accounts of incidents, accidents and injuries encompass a much wider spectrum of society than the chroniclers, providing vivid glimpses of the everyday lives of ordinary people, including children:

> Agnes … was tagging along with other children and playing in the king's highway. She tried to follow the others across a stream and drowned … A girl of two and a half came out of her father's house with a piece of bread in her hand when a small pig came up and tried to take it from her, pushing her into a ditch
>
> *Hanawalt 1986, 180*

> A little girl of four was holding a duck in her hands and wanted to put it in the river … Wiliam Annotson, four and half years old, went to a well and saw his face reflected in its water. When he tried to reach down and touch the face, he fell in
>
> *Hanawalt 1986, 183*

These children only appear because they died an unnatural or suspicious death (Hanawalt 1986, 272), but, nonetheless, coroners' records provide illuminating glimpses of the lives of medieval children. Although they do not generally record emotional responses from parents faced with the accidental death of a child, this does not, of course, necessarily mean that these were not forthcoming, simply that they were not relevant to the coroner's task of ascertaining the circumstances surrounding the incident. Indeed, some accounts demonstrate the lengths parents would go to in attempting to save an endangered child, as in the case of Alice Trivaler who returned to her burning house to rescue her son: 'Alice remembered her son was in the fire within, she leapt back into the shop to seek him, and immediately when she entered she was overcome by the greatness of the fire and choked' (Hanawalt 1986, 184–5).

By meticulously compiling and aggregating snippets of information about children, valuable clues about the perception and experience of medieval children and childhood can emerge. William MacLehose (2006) has recently applied this approach to a range of twelfth- and thirteenth-century texts including medical treatises, religious writings and chronicles, in order to elucidate medieval attitudes to different stages of childhood. This has produced a 'subtle and scholarly study of high medieval discourses on childhood', which provides nuanced and compelling evidence that '[i]n the Western Christian society of the central Middle Ages, the child as a cultural category most certainly existed' (Phillips 2008, 1216). MacLehose has identified a growing anxiety in the twelfth and thirteenth centuries regarding the vulnerability of children, citing Eckbert of Schönau (*c.* 1120–84), who suggested that half of children born did not live to adulthood, as one example of a writer who was 'was preoccupied with the death of infants' (MacLehose 2006, ch. 2, 32). This, MacLehose argues, reflects a pervasive anxiety in the twelfth century over the physical safety of children, shown also in contemporary theological debates about their post-mortem fate, especially of those who died in early childhood (MacLehose 2006, ch. 2, 32–5), before they were old enough to understand Christian teaching. Debate raged as to whether such children were inherently good (because they were incapable of knowing enough to be deliberately evil) or inherently bad (tainted by original sin and the sin their parents committed during their conception). Such debates reveal much about contemporary notions of cognitive development in children, as they often hinged on the age at which children could understand the commitment involved in being baptised into the Christian faith. MacLehose (2006, ch. 2, 33) contrasts neo-Pelagian heretics who 'argued that children were sinless and therefore were already counted among the saved' with orthodox writers such as Peter the Venerable who were forced into 'defending the existence of original sin and … to articulate a negative assessment of the moral world of children' (MacLehose 2006, ch. 2, 33). For the latter, 'childhood appeared to be morally lacking … the child could not understand faith, choose the right path, or actively approach baptism, but he needed all of these things for salvation because his soul was unclean' (MacLehose 2006, ch. 2, 33). Polemicist theologians responded to these interpretations using the Bible 'to show that children had a close connection with piety and purity, and the citation of biblical passages by polemicists of the twelfth and thirteenth centuries could reveal the metaphoric value that their contemporaries placed on children' (MacLehose 2006, ch. 2, 64).

MacLehose also analyses contemporary writers' accounts of children whose murder gave rise to religious cults, such as William of Norwich (d. 1144) and Hugh of Lincoln

(d. 1255). MacLehose (2006, ch. 3, 4) shows that in such circumstances the child could be represented variously as 'a catalyst, a passive object of hatred by the Jews, the object of sadness on the part of the mother, and the object of pathos felt by the Christian crowd' and/or as a symbol of 'sanctity, of simple piety, of innocence, of sacrifice, of human frailty and loss, of an ignorance that unwittingly reveals truth' who could also show 'a carefree playfulness and naïveté'. These perspectives reveal contemporary attitudes pertaining to children and childhood, at a time of growing interest in the cult of the Virgin Mary, idolised as a mother who both nurtured and grieved for her child. These sources connected Mary's specifically maternal functions 'with an increased emotional awareness of, and concern for, the Child and any child'. A change in the role of such tales occurs mid-thirteenth century, when the cult of Hugh of Lincoln extended beyond the merely local (unlike most previous child victims), ultimately receiving English royal approval and leading to the arrest of ninety-three Jews, nineteen of whom were executed (MacLehose 2006, ch. 3, 20). Although Hugh of Lincoln's story was clearly used as propaganda against a group the crown wished to persecute, it is significant that it was the murder of a *child* that was used to fuel popular outrage against English Jews and fatally undermine support for them (see also Hall this volume). Historical analysis, therefore, has the potential, given assiduous persistence and painstaking attention to detail, to reveal not only aspects of the lived experience of medieval childhood, but also, in reading beyond the literal words, to provide new perspectives on contemporary notions of childhood and the ways these could be used to achieve wider social and political aims.

Art History

Art History is the study of the production, techniques, form and role of art in the past, today a wide-ranging discipline with a historico-sociological focus encompassing the role of art in society.[2] Works of art often feature in publications by medievalists (albeit often simply as illustrations), and studies of childhood are no exception.[3] This is despite a commonly held belief that children are rarely represented in medieval art, and then only as miniature adults – an assertion indeed used by Philippe Ariès (1960; 1962) to support his view that there was no notion in the medieval period of childhood as a distinct stage in life. Few would now agree with Ariès, and contextualised analyses of the depiction and presentation of children in the art of the medieval period can, as we shall see, be illuminating.

The very term 'art' of course immediately raises the oft-asked question 'what is art?' (*e.g.* Tolstoy 1995; Gombrich 1950; Pooke and Whitham 2010, 1–25). An object regarded as 'Art' today may not have been perceived as such when it was first made, nor was the person who made it necessarily regarded as an 'artist'.[4] The medieval period was

---

[2] The mission statement of the *Journal of Art Historiography* states that '[c]onsequent to the expansion of universities, museums and galleries, has evolved to include areas outside of its traditional boundaries' (available at http://arthistoriography.wordpress.com/mission-statement (accessed January 18th 2013)).
[3] See for example the paperback editions of Orme 2001 and Heywood 2001, both of which include part of Bruegel's painting of 1560 *Children's Games* on the front cover.
[4] This definition is offered by http://www.arthistory.sbc.edu/artartists/artartists.html accessed 18th Jan 2013.

'saturated with images' (Aston 2003, 68), as a range of artistic media were widely used to convey messages that were both explicit and implicit to a largely illiterate population. These included drawing, painting (of walls and windows as well as notionally portable pieces such as altarpieces), engraving, sculpture, ceramics, jewellery and numerous other decorated artefacts such as reliquaries as well as aspects of architecture. Such art is, of course, always artifice: medieval images were constructed and manipulated to accord with convention and to convey meaning. The pages and margins of devotional books, for example, such as the Luttrell Psalter (Brown 2006) or the Book of Hours of Mary of Burgundy (Miller 1995) include images showing aspects of contemporary life, but such images are complex, and the motivations behind them need to be elicited in order to understand medieval society.

One of the classic art historical sources for information about late medieval/early modern children's play is Pieter Bruegel's *Children's Games*, painted in 1560. This depicts a large number of children playing a wide range of different games, and the level of detail provided can be enticing to the medievalist wishing to know more about the culture of childhood. This, of course, is not an exact representation of a real scene, but a carefully composed and constructed image liable to be misinterpreted if the factors determining the selection and presentation of the images are not understood. This was highlighted more than thirty years ago by Sandra Hindman (1981), before which date *Children's Games* had been interpreted either as a simple visual encyclopaedia of games, or as a more complex allegory (about which opinions varied widely: see Hindman 1981, 448 for relevant bibliography). Hindman analysed the visual structuring of the images, including the placement of the children engaged in different activities relative to each other and to the painting as a whole, as well as the use of colour and images as metaphors, such as masks, symbolising deceit, and an owl, symbolising wisdom, about to be shot by a boy with a pop-gun. Hindman also examined the artistic precedents for *Children's Games* and related artistic traditions in which games and children figure prominently, suggesting that Bruegel's painting represents, in fact, a transformation in the meaning conveyed by images of children (Hindman 1981, 449) from that of innocence to that of folly.

Hindman's discussion of how this allegorical message was structured makes some observations salient to the scholar of late medieval children. Firstly, she firmly dismisses the idea that Bruegel's children are actually miniature adults. She shows them to be wearing garments typical of sixteenth-century northern European children, and engaged in play activities genuinely associated with children of this date (Hindman 1981, 448–9). This was essential for the allegorical message of the painting to work:

> Whatever other meanings it now evokes, *Children's Games* still represents real children playing actual games in front of a believable town hall, a fact that also contributed to the way it was perceived … The interpretation of *Children's Games* … argues for an artist who was intent on depicting the everyday reality of peasant children, while at the same time eliciting verbal allusions, the recognition of which would enhance the richness of the painting
>
> *Hindman 1981, 465, 468*

Hindman's (1981, 449) overall conclusion, that 'Bruegel transformed earlier traditions in which games represented the months or the Ages of Man … [into one in which] children's games [are used] to present the folly of man as a characteristic of adolescence and manhood, as well as of youth and infancy', provides an interesting new perspective on changing contemporary notions of childhood. According to Hindman, Bruegel is conveying (and perhaps even propagating) new northern European adult attitudes to childhood, which were changing from a late medieval notion that childhood represented innocence and even the pre-lapsarian golden age of humanity, to one where childhood is a metaphor for credulous foolishness. This contrasts with views (commonplace and conventional even in those who reject Ariès' thesis) that it was only later – during the Renaissance and the Enlightenment – that adult (and especially parental) attitudes to children became more indulgent, nurturing and engaged, and a culture of childhood developed for the first time (King 2007, 371).

In another art historical discussion, more recently Sophie Oosterwijk (2008, 231) has argued that rather than ignoring children 'medieval artists actually showed a predilection for depicting the births of all kinds of "historical" figures', including the Virgin. Oosterwijk (2008, 232) also notes that the theme of *The Ages of Man*, frequently depicted in medieval art, always includes a childhood stage, while in more extensive versions childhood is even sub-divided into different stages as 'infants are usually shown as swaddled babies, and toddlers try out their first steps in a childwalker while older children play with toys or carry schoolbooks'. Oosterwijk (2008, 232) cites the popularity of the story of the Massacre of the Holy Innocents in medieval art as suggesting that 'medieval people viewed child death with anything but indifference' and goes on to say that the medieval popularity of the image of the Virgin Mary and infant Jesus 'could only have worked if people recognised its fundamental truth: the bond of affection between mother and child' (Oosterwijk 2008, 233).

Oosterwijk has also refuted Ariès' assertion that the absence of tomb effigies for medieval children signifies parental indifference, pointing out that 'although costly burials and monuments were affordable only to the wealthy few, some royal and aristocratic parents seem to have spared no expense in the funerals of their deceased children, who might subsequently be commemorated by costly monuments' (Oosterwijk 2008, 232). One example is Katherine, the disabled daughter of Henry III and Eleanor of Provence, described by Matthew Paris as 'speechless and helpless' who died in 1257 aged just three years (Badham and Oosterwijk 2012, 187–93). While acknowledging that one function of the effort, innovation and cost expended on the design and execution of Katherine's monument was to advertise the status of her parents, Badham and Oosterwijk point out that this was a much-mourned death, referring to Matthew Paris' contemporary records of the grief of the queen who 'as a result of her anguish was seized of a grievous illness that neither physician nor human consolation could alleviate' and John of Oxnead's accounts that the king 'was plunged into such sorrow that he fell ill' (Badham and Oosterwijk 2012, 171; see also Hall this volume).

Oosterwijk gives further consideration to why, on the rare occasions that children appear on medieval funerary monuments, they are typically depicted as adults, which has given rise to the belief that children were regarded in life as 'miniature adults', a notion she rejects (Oosterwijk 2010, 47). For example, the tomb chest of Edward III (d. 1377) depicts his son William of Windsor (who died shortly after birth in 1348) as a 'weeper' – or mourner – of near-adult size and stature. William shares his own tomb in Westminster Abbey with his sister Blanche of the Tower who also died as a baby (in 1342), and both are depicted in effigy as much older children or young adults: 'William is shown in a short tunic and tight hose, Blanche is presented as an elegant female with her hair tied up in fashionable cauls on either side of her face' (Oosterwijk 2010, 53–4). In York Minster, William of Hatfield (another son of Edward III who died in infancy in 1337) is depicted in effigy as 'an elegantly dressed young prince' (Oosterwijk 2010, 54–5). Oosterwijk contends that such effigies are not evidence of a fourteenth-century perception of children simply as adults-in-waiting devoid of their own childish identity and culture, but rather they 'reflect medieval theological thinking about the perfect age of Christ that the blessed would attain in heaven'. That is, the children are shown on monuments as the young adults they would become in heaven, not as the children they had been at death (Oosterwijk 2010, 55–7).

Oosterwijk (2010, 59) concludes that while inclusion of children on funerary monuments is not proof of affection, their absence does not preclude it, and 'it would be wrong to assume that children were neither loved nor remembered. Even the anonymous rows of offspring on [their parents'] monuments suggest that every child counted'. She maintains that the stylised depiction of children, or indeed their apparent absence, is because artists 'had to invent ways of presenting children on tombs in line with patrons' expectations, artistic conventions and religious thinking of the period, resulting in a variety of depictions that are not always immediately recognisable as children to a modern viewer' (Oosterwijk 2010, 59).

The art-historical analyses considered above show how such studies can inform our understanding of childhood, and contemporary perceptions of it, taking us beyond the immediately apparent image to the message and the social context behind the image.

Medieval literature

Medieval literature is another potential source of contemporary information about medieval childhood. Literature has the imaginatively composed artifice of art, but is transmitted through the same textual medium as history, although it is distinct from both of these disciplines. Literature is defined here as formally composed 'imaginative writing' (Eagleton 1996, 1),[5] whether in the form of poetry, drama or prose: this mostly excludes writing that 'may start off life as history or philosophy and then come to be ranked as literature' (Eagleton 1996, 7). A grey area is occupied by medieval texts written as biographical accounts for domestic consumption rather than as history, about people who may even be mythical (*e.g.* biblical characters, heroes from the past) or are members of contemporary (mostly elite) families, the purpose of which may have been to entertain while also recording and drawing attention to family lineages. The

---

[5] Although Terry Eagleton offers this definition simply in order to reject it, it is a useful definition for this consideration of medieval material as it enables a reasonably clear distinction to be drawn between literature and other historical sources – observational, administrative and didactic texts which purport to be factual. Today, to be defined as 'literature' a work usually also needs to be judged to be of some literary merit, which is of course inevitably difficult to define objectively. However, this does not need to be an issue here, as the purpose of this paper is to consider literary scholarship and what it can tell us about medieval childhood.

distinction used here is in the approach – literary rather than historical – which has been used to analyse the texts.

The early study of Middle English literature (dating to 1100–1500 AD) in the nineteenth century was focussed primarily on philological investigation of the history and development of the English language, but attention broadened to encompass wider issues of the development of the literary form after the first world war. Since the 1980s, due to the convergence of these two approaches and increased specialisation within literary studies, 'a more certain and complete picture of the period's literary culture has emerged, not just of the texts themselves, but also of the circumstances of their production, the patterns of their dissemination, and their possible readership' (Scanlon 2009, 5). Eagleton (1996) suggests that reading a work of literature in order to find out about contemporary life is not reading it as literature, but that does not mean that it is not an effective means of advancing knowledge and understanding of medieval childhood. Indeed, as Adrienne Gavin (2012b, 3) points out 'literary depictions of children are not only influenced by views on childhood in their times ... but also reflect and reveal concerns, cultural tendencies, and areas of interest in the period of their composition', while highlighting the important caveat that even if 'inspired by real-life originals or contemporary thought, the child in literature is inarguably a construction of art' (Gavin 2012b, 2).

Relatively little attention has yet been given to children by medieval literary scholars: 'with a few recent exceptions ... literary scholars still seem prone to "the Ariès effect" and have not attended to the widespread appearance of children and childhoods in Middle English texts' (Kline 2012, 21–2). This is beginning to change (*e.g.* Blake 1993; Kline 2005; 2012; Rutter 2007; Chedzoy *et al.* 2007; Knowles 2012), but there is still a striking dearth of research compared to the attention devoted by literary scholars to post-seventeenth-century material for and about children. For example, the survey of literature for children edited by Peter Hunt (1995) included just one chapter on the entire period up to *c.* 1700, while more recently Adrienne Gavin's (2012a) edited volume on the child in British literature from the medieval period onwards includes only two papers on medieval material.

However, that literary analysis can provide new perspectives on medieval attitudes to children and childhood is apparent in some recent studies, such as those addressing the *Pearl* poem, written in Middle English probably in the 1380s or 1390s (Stanbury 2001, 6). The poem recounts the dream of a bereaved father in which he meets his dead infant daughter again as an adult woman in heaven. In his dream the father learns that his daughter's soul is not, like her body, rotting in the ground, but in heaven. He longs to join her there, but when he tries to cross the water that separates them, he wakes abruptly. Ultimately, he finds some consolation in coming to understand that only through religious observance and by going through death, can he and all humans come to the happy state his daughter is now in.

By understanding both the use of a pearl as a literary metaphor for a dead child, it becomes immensely moving:

> Consumed with inconsolable grief for a lost pearl, he seems unable or unwilling to leave the place ... he stays because he believes that his pearl is still there, under the ground, tantalizingly close, yet unreachable. Any reader still unaware of the allegorical dimension of

the pearl is likely to wonder why he does not simply reclaim his lost jewel, since he knows so precisely where it lies. The answer, of course, is that the lost pearl is not lost merely in space but in time: the child whom he remembers belongs to the past, and exhuming her body would hardly remedy his grief. His own literal-mindedness in believing that his pearl is necessarily where he left it traps him by her graveside and prevents him from imagining any other fate, either for her or for himself. Instead, the Dreamer sees the Maiden as irrecoverable, and his sense of hopelessness is underlined by his contemplation of exactly what is happening to his daughter's body

Terrell 2008, 432–3

Reading the language shows the grief of the *Pearl* father to be depicted as uncompromisingly visceral, deep, desperate, agonising, enduring and unbearable. The narrator is 'wounded by love beyond repair' (l. 11), his heart caught in 'chilling care' (l. 50), unmanned by 'bitter grief' (l. 51):

> Are you my pearl for whom I cried,
> For whom I grieved alone at night?
> Much longing I for you have sighed
> Since into grass you left my sight
> *ll 240–4*

Pearl reveals much about parental attitudes to children. Sarah Stanbury (2009, 43) points out that the poem was 'a commissioned work, probably written as a consolatory piece to commemorate the death of a daughter'. Knowing that *Pearl* is not simply the grief-stricken outpourings of a fortuitously gifted literary parent (Stanbury 2009, 8) tells us something about the culture of mourning in relation to children. That such a beautifully crafted, courtly, piece of literature – elegy, eulogy, therapy and religious edification rolled into one – was commissioned about the loss of a child reveals attitudes to children's deaths in the late fourteenth century. We can infer that it was acceptable and even expected that much investment (emotional and financial) might be expended on mourning the death of a child and ultimately, in trying to achieve consolation.

Analysis of the use made of the 'pearl' as a literary metaphor also enhances our understanding of the perception of children. At its simplest level, the pearl represents the dead child: the reader, after being briefly lured into supposing it is simply a dropped gem which has 'slipped through the grass', soon realises that what the narrator seeks is, in fact, his two-year-old daughter who is buried under that grass. The pearl metaphor works at one level to show how the father valued his daughter, but also how he saw her as an innocent, pure, perfect unblemished beauty. The pearl metaphor also associates other concepts with the dead child: it '*is* a gem, *is* a two-year old child, *is* a beautiful young woman, *is* the immortal soul, *is* the heavenly city – as well as a collective of the properties that inhere to each term singly' (Stanbury 2001, 3). Here we see something of the ways in which young children could be perceived in later fourteenth-century England.

The pearl metaphor works at other levels as well, as Katherine Terrell points out, helping the fourteenth-century reader to understand the central message of the poem, that through religion there is hope after death, even that of a child:

The pearl was traditionally believed to be incorruptible, and thus the description of a rotting pearl goes against all conventional wisdom – suggesting that the Dreamer is wrong either in his apprehension of his child as a pearl or in his conception of the way in which she has become 'spotte[d]' through her death and burial .... [But] applied to a human soul, sullied by sin and purified through confession, the metaphor is an apt one. The Dreamer's mistake, clearly, is in attempting to apply the pearl metaphor to the corruptible body rather than the immortal soul

Terrell 2008, 438

A further demonstration of the skill of the author, is the way the word 'spot' is used punningly to link the location of the buried child and the discolouration of physical decay: 'In its dual senses of "defilement" and "location", the repeated word echoes the Dreamer's circling thoughts, associating the physical site of the grave with the decay that takes place there and emphasising the Dreamer's anguished obsession with the location of the grave and with the body that lies within' (Terrell 2008, 435). These metaphors are intricately woven through the poem to encourage the reader to empathise with the narrator, enhance the poem's impact and drive home its message: 'Pearl uses a dizzying punnology, embedded within concepts, words and grammatical structures and even within the system of its meter and rhyme, as if in invitation to engage with language as an encounter with haunting and repetition' (Stanbury 2001, 3–4).

The poem addresses at length the bitter, tortuous (in both senses of the word) controversy of the period: whether children too young to understand the Christian creed could or should be baptised, and, accordingly, be able get to heaven. The concept of *Limbo Puerorum*, which had been part of the theological canon since the mid-thirteenth century, spared unbaptised children Hell, but theologians were still in disagreement about whether children should be able to get to heaven (seen as being in the presence of God) if they had died before they were old enough to understand Christian teaching. This problem is articulated by the bereaved *Pearl* father who struggles to accept his transfigured daughter's explanation of the contrived rules allowing her to enter heaven when she had died before her second birthday:

> You lived not two years in our land,
> How to please God you never know,
> Nor Creed nor prayers could understand;
>
> *ll 482–4*

The daughter patiently explains to her father the compromise that allowed the Church to avoid alienating those who did not want to believe their dead children were consigned to an eternity barred from heaven.

Further analysis shows that the message of hope, the consolation the poem seeks to offer, is subtly reinforced in the structure of the poem:

Comprising twenty sets of five, the stanzas are grouped to add up to 100, a number of perfection. This symmetry is offset, however, by the curious addition of an extra stanza in the fifteenth set – with the result that the stanzas total 101. One hundred and one, a strong number that suggests new beginning after return, is doubtless no accident

Stanbury 2001, 4

Thereby the poem enhances both its technical mastery and its impact as an allegory on divine salvation. '[O]n an individual level, *Pearl* describes the difficulties of the individual who we might say is "working through" grief with the aid of devotional psychology. On the collective level, *Pearl* offers the promise that the particular accommodation represented in the vision, the maiden one of 144,000 brides of Christ, can be available to all' (Stanbury 2001, 12).

This beautifully structured, complex, multi-layered theological message is delivered through the story of the death of a child who did not live to see her second birthday, and this again hints at late fourteenth-century attitudes to children which are tellingly different from the apparently austere, emotionless, child-denying funerary monuments. Even if the *Pearl* poem is a metaphor for something other than the death of a child, as some scholars have suggested,[6] it is still the case that, for the spiritual and/or allegorical message of the *Pearl* poem to work, the grief of the father would have to be recognisable and realistic to readers. He has to be not some uniquely deranged individual, but any parent, 'everyparent': 'the poem is addressing the complex work of human mourning rather than dealing exclusively in doctrinally correct consolation. The poem recognises that the Dreamer cannot simply set aside his mourning and alter his worldview because he is told that he should; instead, he can accept the Maiden's teachings only by slow degrees' (Terrell 2008, 432).

Turning to another very different case study, James Schultz's (1995) examination of Middle High German (MHG) literature constitutes a rare example in literary scholarship of an entire volume dedicated to medieval childhood. Schultz is aware of the limitations of such material, pointing out that the texts are 'profoundly shaped by literary tradition, by the circumstances of their patronage and performance, and by a host of other factors that make it absurd to suppose they might somehow offer an accurate representation of extraliterary childhood' (Schultz 1995, 13).[7] In addition, Schultz (1995, 13) points out that the MHG texts are restricted in their focus, with most of the children featured in the texts being idealised high-status males. The reason for this lies in their being almost exclusively written and commissioned 'by men and, less frequently, women of the nobility and the church, themselves usually of noble birth, who regarded literary patronage as a way of glorifying themselves and legitimating their power' (Schultz 1995, 13). Accordingly, Schultz (1995, 263) concludes that 'any attempt to read historical childhood out of literary texts must be highly problematical'.

This does not sound encouraging for present purposes, but in admitting that 'it would be foolish to think that they represent the real children of the German Middle Ages', Schultz (1995, 13) also points out that the MHG texts are, nonetheless, the best source available as 'the more usual kinds of historical sources waste hardly a word on children' (a familiar problem). More significantly, he goes on to make two important points about the value (rather than the simple necessity) of such literary sources for the study of medieval childhood, commenting that MHG texts are privileged:

---

[6] Various scholars have suggested that *Pearl* may be an allegory on baptism or entrance into a nunnery (Stanbury 2001, 8).

[7] This, of course, is true of medieval literature in other languages, including Middle English, and much other documentary evidence besides.

first, because the knowledge of childhood is the culturally constructed *meaning* of childhood, and literary texts are a rich source of cultural meaning... Second, the representation of children in the literary texts are themselves part of the historical knowledge of childhood. They rely on that knowledge and incorporate elements of it – otherwise they would have been incomprehensible

Schultz 1995, 225

In addition, some of the statistics that emerge from Schultz's work are alone worth knowing: for example, the entire cannon of MHG texts between 1100 and 1350 refers to just 375 children, 94% of which were of noble or high birth (Schultz 1995, 59).

Analysis of these texts allows Schultz to propose a succession of distinctive phases in the literary portrayal of children in German language literature. From 1100–1150, childhood rarely features and is limited to a few religious figures, such as Jesus, Moses and John the Baptist (Schultz 1995, 200–1). From 1150–1200 a larger number of saints and martyrs appear, while secular children make a first appearance, with childhood represented as a period of preparation for adulthood (mostly knighthood) 'an age of discipline and determination, the heroic age of the knightly child' (Schultz 1995, 208). Between 1200 and 1250, descriptions of secular childhoods become more common, reflecting 'a general desire for completeness, biographical and genealogical' (Schultz 1995, 209–19). These accounts of childhood are more sentimental with children represented as loving and being loved (by parental figures and by other children) and as behaving in child-like ways such as by crying and playing with toys and pets. They are described acting naively and innocently, while in pursuit of worthy aims. This 'Golden Age of secular Childhood' (Schultz 1995, 209) in the literature does not last, with the period 1250–1300 showing a decline in interest in stories of secular childhoods, attention turning back to stories of saints, and the first appearance of negative views of childhood in the literature (Schultz 1995, 219–35): '[t]here is no child so small that he does not want to squander his time in mockery, abuse, cursing, swearing, insults, games, gluttony and all sort of loose living' (Schultz 1995, 225). This pattern continues between 1300 and 1350, when a loss of literary interest in children is shown by a 50% reduction in the number of childhood narratives, most of which Schultz (1995, 235) considers, in any case, to be 'derivative, cursory, fragmentary, or partial'.

Such observations are primarily socio-historical rather than literary, but Schultz also shows the potential of linguistic analysis to illuminate contemporary perceptions of children. Terms referring to babies are used very little; '*kindelin*' (the diminutive of '*kint*' meaning child) is not used exclusively for infants, and is in fact less commonly used for this age group than '*kint*' (Schultz 1995, 23–4). The words used by MHG writers to designate children are those also used for servants or attendants, suggesting that contemporary perceptions of children were rooted in their lack of autonomy and status (Schultz 1995, 247). The use of language also reveals perceptions of gender in childhood (Schultz 1995, 21–42), as the word '*kint*' is used to describe children of either biological sex from birth, but its use is differentiated by gender as children age. The word '*kint*' refers to males throughout their childhood until they came of age as adults (aged fourteen to eighteen), but when used of them thereafter (which is rare) it is explicitly to signify their relative youth (Schultz 1995, 23–4). Of females, '*kint*' ceases to be used at a much younger age (around seven to ten), and certainly as soon as a girl in the narrative has any contact with strangers/suitors. In the rare instance where *'kint'* is used to refer to older females it is used, unlike in males, to signify their virginity (Schultz 1995, 24–5). Thus, we see that the essence of German high medieval perceptions of gendered male childhood identity lies in youth, whereas gendered female childhood identity is rooted in virginity. By implication, a boy's cultural identity as a male focusses on age, an attribute which is naturally and inevitably acquired, whereas a girl's gendered identity relied on virginity, a much more culturally nuanced characteristic and one whose retention or loss is not a natural process but one that is consciously enacted. Another telling linguistic perspective on gendered contemporary perceptions of children is the use of only one term, *'maget'* (virgin/maiden) to denote female gender in children, whereas several terms are used to denote male gender (Schultz 1995, 256).

There is much more that is of interest in Schultz's research, but it is interesting to note that some of his conclusions would have been welcomed by Ariès:

> Probably the German nobility of the thirteenth century did believe that children were deficient, that childhood should be focused on adulthood, that the immutable nature of the individual was revealed during childhood, that no amount of childhood dislocation could prevent the noble nature from attaining its proper place in society, that the childhood of maidens was fundamentally different from that of youths, and that childhood was more important in secular than in religious contexts
>
> *Schultz 1995, 264*

Notably, while accepting that the texts are artificial constructs, not mirrors of everyday life, Schultz is clear that they do provide evidence of contemporary attitudes to children and childhood:

> The MHG narratives were inevitably part of the larger cultural discourse on childhood in medieval Germany. On the one hand, they would have been meaningless to their contemporary audiences if they had not incorporated common assumptions about childhood. On the other, the textual representation of childhood must have affected the ideas about childhood, even the treatment of children, among those who were familiar with the stories
>
> *Schultz 1995, 263*

These examples of literary analysis used to illuminate aspects of medieval childhood show how such work can produce nuanced perspectives which complement and extend those from other approaches. Not least, we can see how representations of children can be manipulated in order to elicit diverse responses from audiences, leaving us to wonder how such manipulation might affect what we find in the archaeological record.

Folklore Studies

Folklore can be defined as 'whatever is voluntarily and informally communicated, created or done jointly by members of a group (of any size, age, or social and educational level): it can circulate through any media (oral, written, or visual) … The essential criterion is the presence of a group whose joint sense of what is right and appropriate shapes the story, performance or custom – not the rules and teachings of any official body' (Simpson and Roud 2000, v). Folklore can include traditions, beliefs, superstitions, myths, legends, songs, rhymes, pastimes, games and much else. Folklore is transmitted primarily either by verbal recounts of beliefs, traditions or stories, or by observation of or participation in activities. Written descriptions were rare until intellectual interest in the subject began to develop in the nineteenth century when many folklore collections were made, mostly by individuals with a personal interest and little or no pretension to academic status. Folklore provides a counterpoint to historical evidence (as it is not usually transmitted by being written down), to literature (as it is not usually formally composed) and to art history (as it is enacted and transmitted by participation, not by viewing). Of all of these four disciplines, folklore suffers least from being biased towards the activities and interests of the elite and the educated, and as such, despite the difficulties inherent it using it in the study of medieval childhood, it deserves serious consideration.

However, of all the disciplines considered in this chapter, folklore studies (especially those focussed on the past) present the most frustrating challenge for the scholar of medieval childhood. This is because while the potential value of evidence about 'traditions that are learned, performed and transmitted by children without the influence of adult supervision or instruction' (McCormick and White 2011, 264) is clearly immense (as there are so few other sources for this sort of evidence, which is by definition rarely written down), its reliability and temporal stability can be questionable. Here, academic folklorists admit that they suffer more than most from what Brian Sutton-Smith (1970, 4–5) so elegantly termed the 'triviality barrier'; that is, the reluctance of scholars in other disciplines to take their research seriously as 'English academia has almost universally turned a blind eye' (Simpson and Roud 2000, vi). This is partly because the usual robustly reflexive process of scholarly knowledge generation, which involves collecting and analysing evidence in order to develop inferences and test them against other evidence, is less easy to achieve within folklore studies. It is not alone in this, of course, but folklorists suffer from being subject to key problems inherent both in historically-based research (that direct 'live' observation, interrogation and cross-examination are not possible) and in social sciences (that the subject may not be providing an accurate, reliable, objective or complete testament).

Brian Sutton-Smith (1970, 4–6) considers those dealing with the folklore of children in particular to be particularly disadvantaged with regard to the triviality barrier. But folklorists are notable for their interest in children and their folklore, and for accepting child-related matters more readily as worthy of study in their own right (rather than an adjunct of an older or more sophisticated body of informants) than many other disciplines within the humanities and social sciences. This is another reason why archaeologists interested in medieval childhood should be critically aware of folklore studies, despite the fact that achieving temporal depth is challenging and requires folklorists to rely either on 'historic' accounts (collected when standards of scholarship were very different), or on back-projection of modern or historic accounts.

As few accounts of child-related folklore survive from the medieval period, one of the most vexed questions for medievalists when looking at folklore is, inevitably, the extent to which such back projection can elucidate the traditions of earlier centuries. Folklore studies started on an optimistic note in this respect, as 'early folklorists took it as read that children preserve in their games and rhymes the serious practices of previous adult generations, and were thus quick to see survivals of bride-capture, funeral customs, or foundation sacrifice' (Simpson and Roud 2000, 59). As a corollary, many early folklorists believed that there was a high degree of conservatism in children's enaction and transmission of games and traditions: Alice Gomme (1853–1938), in the introduction to her pioneering 1894 collection of children's games and rhymes, commented that '[a]lthough none of the versions of the games now collected together are in their original form … it cannot, I think, fail to be noticed how extremely interesting these games are … as a means of obtaining an insight into many of the customs and beliefs of our ancestors. Children do not invent, but they imitate or mimic' (Gomme 1894, x). Indeed one of Gomme's priorities in presenting her accounts of children's games was 'to deduce from the evidence thus collected suggestions as to the probable origin of the game' (Gomme 1894, ix). Although her work has been criticised in recent years (see below), in fairness to her it is extremely useful that she saw fit to include 'such references to early authorities and other facts bearing upon the subject as help to elucidate the views expressed' (Gomme 1894, ix; see also Gomme 1898). Nonetheless, amongst folklorists today the notion that children's folklore is likely to represent survival of much earlier traditions is widely doubted (Simpson and Roud 2000, 59).

Helpfully, folklorists' interest has now shifted away from attempts to use children's folklore to identify other (adult) traditions and towards exploring children's culture itself. In the mid-twentieth century, Iona and Peter Opie, the best-known twentieth-century folklorists of childhood, published two extensive collections of games and rhymes (1959; 1969), which constitute an invaluable reservoir of knowledge about children's culture, encompassing material mediated by adults as well as that which was more child-derived and transmitted. The Opies were less concerned with eliciting earlier traditions, and focussed instead on the children's games in their own right. This is, of course, potentially a much more useful perspective for those interested in medieval childhood, although doubts remain as to what time depth children's folklore has. In 1969 the Opies (1969, 6–10) were confident that children's games, while subject to innovation and change were also prone to considerable levels of persistence over centuries. But by 1995 Brian Sutton-Smith (1995, 20) was less certain, emphasising that '[c]hildren's folklore is not immutable and unchanging', while, in the same volume, John McDowell applied concepts of 'mutation' and 'emergence' in exploring change in folklore and pointed out that scholars have highlighted the 'unique, unpredictable quality of any given instance of folklore transmission' (McDowell 1995, 51). No firmer conclusions have since been reached, although Charlie McCormick and Kim Kennedy White (2011, 261) are more optimistically prepared to assert that folk traditions can persist over centuries, including children's folklore which they suggest 'has remarkable stability over long periods of time'. The position remains largely as McMahon and Sutton-Smith (1995, 293) stated it: 'The field of folklore began with an interest in origins, with survivals, and with history, and this interest will probably continue; many of the problems of historical origins and historical change have not been solved'.

McCormick and White also provide an overview of, and commentary on, current thinking in folklore studies, including that relating to children, whose folklore they view as no less valid than any other sector of society and as containing 'practically all of the principal genres of tradition, including games, narratives of many kinds, songs, customs, and material culture' (McCormick and White 2011, 265). Their comments reveal that the social context of enacted traditions is increasingly of interest, something recognised in Damian Webb's comments in his introduction to the 1984 edition of Gomme's opus: 'None of these sources gives specific details: what sort of children were playing the games in what sort of place and what were their ages? Were they the urban poor singing in dancing in their own back yards or were they organised groups of children playing under adult supervision?' (Webb 1984, 70). McCormick and White (2011, 265) echo this point, adding that 'analyzing the social interactions in which the games are embedded as at least as important as documenting the exact texts and tunes of the songs children sing or the rhymes they recite during hand-clap routines'. Their perspective on this problem reflects much current thinking within psychology and anthropology on child socialisation:

> childhood traditions are an integral part of the overall enculturation process because through mastering the rules of the games or the literary structure of oral genres such as riddles and rhymes, children learn some of the fundamental aspects of cooperation and strategy that are so integral to contemporary Western society. Furthermore, much of the interaction that takes place when children play games together involves negotiation of rules and the status of various players more than the actual performance of the game itself. Many researchers believe that analyzing the social interactions in which the games are embedded as at least as important as documenting the exact texts and tunes of the songs children sing or the rhymes they recite during hand-clap routines
>
> *McCormick and White 2011, 265*

Turning to one specific folklore study linked to the late medieval period, Malcolm Comeaux (2005) recalls two games, 'roly poly' and 'horse', from his childhood in the Cajun area of southwest Louisiana in the late 1940s and early 1950s. Comeaux (2005, 50–5) states that one of his aims is simply to put these on record, but he also feels that they should be 'compared with how these games were played elsewhere and at other times', and in doing so he sees similarities with some of Bruegel's images in *Children's Games*:

> The scene of the boys playing roly poly in the Bruegel painting is an accurate depiction of the game known to the author as both roly poly and pique partout, and obvious to anyone who has ever played the game. It has, however, sometimes been misidentified as marbles or skittles. The size of the ball used by the boys in the Bruegel painting, the line of holes facing the boy about to release the ball, and the position of the boys around the holes, clearly indicate that roly poly is being played, not marbles.

In support of his identification, Comeaux cites Jeanette Hills who in 1950 identified the game by its Dutch name 'petjeball' ('hole ball') and then provides 'a good description of how to play roly poly, complete even to the point that the loser must pay a penalty'. Comeaux (2005, 63) goes on to say that 'The game of horse could be played in many variations, but still can be clearly recognised in the Bruegel painting. The painting of the boys playing roly poly, however, although done in 1560, could just have easily been painted in 1950 in South Louisiana, and without any marked changes, save for clothing styles'.

Having established to his own satisfaction that the games depicted by Bruegel are likely to have been similar to his 'roly poly' and 'horse', Comeaux comments, from personal experience, on the violent nature of both games, where children could be, and frequently were, hurt. In his experience, girls were excluded from both games, weaker or more timid boys were not allowed to play 'horse' (not out of concern for their welfare but because they might jeopardise the team which was only as strong as its weakest player) and younger boys were only allowed to play 'roly poly' if they were prepared to accept the painful consequences of loss when projectiles would be hurled at them (this is implied in one of its other names *'pique partout'* (meaning 'sting everywhere')). Comeaux (2005, 63) goes on to suggest that the playing of these games in the sixteenth century may 'reflect a time when might made right, when issues of equality, or fairness, carried much less weight'. He suggests that the games reflect medieval society, which was 'a time of pomp and ceremony, as well as chivalry, but [it was] also a time of cruelty and early death. In life, no quarter was asked and none given, and these games mirror this attitude'. Comeaux suggests that in the medieval context horse served 'to identify the strong and the reliable, attributes critical in warfare and life in general', while roly poly 'was a game whose aim was to inflict pain and punishment. Here strength and size counted for less, and what was important was the "heart" a boy had – whether or not he was willing to accept pain and punishment stoically'.

Folklore is a difficult subject for the medievalist interested in childhood, but the study outlined above is one example which shows its potential to illuminate aspects of past life which may otherwise be lost.

Analysis

There has been space to examine only a few case studies from each of the disciplines considered above, which were selected to illustrate the potential that different analytical techniques have for advancing the study of medieval childhood, and in the hope that they will inspire further exploration of reading across other disciplines. It is apparent, however, even from a cursory survey, that such potential is very high. For example, the literary and art historical studies discussed above leave one surprised that an historian writing as recently as 2007 should be able to suggest that it was not until the seventeenth or eighteenth centuries that 'obstetrical science trumped old wives' tales, the children's book industry was born – along with children's clothing, children's furniture, and children's games – and middle-class parents, publicly expressing their love for children and their grief at child death, dedicated themselves to the welfare and advancement of their offspring' (King 2007, 371). As we have glimpsed, research in History, Literature, Art History and Folklore, as well as Archaeology, have generated evidence to question, even to downright contradict, almost every one of these assertions, but this information does not seem to be penetrating as widely or as rapidly as scholars of medieval childhood might have hoped or expected. So the case for greater inter-disciplinary awareness clearly still needs to be made.

Presented together, these case studies reveal what a rich perspective different approaches can provide, and how inferences and ideas from one discipline can support, substantiate or illuminate those from other disciplines. For example, the boys in

Bruegel's *Children's Games* are playing a game that Comeaux's folklore study suggests to be 'roly poly', in which 'small, plucky boys were always welcome' (Comeaux 2005, 52), while dressed in clothes Hindman (1981, 449) identifies as those worn by younger boys aged five to eleven years. Similarly, the boys Comeaux (2005, 54) identifies as playing 'horse' which 'small boys would often not be permitted to play' are dressed by Bruegel as older boys aged over eleven (Hindman 1981, 449). Realising that Hindman's older boys are playing Comeaux's older boys' game not only supports Comeaux's linking of his games with those depicted by Bruegel, but also supports Hindman's assertion that Bruegel's depictions are accurate images of real children. Interdisciplinary study strengthens research findings by providing external data against which observations can be assessed, a means of resolving the 'taphonomic conundrum' (see above p. 145). Hindman herself uses a knowledge of Flemish folklore to support her interpretation of the allegorical meaning of *Children's Games*: the Flemish proverb 'to put a blue cloak on someone' (referring to the action of an unfaithful wife) is used to identify blue as a colour associated with deceit and infidelity, used by Bruegel to link the games of blind man's buff with the marriage and baptismal processions, thereby associating marriage with folly (Hindman 1981, 451–5).

In a different vein, evidence that a culture of mourning extended to dead children, evidenced by Stanbury's and Terrell's literary analyses of the *Pearl* poem, supports Oosterwijk's suggestion that the apparently austere style of medieval funerary monuments for children are not evidence of any lack of emotion, but determined by social conventions in which mourning was expressed in other ways. The close dating that written documents (historical, literary or both) can provide allows us to see how short-lived some twists and turns in the representation of children are in different media in different places at different times, as Schultz has shown. Generally, it is salient to note again and again the view that representations of or about children, whether conveyed via literature, historical text or art, must be realistic in order for the originator's message to be meaningful to his or her audience.

Archaeology, a discipline which seeks to understand the past based on analysis of its physical remains, has, like the other disciplines reviewed here, come relatively late to the study of childhood (Crawford and Lewis 2008; and see also the introduction to the present volume). In the eighteenth and nineteenth centuries, interest was influenced by the classical and religious education which early antiquarians received, and relatively little attention was given to areas of study not given to advancing understanding of the civilisations of ancient Greece, Rome or the Bible. Children, of any period, were of little or no interest. In the mid-nineteenth century, publication of books such as Charles Lyell's *Principles of Geology* (1830–3) and Charles Darwin's *On the Origin of Species* (1859) attracted attention to prehistory, with the medieval period commonly dismissed as the preserve of historians and/or Gothically-inclined aesthetes. In the mid-twentieth century, a processual focus on data-gathering and systemic 'longue dureé' explanations also left little space for an interest in children. More recently, however, interest has broadened, and since the late twentieth century archaeological scholarly enquiry has become more inclusive and holistic, recovery processes are ever more thorough and comprehensive, while analytical techniques are increasingly innovative, broad-ranging and finely honed. Post-modernism has led to post-processual and post-colonial approaches which have focussed attention on the impact of individuals and championed the cause of multi-vocality in reconstructing the lives of those whose voices have been lost. These developments should have benefited the study of childhood, and the extent to which this has, indeed, happened is reflected in a number of publications on the archaeology of childhood in the last twenty years (Moore and Scott 1997; Baxter 2005; Wileman 2005; Crawford and Shepherd 2007; Lillehammer 2010; see also the introduction to the present volume).

Nonetheless, archaeology still struggles to put children into its pictures of the past and medieval children have fared particularly badly, with the period receiving relatively little attention in publications on the archaeology of childhood (see also Crawford this volume). With a few notable exceptions (*e.g.* Forsyth and Egan 2005; Mays *et al.* 2007), childhood is only minimally present (if at all) in surveys of medieval archaeology. When thinking about the reasons why medieval archaeology is not good at putting children into its reconstructions of the past, it becomes ruefully apparent that this is not least because it is still not very good at putting people *per se* into the past. Excavation reports focus on the physical record of construction, deposition and disposal (a 'stones, bones, bricks and sticks'-based approach), while synthesising work commonly takes a long view in which the individual lived life, and especially that of the child, tends to get lost. Although this is beginning to change (*e.g.* Gilchrist 2012; and papers in the present volume), it is epitomised by reconstruction drawings of almost any medieval site, where human figures are included (if at all) in much smaller numbers than would have been present in reality.[8]

Greater cross-disciplinary awareness has considerable potential to advance the investigation of archaeologically-derived phenomena (Crawford and Lewis 2008). For example, MacLehose's historical analyses of medical texts, annals and theological treatises show the potential of such sources as a mine of information for osteologists, even down to details of children's development and diet, such as Aldobrandino of Siena's late thirteenth-century injunction 'that children between the ages of seven and fourteen must not drink cold water with meat, "since that could aggravate them too much"' and advice against giving children 'milk, fruit, and cheese "as much as you can", for fear of generating stone' (MacLehose 2006, 29). Palaeo-demographers exploring medieval child mortality levels and under-representation in cemetery populations will be interested to know that in the twelfth century Eckbert of Schönau commented that 'scarcely one half of [all] humans arrives alive at those days when they can know what to believe and what not' (MacLehose 2006, 66). An awareness of fourteenth-century attitudes to child death elicited by art historical and literary analysis must open the eyes of anyone working on cemetery assemblages of this date.

A small number of archaeological studies have successfully used material from other disciplines to add depth or perception to their research into aspects of childhood, demonstrating the value of this strategy. The present author has woven together evidence from History, Folklore and Art History to explore ways in which medieval children's play might appear in the archaeological record (Lewis 2009; see also the

---

[8] Examples chosen entirely at random to illustrate this point are no worse than any others but simply happened to be on my desk when I was writing this paper and include Brown, N. C. 2006. *A Medieval Moated enclosure by the Thames Estuary* and Thomas. G. 2010. *The Later Anglo-Saxon Settlement at Bishopstone: A Downland Manor in the Making.* Cessford, C., Alexander, M. and Dickens, A. 2006. *Between Broad Street and the Great Ouse: waterfront archaeology in Ely* is a rare but honourable exception to this rule.

introduction to the present volume), while another example is by Stig Welinder, Anna Kjellström and colleagues who found in Folklore an explanation for their discovery of seventeen deciduous (milk) teeth in a fourteenth-century log house at Tibrandsholm in Sweden (Olofsson and Welinder 2004; Kjellström *et al.* 2011). Excavation showed that the teeth were all found along the southern and western walls of the house (Kjellström *et al.* 2011, 153–4), suggestive of deliberate, structured deposition. In an attempt to find an explanation, early twentieth-century folklore collections from Norway and Sweden (Kjellström *et al.* 2011, 155) were examined for beliefs pertaining to lost deciduous teeth. These revealed a number of traditions intended to prevent teeth from falling into malign supernatural hands (which was widely considered likely to harm the child if it happened). One practice involved wedging the shed teeth into the timbers of house walls (Kjellström *et al.* 2011, 156, citing Tillhagen 1983 and Rooth 1982): this fitted perfectly with the observed locations of the Tidbrandsholm teeth. Although this tradition had been claimed by folklorists as of probable early origin, such claims had lapsed in recent years in line with recent academic scepticism (as discussed in this chapter, pp. 159–60). This scepticism appears to be refuted by this interdisciplinary research at Tidbrandsholm, which has not only identified the possible reasons behind an archaeologically-observed phenomenon, but also demonstrated the likely antiquity of a recently documented folk tradition: the Tidbransholm teeth were certainly deposited by the seventeenth century, and possibly as early as the fourteenth century.

While being excited by the visions that non-archaeological techniques can provide, it should also be recognised, of course, how much archaeology can contribute to broadening and advancing knowledge and understanding of medieval children in its own right. Among other virtues, archaeology is less socially-restricted than most historical evidence, less consciously mediated by artifice than composed works of literature or art, and more dateable than folklore. Archaeological analysis can be conducted at varying scales, exploring entities as large as landscapes or as small as individual cells, time periods as long as millennia or as short as days. Archaeology is, of all the disciplines reviewed here, the only one in which new sources of evidence are still constantly being discovered, and in which we must always be aware that only a tiny percentage of the existing evidence has yet been investigated in detail. Scientific analytical techniques are becoming ever more sophisticated, increasing the information that can be elicited from archaeological material, old or new. Archaeology is capable of providing information about intimate details of individual lived lives which may not even have been known to the individual themselves, which can, furthermore, be aggregated to generate population-level long-term studies. Simon Mays' analyses of the human remains from Wharram Percy (north Yorkshire) (Mays *et al.* 2007; Mays 2010), which include 312 individuals aged under about sixteen years (45% of the total) (Mays 2007, 89), provide just one compelling example of what archaeological investigation can reveal about a rural medieval community for whom no other substantive historical, literary, artistic or folklore evidence survives. While Judith Bennett commented in 1987 that 'the first dozen years of life in the medieval countryside defy historical reconstruction' (Bennett 1987, 68), it is certainly not the case that these years defy archaeological reconstruction, let alone interdisciplinary reconstruction.

The four disciplines reviewed above are all very different, but common themes emerge. Post-modernism has impacted on all (Thomas 1994, 12; Scott 1997, 4–5) and the whiff of Keith Thomas' 'death of certainty' is certainly evident, in some more than others, although it has not wreaked the havoc that was once feared. The study of children and childhood is benefiting in all disciplines from the post-modern interest in multiple narratives and under-represented sectors of society. Another welcome consequence of post-modernism is the broadening out of scholarly interests from inward-looking source-centred studies towards a more sociologically-orientated concern with what the source material can reveal about the societies that produced it, even if confidence in the possibility of making useful progress is sometimes low: all disciplines recognise that their evidence is partial and biased. However, scholars in each of the disciplines reviewed above are of the opinion that while the message of their sources is inevitably mediated by cultural transmission, our interest in the meaning behind the mediation (as well as the presented meaning) justifies our use of the source material, although it does inevitably make it more difficult to understand. Ontological and hermeneutic analyses in each discipline have suggested that while cultural transmissions may not represent literal facts, the tropes presented must have been recognisable by contemporary audiences as close to reality in order for them to perform the purposes for which they were created.

As a result of these developments, the aims and principles of History, Art History, Literature, Folklore Studies and Archaeology (and indeed many other social sciences) are closer than ever before, which advances the potential for greater inter-disciplinarity. Indeed, it is apparent from the inter-relatedness of the case studies discussed above that any source, any idea, should be read and explored using whatever techniques and approaches are best suited to advancing knowledge and understanding. Source material, along with spheres of interest, should not occupy a single ascribed disciplinary pigeonhole, but a fuzzily-bounded zone within a multi-dimensional disciplinary spectrum, having aspects which may be susceptible to (and benefit from) analysis or interpretation using different techniques.

Conclusion

This chapter has aimed to show how analyses from different disciplines can advance knowledge and understanding about medieval children, and inform and support each other, by opening the closed circles of taphonomic conundrums. While it is impossible for today's researcher to be the perfect Renaissance scholar, comprehensively knowledgeable across a range of subjects, it is hugely advantageous that those interested in medieval childhood know as much as possible about the potential inherent in other disciplines. We must also, of course, ensure we are aware of the limitations of the evidence we are exploring and the reliability of the scholar who presents it, being aware that we all suffer the problem that '[n]othing we do … can be done with certainty' (Schultz 1995, 263). But thus armed, we should be willing and able to proceed, in informed acceptance of the difficulties 'because we think we can learn something we want to know … if we refuse out of methodological squeamishness to speculate on what it might be able to tell us about the lives of real children, then we will be left knowing almost nothing about them at all' (Schultz 1995, 263).

The range of different sources and analytical techniques available to the study of medieval children gives this period great potential strengths, but also presents challenges, as interdisciplinary awareness of the type it requires, and merits, is always difficult. But it also creates opportunities to generate new knowledge and understanding of the experience of childhood and its impact on society which is robust, compelling and nuanced because it is inter-disciplinarily derived. The study of medieval childhood is growing in vigour and confidence in its many separate disciplines, but to fulfil its potential this multi-disciplinary subject should strive for ever greater inter-disciplinary cooperation.

Bibliography

Ariès, P. 1960. *L'enfant et la vie familiale sous l'ancien régime*. Paris: Librairie Plon (English translation Baldick, R. 1962. *Centuries of Childhood*. London: Jonathan Cape).

Aston, M. 2003. The use of images, pp. 69–73 in Marks, R. and Williamson, P. (eds), *Gothic: art for England 1400–1547*. London: V&A Publications.

Avery, G. 1995. The beginnings of children's literature to c.1700, pp. 1–25 in Hunt, P. E. (eds), *Children's Literature: an illustrated history*. Oxford: Oxford University Press.

Badham, S. and Oosterwijk, S. 2012. The monument of Katherine (1253–7), daughter of Henry III and Eleanor of Provence. *Antiquaries Journal* 92, 169–96.

Baxter, J. E. 2005. *The Archaeology of Childhood: children, gender and material culture*. Walnut Creek: Altamira Press.

Bennett, J. M. 1989. *Women in the Medieval Countryside. Gender and household in Brigstock before the plague*. Oxford: Oxford University Press.

Blake, A. 1993. Children and suffering in Shakespeare's plays. *The Yearbook of English Studies* 23, 293–304.

Brown, N. C. 2006. *A Medieval Moated Enclosure by the Thames Estuary: excavations at Southchurch Hall, Southend, Essex* (East Anglian Archaeology 115). Norwich: East Anglian Archaeology.

Cannadine, D. (ed.) 2002. *What is History Now?* London: Macmillan.

Carr, E. H. 1961. *What is History?* London: Random House.

Cessford, C., Alexander, M. and Dickens, A. 2006. *Between Broad Street and the Great Ouse: waterfront archaeology in Ely* (East Anglian Archaeology 114). Norwich: East Anglian Archaeology.

Chamberlain, A. T. 1997. Commentary: missing stages of life – towards the perception of children in archaeology, pp. 248–50 in Moore, J. and Scott, E. (eds), *Invisible People and Processes: writing gender and children into European Archaeology*. London: Leicester University Press.

Chedzoy, K., Greenhalgh, S. and Shaugnessy, R. (eds) 2007. *Shakespeare and Childhood*. Cambridge: Cambridge University Press.

Comeaux, M. L. 2005. What games can say: two medieval games from French Louisiana. *The Journal of the Louisiana Historical Association* 46 (1), 47–63.

Crawford, S. and Lewis, C. 2008. Childhood studies and the Society for the Study of Childhood in the Past. *Childhood in the Past* 1, 5–16.

Crawford, S. and Shepherd, G. (eds) 2007. *Children, Childhood and Society* (British Archaeological Reports International Series 1696). Oxford: Archaeopress.

Cunningham, H. 2005. *Children and Childhood in Western Society since 1500*. Harlow: Longman.

deMause, L. (ed.) 1974. *The History of Childhood*. New York: Psychohistory Press.

Eagleton, T. 1996. *Literary Theory: an introduction* (second edition). Oxford: Blackwell.

Forsyth, H. and Egan, G. 2005. *Toys, Trifles and Trinkets: base-metal miniatures from London 1150–1800*. London: Unicorn Press.

Gavin, A. E. (ed.) 2012a. *The Child in British Literature: literary constructions of childhood, medieval to contemporary*. London: Palgrave Macmillan.

Gavin, A. E. 2012b. The child in British literature, pp. 1–19 in Gavin, A. E. (ed.), *The Child in British Literature: literary constructions of childhood, medieval to contemporary*. London: Palgrave Macmillan.

Gilchrist, R. 2012. *Medieval Life: archaeology and the life course*. Woodbridge: Boydell.

Giles, J. A. (ed.) 1847. *William of Malmesbury's Chronicle of the Kings of England*. London: Henry G. Bohn.

Goldberg, J. P. J. 1992. *Women, Work and Life Cycle in a Medieval Economy. Women in York and Yorkshire, c. 1350–1520*. Oxford: Oxford University Press.

Gombrich, E. H. 1950. *The Story of Art*. London: Phaidon.

Gomme, A. 1894. *The Traditional Games of England, Scotland and Ireland Volume 1*. London: D. Nutt.

Gomme, A. 1898. *The Traditional Games of England, Scotland and Ireland Volume 2*. London: D. Nutt.

Hanawalt, B. 1986. *The Ties That Bound. Peasant families in medieval England*. Oxford and New York: Oxford University Press.

Hanawalt, B. 1993. *Growing Up in Medieval London: the experience of childhood in history*. Oxford: Oxford University Press.

Heywood, C. 2001. *A History of Childhood*. Oxford: Blackwell.

Hills, J. 1957. *Das Kinderspielbild von Pieter Bruegel d. A., 1560: eine volkskundliche Untersuchung*. Vienna: Osterreichischen Museums für Volkskunde.

Hindman, S. 1981. Pieter Bruegel's *Children's Games*, folly, and chance. *The Art Bulletin* 63 (3), 447–75.

Jenks, C. 1996. *Childhood*. London: Routledge.

King, M. L. 2007. Concepts of childhood: what we know and where we might go. *Renaissance Quarterly* 60 (2), 371–407.

Kjellström, A., Olfsson, C., Stenbäck Lönnquist, U. and Welinder, S. 2011. Living children, pp. 152–61 in Lally, M. and Moore, A. (eds), *(Re)Thinking the Little Ancestor: new perspectives on the archaeology of infancy and childhood* (British Archaeological Reports International Series 2271). Oxford: Archaeopress.

Kline, D. T. 2005. *Medieval Literature for Children*. London: Routledge.

Kline, D. T. 2012. 'The child may doon to fadres reverence': children and childhood in Middle English literature, pp. 21–37 in Gavin, A. E. (ed.), *The Child in British Literature: literary constructions of childhood, medieval to contemporary*. London: Palgrave Macmillan.

Knowles, K. 2012. Shakespeare's 'terrible infants'? Children in *Richard III, King John* and *Macbeth*, pp. 38–55 in Gavin, A. E. (ed.), *The Child in British Literature: literary constructions of childhood, medieval to contemporary*. London: Palgrave Macmillan.

Labarge, M. W. 1986. *Women in Medieval Life*. London: Penguin.

Lewis, C. 2009. Children's play in the later medieval English countryside. *Childhood in the Past* 2, 86–108.

Leyser, H. 1995. *Medieval Women*. London: Weidenfeld and Nicholson.

Lillehammer, G. 1989. A child is born. The child's world in archaeological perspective. *Norwegian Archaeological Review* 22 (2), 91–105.

Lillehammer, G. (ed.) 2010. *Socialization. Recent research on childhood and children in the past*. Stavanger: Stavanger Museum.

Lyell, C.

MacFarlane, A. 1985. *Marriage and Love in England: modes of reproduction, 1300–1840*. Oxford: Blackwell.

MacLehose, W. 2006. *A Tender Age: cultural anxieties over the child in the twelfth and thirteenth centuries*. New York: Columbia University Press.

McCormick, C. T. and White, K. K. 2011. *Folklore: an encyclopedia of beliefs, customs, tales, music and art*. Santa Barbara: ABC-CLIO.

McDowell, J. 1995. The transmissions of children's folklore, pp. 49–62 in Sutton-Smith, B., Mechling, J., Johnson, T. W. and McMahon, F. R. (eds), *Children's Folklore: a sourcebook*. New York: Garland Press.

McMahon, F. and Sutton-Smith, B. 1995. The past in the present: theoretical directions for children's folklore, pp. 293–308 in Sutton-Smith, B., Mechling, J., Johnson, T. W. and McMahon, F. R. (eds), *Children's Folklore: a sourcebook*. New York: Garland Press.

Mays, S. 2012. The effects of infant feeding practices on infant and maternal health in a medieval community. *Childhood in the Past* 4, 63–78.

Mays, S., Harding, C. and Heighway, C. (eds) 2007. *The Churchyard. Wharram. A study of settlement on the Yorkshire Wolds. Volume XI*. York: York University Publications.

Miller, H. (ed.) 1995. *The Hours of Mary of Burgundy* (facsimile edition with a commentary by E. Inglis). London: Harvey Miller Publishers.

Olofsson, C. and Welinder, S. 2004. Historiens avfall, pp. 7–21 in Kjellson, C., Olofsson, S. and Sörlin, P. (eds), *Blickar bakåt. Elva uppsatser om ett förgånget nu*. Härnösand: Mitthögskolan, Institutionen för humaniora.

Oosterwijk, S. 2008. The medieval child: an unknown phenomenon?, pp. 230–5 in Harris, S. J. and Grigsby, B. (eds), *Misconceptions about the Middle Ages*. New York and London: Routledge.

Oosterwijk, S. 2010. Deceptive appearances: the presentation of children on medieval tombs. *Ecclesiology Today* 43, 45–60.

Opie, I. and Opie, P. 1959. *The Lore and Language of Schoolchildren*. Oxford: Oxford University Press.

Opie, I. and Opie, P. 1969. *Children's Games in Street and Playground*. Oxford: Oxford University Press.

Orme, N. 1973. *English Schools in the Middle Ages*. London: Methuen.

Orme, N. 1989. *Education and Society in Medieval and Renaissance England*. London: Hambledon Press.

Phillips, K. M. 2008. Review of William F. MacLehose, *A Tender Age: cultural anxieties over the child in the twelfth and thirteenth centuries. American Historical Review* 113 (4), 1216–17.

Pooke, G. and Whitham, G. 2010. *Understand Art History* (second edition). London: Hodder Education.

Porter, R. 1997. *The Greatest Benefit to Mankind. A medical history of humanity from Antiquity to the present*. London: Harper Collins.

Postman, N. 1995. *The Disappearance of Childhood*. London: Vintage Books.

Rawcliffe, C. 1995. *Medicine and Society in Later Medieval England*. Sutton: Stroud.

Rooth, A. B. 1982. *The 'offering' of the first shed tooth and the tooth-formula: A study of a physiological custom*. Uppsala: Etnologiska institutionens Småskriftserie 30.

Rosenthal, J. T. 2007. *Essays on Medieval Childhood: responses to recent debates*. Donnington: Shaun Tyas.

Rutter, C. C. 2007. *Shakespeare and Child's Play: performing lost boys on stage and screen.* Abingdon: Routledge.

Schultz, J. 1995. *The Knowledge of Childhood in the German Middle Ages 1100–1350.* Philadelphia: University of Pennsylvania Press.

Scott, E. 1997. Introduction, pp. 1–12 in Scott, E. and Moore, J. (eds), *Invisible People and Processes: writing gender and childhood into European prehistory.* London: Leicester University Press.

Shahar, S. 1990. *Childhood in the Middle Ages.* London: Routledge.

Simpson, J. and Roud, S. 2000. *A Dictionary of English Folklore.* Oxford: Oxford University Press

Stanbury, S. (ed. and trans.) 2001. *Pearl.* Western Michigan University: Medieval Institute Publications.

Stanbury, S. 2009. The Gawain poet, pp. 139–51 in Scanlon, L. (ed.), *The Cambridge Companion to Medieval English Literature 1100–1500.* Cambridge: Cambridge University Press.

Stone, L. 1977. *Family, Sex and Marriage in England 1500–1800.* London: Weidenfeld and Nicholson.

Sutton-Smith, B. 1970. Psychology of childlore: the triviality barrier. *Western Folklore* 29, 1–8.

Sutton-Smith, B. 1995. Introduction: what is children's folklore?, pp. 3–10 in Sutton-Smith, B., Mechling, J., Johnson, T. W. and McMahon, F. R. (eds), *Children's Folklore: a sourcebook.* New York: Garland Press.

Sutton-Smith, B., Mechling, J., Johnson, T. W. and McMahon, F. R. (eds) 1995. *Children's Folklore: a sourcebook.* New York: Garland Press.

Terrell, K. T. 2008. Rethinking the 'Corse in Clot': cleanness, filth, and bodily decay in 'Pearl'. *Studies in Philology* 105 (4), 429–47.

Tillhagen, C.-H. 1983. *Barnet i folktron. Tillblivelse, födelse och fostran.* Stockholm: LTs förlag.

Thomas, K. 1994. The death of certainty. *The Guardian* 6th September, 12.

Tolstoy, L. 1995. *What is Art?* (translated from 1896 Russian edition by R. Pevear and L. Volokhonsky). London: Penguin.

Webb, D. 1984. Introduction, pp. 5–15 in Gomme, A. *The Traditional Games of England, Scotland, and Ireland* (reprint of 1894 and 1898 editions). London: Thames and Hudson.

Wileman, J. 2005. *Hide and Seek: the archaeology of childhood.* Stroud: Tempus.